ADVANCE PRAISE FOR

LITERARY IMAGINATION
KNOWLEDGE: USING LITE
EDUCATION

"Praise for this compelling compilation of creative teaching lessons and ideas to captivate and renew interest in teaching with literature! Teachers will be motivated to use the powerful themes of such classics as Milton's *Paradise Lost*, Dickens' *Great Expectations*, and William Blake's lyric poetry, but they will also be mesmerized by the many learning connections to the heart wrenching memoir by Isabelle Allende *The Sum of Our Days*, the delightful multi-cultural children's read aloud *My Name is Maria Isabel*, and "For Every One," a poem by the very popular Young Adult (YA) writer Jason Reynolds...and more!"

Laura Staal, PhD
Professor of Education,
Department of Leadership and Educational Specialties
University of North Carolina at Pembroke

"*Literary Imagination and Professional Knowledge: Using Literature in Teacher Education* is a gift for educators. This book highlights the power of literature as a source for lessons in identity, resilience, human development, the journey of an adolescent's life, and much more. Reading each chapter's valuable lessons interwoven with fantastic literary examples made me wish I had this book while on my teacher education journey, but so thankful that it is available now for all!"

Robyne Elder, EdD
Editor, *The Journal of Educational Leadership in Action*
Head of Academic Effectiveness
Lindenwood University

"For far too long, teacher education has been trapped in a professionalization feedback loop which focuses on concepts, methods, and hot-button issues in a piecemeal fashion. Dr. McLaughlin's edited volume reminds us of something that most teacher educators have forgotten, that reading good literature is key to developing the consciousness of the teacher workforce. Teacher education programs typically present students with a myriad of topics through dry textbooks and classes that emphasize concepts outside of a compelling narrative. We try to train teachers at the risk of graduating future schoolteachers who aren't educated. We may claim that students "get" literature in general education courses, but these are often larger survey courses. An elementary education major, for example, may only take a single 100 level literature course in college.

Dr. McLaughlin presents us with a compelling solution, that we should incorporate literature, poetry and compelling prose within teacher education courses so that narratives can shift the consciousness of future teachers. Stories which build upon what Dewey referred to as "the sympathetic imagination" form rich, compelling backdrops for aspiring teachers to shift their own thinking. What is impressive about Dr. McLaughlin's edited volume is the variety of classical and contemporary literature and poetry presented by its diverse contributors. The authors clearly demonstrate that literature has a power that textbooks lack. By assimilating the struggles of protagonists, future educators will see problems through new lenses. Lines of poetry can foster existential moments. Beautiful prose can carry students away from the mundane into a realm of humanistic evolution. The authors' use of Milton, Blake, Dickens, Homer, Allende, and Dante bring us all back to the great minds of the past who shifted human consciousness for the better. Teachers, above all others, should be privy to such greatness.

We should all thank Dr. McLaughlin for reminding us that great minds can make great teachers."

Matthew V. Schertz, EdD
Professor, Department of Teaching and Learning
Phyllis J. Washington College of Education
University of Montana

LITERARY IMAGINATION
AND PROFESSIONAL KNOWLEDGE

THE ACADEMY FOR EDUCATIONAL STUDIES SERIES

EDITED BY STEVEN P. JONES AND ERIC C. SHEFFIELD

The *Academy for Educational Studies Series* focuses serious attention on the often-missed nexus of educational theory and educational practice. The volumes in this series, both monographs and edited collections, consider theoretical, philosophical, historical, sociological and other conceptual orientations in light of what those orientations can tell readers about successful classroom practice and sound educational policy. In this regard, the *Academy Series* aims to offer a wide array of themes including school reform, content specific practice, contemporary problems in higher education, the impact of technology on teaching and learning, matters of diversity, and other essential contemporary issues in educational thought and practice.

Books in the Series:

Why Kids Love (and Hate) School: Reflections on Difference
edited by Steven Jones and Eric Sheffield (2018)

Why Kids Love (and Hate) School: Reflections on Practice
edited by Steven Jones and Eric Sheffield (2018)

A Case for Kindness: A New Look at the Teaching-Ethic
by Steve Broidy (2019)

Making Sense of Race in Education: Practices for Change in Difficult Times
edited by Jessica A. Heybach and Sheron Fraser-Burgess (2020)

John Dewey's Imaginative Vision of Teaching: Combining Theory and Practice
by Deron Boyles (2020)

Literary Imagination and Professional Knowledge: Using Literature in Teacher Education
edited by Jeff McLaughlin (2023)

What Do We Mean by That? Interrogating Familiar Expressions in Education
edited by Laura Rychly (2024)

Steven P. Jones is a professor in the College of Education at Missouri State University and Executive Director of the Academy for Educational Studies. He is author of *Blame Teachers: The Emotional Reasons for Educational Reform*—a book that investigates how and why so many people try to justify educational change by deriding the efforts and effectiveness of our public-school teachers. A former high school English teacher in Jefferson County, Colorado, Jones received his B.A. in English from the University of Denver, his M.A. in Educational Administration from the University of Colorado (Boulder), and his Ph.D. in Curriculum and Instruction from the University of Chicago.

Eric C. Sheffield is Professor and Department Chair of Educational Studies at Western Illinois University in Macomb. He is also founding editor of the Academy for Educational Studies' peer reviewed journal, *Critical Questions in Education*. A former English teacher in Putnam County Florida, Sheffield received his B.A. in Philosophy from Illinois College, and his M.Ed (English Education) & Ph.D (Philosophy of Education) from the University of Florida.

The editors of The Academy of Educational Series are interested in reviewing manuscripts and proposals for possible publication in the series. Scholars who wish to be considered should email their proposals, along with two sample chapters and current CVs, to the editors. For instructions and advice on preparing a prospectus, please refer to the Myers Education Press website at http://myersedpress.com/sites/stylus/MEP/Docs/Prospectus%20Guidelines%20MEP.pdf.

You can send your material to: Steven P. Jones & Eric C. Sheffield
academyedbooks@gmail.com

LITERARY IMAGINATION AND PROFESSIONAL KNOWLEDGE

❧ Using Literature in Teacher Education

EDITED BY JEFF MCLAUGHLIN

Myers Education Press

Gorham, Maine

Copyright © 2023 | Myers Education Press, LLC
Published by Myers Education Press, LLC
P.O. Box 424
Gorham, ME 04038

All rights reserved. No part of this book may be reprinted or reproduced in any form or by any electronic, mechanical, or other means, now known or hereafter invented, including photocopying, recording, and information storage and retrieval, without permission in writing from the publisher.

Myers Education Press is an academic publisher specializing in books, e-books and digital content in the field of education. All of our books are subjected to a rigorous peer review process and produced in compliance with the standards of the Council on Library and Information Resources.

Library of Congress Cataloging-in-Publication Data available from Library of Congress.

13-digit ISBN 978-1-9755-0530-1 (paperback)
13-digit ISBN 978-1-9755-0531-8 (library networkable e-edition)
13-digit ISBN 978-1-9755-0532-5 (consumer e-edition)

Printed in the United States of America.

All first editions printed on acid-free paper that meets the American National Standards Institute Z39-48 standard.

Books published by Myers Education Press may be purchased at special quantity discount rates for groups, workshops, training organizations and classroom usage. Please call our customer service department at 1-800-232-0223 for details.

Cover design by Teresa LaGrange.

Visit us on the web at **www.myersedpress.com** to browse our complete list of titles.

Contents

Acknowledgments	ix
Introduction	xi

ONE	"A Fire Was In My Head": Using Classic Stories to Teach the Ecstasies of Adolescence, with a Purpose *Mark D. Beatham*	1
TWO	Teacher Resilience and the Lessons of *Great Expectations* *Frank Giuseffi*	17
THREE	"A Mighty, Mighty Thing": Jason Reynolds' Poem *For Every One* as a Framework for Examining Adolescent Identity Development and Teacher Identity Development *Erin Hill*	33
FOUR	John Milton's *Paradise Lost*: Eve's Construction of Knowledge, Identity, and Morality *Anna Gallagher*	49
FIVE	The Crooked Roads of Genius: William Blake and Educational Psychology *Jeff McLaughlin*	71
SIX	Gilgamesh, Enkidu, and Ishtar: Lessons on Living for Incarnated Souls *Margarita García-Notario*	93

SEVEN	O Brave New World, That Has Such People In't! *Cory Glenn*	101
EIGHT	Homer, *The Odyssey*, and Resilience in Education *Lynanne Black*	119
NINE	Developing Preservice Teachers' Beliefs About Cultural Diversity Through Multicultural Children's Literature *Brian Hibbs*	143
TEN	Circles of Learning: Teaching with Dante's *Inferno* *Lochran C. Fallon*	163
ELEVEN	Isabel Allende's *The Sum of Our Days*: Discovering the Extraordinary Through the Ordinary *Margarita García-Notario*	179

About the Authors — *187*

Index — *191*

Acknowledgments

I WANT TO FIRST EXPRESS SINCERE gratitude to Steven Jones, from the Academy for Educational Studies, for his early support of this project and his encouragement to take the initial steps down the road to publication. And I am equally thankful for my dear friend Anna Gallagher, who—reflecting upon our parallel interests in William Blake and John Milton—said something like, "Yes, this could be a book," and who subsequently offered her own chapter as a contribution to this edited volume.

Of course, it's the individual chapter authors—so varied and so uniquely gifted—who represent the very heart and soul of this book, and I am filled with gratitude for each of them. Thanks for your hard work, your patience through revisions, your willingness to share ideas during our Zoom meetings, your continued patience through yet more revisions, and your persistence through the whole journey from idea to final manuscript. I am immensely proud to have my name on the cover of this book and it is your expertise and your insights that justify that pride on my part.

Once the project was underway, Chris Myers and Stephanie Gabaree from Myers Education Press were more than gracious with their ongoing assistance and gentle guidance along this journey through the publishing labyrinth. Many thanks to them, and to others involved in the process that I did not meet personally along the way.

The conceptual genesis for this book must be attributed to the students—undergraduate and graduate—at West Chester University of Pennsylvania who patiently tolerated my tendency to introduce topics in educational psychology with (perhaps, at times, ambiguous) references to great literature from the likes of William Blake, Flannery O'Connor, and Voltaire. And while mentioning West Chester University, I am reminded of the great debt I owe to my colleagues in the Department of Educational Foundations and Policy Studies who, under the able and consistent leadership of Dr. John Elmore, have maintained an academic environment conducive to professional imagination, critical thinking, and pedagogical innovation.

Finally, I offer a shout-out to my two amazing children, Iris and Sam, who—now on their own out in the world—nevertheless continue to renew my joy as a parent and as an educator and, more importantly, as a "perpetual beginner" in both of those areas. Thanks to both of you for keeping me young and humble! And let me add to this blessed mix my daughter-in-law Stephanie and my brand new (and first) grandchild, Dimitri, who is destined for an inspired life immersed in great books and enriched with the wonders of imagination.

Introduction

Jeff McLaughlin, West Chester University of Pennsylvania

At present, there is a limited resource base for using literature (e.g., fiction, poetry, and other narrative writing) as a pedagogical resource in college-level teacher education classrooms. While grade-level-appropriate literature is routinely utilized in teacher education programs, the goal is typically to familiarize future teachers with resources they will eventually include in their own classrooms. However, the explicit use of literary works to reinforce teacher education content is less common. The purpose of the present volume is to address this shortcoming.

Over the years, there have been a variety of published calls for the inclusion of literature in teacher education courses. Roberts, Jensen, and Hadjiyianni (1997) explored the use of literature study groups as a way to help preservice teachers develop sensitivity to student diversity. While the results were encouraging, the books used in this study were strictly education-related nonfiction works. In similar research in college classrooms, literature has been suggested as a means of facilitating cultural sensitivity and awareness of student differences by Beecher and Darragh (2011), Escamilla and Nathenson-Mejía (2003), Harris (2014), Nathenson-Mejía and Escamilla (2003), and Pytash (2013). In these cases, the objectives of instruction were more affective and attitude-based than related to content-related objectives of the courses themselves. While sensitivity and empathy are, of course, critical dispositions for future teachers, it is the latter types of course-related objectives that are addressed in the present volume.

Kate Marek (2006) has advocated for the inclusion of literature in graduate-level library science curricula as a way to prepare college librarians as literary resources across a variety of college programs, including teacher education. In establishing her theoretical foundation, Marek draws upon the work of Robert Coles (1989), who advocated strongly for the inclusion of quality literature across the curriculum from elementary through graduate school.

About 35 years ago, Lyle Grant (1987) surveyed college courses that combined literature and psychology, discovering that the majority of these course offerings were taught in literature (as opposed to psychology) departments. In other words, it is more common for literature courses to incorporate concepts from psychology than it is that psychology courses would make use of literature as part of the pedagogical process.

A number of examples of using literature in psychology-related curricula have been documented, including for courses in introductory psychology (Schwartz, 1980), developmental psychology (Boyatzis, 1992), humanistic psychology (Jayawickreme & Forgeard, 2011), and psychiatry (Clarke, 2011). Bolton-Gary (2013) has suggested the use of children's literature in the teaching of educational psychology as a way to help preservice teachers "construct theoretical knowledge with familiar, identifiable, and entertaining characters and situations" (p. 387). Proposed benefits of using literature in psychology courses include the reinforcement and application of concepts through supplemental literary readings (Boyatzis, 1992; Jayawickreme & Forgeard, 2011; Schwartz, 1980), improvement of writing skills by example (Chrisler, 1990), encouragement of critical thinking (Bowman, 2009), and the provision of meaningful and relatable assessment tools (Connor-Greene et al., 2005).

Other disciplines, such as criminal justice (Bowman, 2009), cross-cultural studies (Sreenivas, 2011), and gender studies (Lips, 1990) have also been presented as instances where literature could enhance the educational experience. Despite the reported benefits of using literature across college disciplines, there is a notable absence of proposals for using literature across the scope of teacher education programs, whether in required teacher education courses or in courses offered as social science options to meet general education standards. Further, while the proposals referenced above include discrete examples of using literature in college courses, there is a lack of recommendations for using literature in a more comprehensive way, to expand upon specific concepts and encourage critical thinking within specific (nonliterary) disciplines. This volume is intended to address this shortage, specifically in teacher education, by detailing how specific literary works and writers can be integrated into curricula designed for preservice teachers.

Jessica Hooten Wilson (2022), writing from outside the pedagogical realm, describes the power of fiction to combine imagination and intellect (a false dichotomy in the first place, in her view). In her view, fiction provides models and images that are inaccessible by reason alone. As we "live through another's eyes and experience their struggles and victories," our imaginations

Introduction xiii

can generate a new sense of mission in our own worlds of living and working (p. 13). To put this in the terminology of teacher education, the imaginative reading of literature can serve as a gateway to professional development.

An additional rationale for this volume is to establish a foundation for further examination of the outcomes of using literature in teacher education curricula. It is hoped that the concepts and methods contained in the following chapters will provide a basis for further field testing and evaluation of the proposed strategies in actual college classrooms. It would be useful to determine, using both qualitative and quantitative methodology, whether literature can enhance students' understanding of concepts and facilitate critical thinking within the field of their professional preparation. And for students pursuing other (noneducation) courses of study, literature may provide unique supplementary benefits that enhance their understanding of pedagogical issues and perspectives.

A large part of the motivation for this enterprise comes from my own classroom experience as a professor of educational psychology. As I have found ways to incorporate literature into coursework, I have perceived, at an anecdotal level, how literature can be used to illuminate subject matter dealing with educational psychology, human development, and educational assessment. Whether students are directed to choose their own literature or required to read assigned literary texts, the resulting connections have consistently served to enhance student understanding and critical thinking. Further, classroom discussions are greatly enhanced, in both quality and scope, when literary excerpts are incorporated into the presentation of content.

This book is intended to provide specific suggestions and outlines for incorporating literature (e.g., fiction, poetry, and narrative) in teacher education courses. A variety of genres, historical contexts, and specific applications are represented. In Chapter One, Mark Beatham describes how classic stories (principally folk and fairy tales) can be used to illustrate aspects of children's cognitive, emotional, moral, and social growth, helping future teachers to appreciate the nuances and complexities of child development. Frank Giuseffi, in Chapter Two, describes connections between *Great Expectations* by Charles Dickens and issues in educational foundations, beginning with the questions, "What 'great expectations' should future teachers have about their careers?" and "How are these expectations likely to be reevaluated over time?" Chapter Three, by Erin Hill, connects the poetry of Jason Reynolds (specifically his poem *For Every One*) to adolescent identity development, highlighting several prominent theorists in the area; she also relates the poetry to aspects of teacher identity construction.

Anna Gallagher, in Chapter Four, proposes the use of John Milton's *Paradise Lost*, specifically Eve's role in the epic poem, to reinforce topics such as knowledge construction, memory, attribution theory, misogyny, and critical thinking. Chapter Five, by Jeff McLaughlin, describes how the writings of William Blake (who wrote in the century following *Paradise Lost* and was influenced by Milton) can be used to introduce and develop concepts in educational psychology, such as constructivism, information processing, identity formation, and creative thinking. Chapter Six, by Margarita Garcia-Notario, explores Gilgamesh and other ancient texts for insights into moral judgment and professional identity as they relate to teacher development. Aldous Huxley's *Brave New World* is the subject of Chapter Seven, wherein Cory Glenn describes applications of the novel to topics in a typical educational foundations course, such as societal and political influences, instructional design, and the purpose of education.

Lynanne Black, in Chapter Eight, incorporates Homer's *The Odyssey* as an example of education in practice, encouraging teachers to enhance student success by fostering the very skills and characteristics that made Odysseus successful (e.g., persistence, goal setting, delay of gratification, and progress monitoring). Chapter Nine combines pedagogy and research with an investigation by Brian Hibbs of the influence of multicultural literature on preservice teachers' personal and professional beliefs about cultural diversity. In Chapter Ten, Lochran Fallon offers Dante's *Inferno* as a model text for exploring cross-disciplinary learning and reflection, cultural values, project-based learning, and multimedia literacy. In Chapter Eleven, Margarita Garcia-Notario's second contribution to this volume, Isabel Allende's *The Sum of Our Days* is employed to nurture future teachers' appreciation of cultural diversity, both by embracing their own heritage and by appreciating the identities of others.

As the above summaries make clear, this is a wide-ranging and diverse collection of pedagogical insights into the use of literature in teacher education. In addition to providing practical ideas and approaches for incorporating literature in the college classroom, it is hoped that a foundation will be provided for further creative work by those who design and teach college-level courses in educational foundations, psychology, teaching methods, and related areas. Hopefully, these chapters represent a variety of paradigms for additional course design and for research on the effectiveness of the individual approaches.

References

Beecher, C. C., & Darragh, J. J. (2011). Using literature that portrays individuals with autism with pre-service teachers. *The Clearing House, 84*, 21–25.

Bolton-Gary, C. (2013). Pooh's corner: Teaching educational psychology at the intersection of children's literature and technology. *Childhood Education, 89*(6), 387–391. https://doi.org/10.1080/00094056.2013.854128

Bowman, B. A. (2009). Classical literature for the criminal justice classroom. *Journal of Criminal Justice Education, 20*(1), 93–108. https://doi.org/10.1080/10511250802680365

Boyatzis, C. J. (1992). Let the caged bird sing: Using literature to teach developmental psychology. *Teaching of Psychology, 19*(4), 221–222. https://doi.org/10.1207/s15328023top1904_5

Chrisler, J. C. (1990). Novels as case-study materials for psychology students. *Teaching of Psychology, 17*(1), 55–57. https://doi.org/10.1207/s15328023top1701_14

Clarke, L. (2011). Mental health problems in works of literature. *Mental Health Practice, 14*(6), 12–16. https//doi.org/10.7748/mhp2011.03.14.6.12.c8364

Coles, R. (1989). *The call of stories*. Houghton Mifflin.

Connor-Greene, P. A., Murdoch, J. W., Young, A., & Paul, C. (2005). Poetry: It's not just for English class anymore. *Teaching of Psychology, 32*(4), 215–221. https://doi.org/10.1207/s15328023top3204_2

Escamilla, K., & Nathenson-Mejía, S. (2003). Preparing culturally responsive teachers: Using Latino children's literature in teacher education. *Equity & Excellence in Education, 36*, 238–248. https://doi.org/10.1080/10665680390246275

Grant, L. (1987). Psychology and literature: A survey of courses. *Teaching of Psychology, 14*(2), 86–88. https://doi.org/10.1207/s15328023top1402_4

Harris, K. L. (2014). The unexpected journey shared by families: Using literature to support and understand families raising a child with disabilities. *Early Childhood Education, 43*, 473–484. https://doi.org/10.1007/s10643-014-0682-1

Jayawickreme, E., & Forgeard, J. C. (2011). Insight or data: Using non-scientific sources to teach positive psychology. *The Journal of Positive Psychology, 6*(5), 499–505. https://doi.org/10.1080/17439760.2011.634819

Lips, H. M. (1990). Using science fiction to teach the psychology of sex and gender. *Teaching of Psychology, 17*(3), 197–198. https://doi.org/10.1207/s15328023top1703_17

Marek, K. (2006). Using literature to teach in LIS education: A very good idea. *Journal of Education for Library and Information Science, 47*(2), 144–150.

Nathenson-Mejía, S., & Escamilla, K. (2003). Connecting with Latino children: Bridging cultural gaps with children's literature, 27(1), 101–117. https://doi.org/10.1080/15235882.2003.10162593

Pytash, K. E. (2013). Using YA literature to help pre-service teachers deal with bullying and suicide. *Journal of Adolescent and Adult Literacy, 56*(6), 470–479.

Roberts, S. K., Jensen, S. J., & Hadjiyianni, E. (1997). Using literature study groups in teacher education courses: Learning through diversity. *Journal of Adolescent and Adult Literacy, 41*(2), 124–133.

Schwartz, L. L. (1980). Tying it all together: Research, concepts, and fiction in an introductory psychology course. *Teaching of Psychology, 7*(3), 192–193. https://doi.org/10.1207/s15328023top0703_24

Sreenivas, D. (2011). Possible childhoods in children's literature. *Childhood, 18*(3), 316–332. https//doi.org/10.1177/0907568211407531

Wilson, J. H. (2022). *The scandal of holiness: Renewing your imagination in the company of literary saints.* Brazos Press.

ONE

"A Fire Was In My Head": Using Classic Stories to Teach the Ecstasies of Adolescence, with a Purpose

Mark D. Beatham

Adolescence is the greatest natural developmental transformation in a person's life—physically, sexually, neural-cognitively, socially, emotionally, and spiritually. Adolescents acquire new bodies, hearts, and heads. Life is enlarged and surging. The highs are higher and the lows lower. It is the Great Ecstasy (defined as a state of overwhelming emotion, especially rapturous delight or a state of being beyond reason and self-control, from Greek *ekstasis*, meaning "standing outside oneself"). According to Erikson (1980), the developmental question "Who am I?" signals a great disruptive adventure. That adventure is met by a cataclysm from the outside. "Things fall apart; the centre cannot hold" (Yeats, 1920, p. 158). Nor can modern schooling hold these ecstasies.

For most of human history, cultures have conducted elaborate festivals and rites of passage to teach children to discipline and focus their newfound energies, powers, and perspectives. They send them on vision quests, isolate them in sacred spaces with minimal provisions, and subject them to harrowing physical, mental/emotional, and spiritual trials (Gennep, 1960; Turner, 1969). And they tell them *stories*, special stories, great, heroic stories of young people answering the call to transform themselves into better, smarter, stronger, and braver people, to save their families, their communities, the world, even other worlds. These are stories strung at the same high pitch as adolescent energies (Jones, 2003; Kendrick, 1991; Von Franz, 1995; Warner, 2014).

Modern technological cultures, however, have banished nearly all ancestral traditions and diminished what remains: team sports, prom, quinceañera, bah/bat mitzvah, and sex ed/health class. Adolescent development is taught reductively, in scientific and social scientific branches—physical, cognitive/neural, social/emotional, and moral—without a view of this lustrous tree and its place in the forest, or recognition of the accumulated cultural wisdom to teach how to distinguish means and ends. Science and social science are weak guides with bad memories. But ancestors' classic stories (and rituals) have a higher development in mind, something to fire the imagination and lift the spirit up. They advise children about impending, drastic changes, lurking dangers, and higher callings, and they encourage a seize-the-moment character development to suit the call. Teachers can better educate adolescents for their futures by using classic stories to explore adolescents' deepest existential concerns and challenges. Classic stories can complement the facts and civic exercises common to modern schooling, K-college.

This chapter makes the case that classic stories are important components in exploring and understanding the *ecstasies* of adolescent development, especially for their transcendent and transformative elements. They describe and prepare children for development, by displaying their challenges and opportunities, providing direction and purpose, and furnishing the imagination with higher possibilities resolved on a higher plane. After the case is made, classic stories will be described and discussed in terms of the major topics and themes that address development in existential contexts, with explicit examples to illustrate their usefulness in teacher education classrooms,

Here, classic stories are principally folk and fairy tales, with some tragedies and myths included. They are classic because they have been revered, told, and retold for generations; they live in and order the conscious and subconscious. Like memes, their success is measured by their persistence. They are favorites for good reasons, even if those reasons are ineffable. The stories most relevant are those principally about growing up, managing new realities, and preparing for transformation. Some examples are *Pinocchio* (Collodi, 1995), *Snow White* (Grimm & Grimm, 2019), *Gilgamesh* (Kovacs, 1998), *Cinderella* (Perrault, 1954), *The Hobbit/Lord of the Rings* (Tolkien, 2020), *Bluebeard/Beauty and the Beast* (Villeneuve, 2017), *Moana* (Clements & Musker, 2017), *Rapunzel* (Grimm & Grimm, 1997), *The Lion King* (1994), *King Lear* (Shakespeare, 1994), *Jungle Book* (Taylor & Favreau, 2016), *Aladdin* (Houseman, 2019), *Peter Pan* (Barrie & Unwin, 1950), *Huckleberry Finn* (Twain, 1996), *To Kill a Mockingbird* (Lee, 1983), and *Star Wars* (Lucas, 2004). (As these stories are discussed throughout this chapter, the specific references are not—for the sake of clarity—repeated in each case; however, all titles can be found in the References at the end of the chapter.)

The Case for Classic Stories

Why stories and why classic stories? According to Angus Fletcher (2021), a professor of story science, humans think and coordinate their behaviors by narratives. Plots order the consciousness to think of what happens next, a sine qua non of development. And consciousness orders itself in plot points, providing meaning, purpose, and antagonists, and by anticipating challenges, rewards, and consequences of failure. Stories map the known territory, including the immaterial domains of principles, goals, morals, values, and habits, which means they tap into the subconscious, that most ancient human agent. Ultimately, stories are more fully furnished than the scientific/clinical orientation can grasp. Humans live *whole* lives, not in parts (which school curricula imply), with everything connected. Stories enrich and better align with human sensibilities by adding back in several dimensions.

The right kinds of stories can aid learning by forcing the brain to suspend judgment and to look for more details (Fletcher, 2021). The Anterior Cingulate Cortex (ACC), surrounding the frontal part of the corpus callosum, is responsible in part for emotional expression, attention allocation, and mood regulation. The ACC hits pause on snap judgments when there is too much or inscrutable information (something felt when visiting a very foreign place). By suspending judgment, we search for more information and *learn*. Jonathan Swift's *Gulliver's Travels* (1997) is a classic example of the story that keeps the reader dizzy with uncertainty and unlikely to judge too quickly. The off-kilter, bizarre story is manna for the adolescent brain.

But why *classic* stories, especially in terms of adolescent development? First, they are what ancestors have treasured and told for generations, and therefore an adolescent's rightful heritage. As she moves naturally past primary attachments (to parents and family) to secondary attachments (friends and the wider community), knowing her greater heritage gives her a more substantial sense of place, in "the circle of life," which grounds her energies. The ancestors' stories train the imagination by multiple means—such as archetypes, metaphors, and symbols—to advise adolescents about coming existential challenges and the necessity of transformation.

Second, the stories can *teach against the times*, which is often necessary. As adolescents turn toward the wider world, they are looking for new authorities. As discussed below, that makes them vulnerable to nefarious forces seeking to exploit them. And too often, those forces can be inept or ideological "authorities." C. S. Lewis describes this predicament in *The Abolition of Man* (1943/2017), when he contrasts the cynical teacher to his teaching:

> My own experience as a teacher tells an opposite tale. For every one pupil who needs to be guarded from a weak excess of sensibility there are three who need to be awakened from the slumber of cold vulgarity. The task of the modern educator is not to cut down jungles but to irrigate deserts . . . By starving the sensibility of our pupils, we only make them easier prey to the propagandist when he comes. For famished nature will be avenged and a hard heart is no infallible protection against a soft head. (p. 699)

Today, those who "starve the sensibilities of pupils" through teaching only the shibboleths and slogans of their age are the rank materialists, the political propagators, and the reductionists depicting adolescence as mere hormone bursts (or worse, *elective*). Tomorrow, they will be onto something else. These modernists, living in the era of "Psychological Man," espouse "Expressive Individualism" (Trueman, 2020a), characterized by "notions that human flourishing is found primarily in an inner sense of well-being, that authenticity is found by being able to act outwardly as one feels inwardly, and that who we are is largely a matter of personal choice not external imposition" (Trueman, 2020b). These notions would have been nonsense in earlier ages in the West: Political Man (Ancient Greece), Religious Man (Medieval Europe), and Economic Man (with the rise of the market economies). The genius of any culture is its ability to competently propagate itself *in spite of* the limitations of its members in any particular era. Classic stories can supplement the modernists. They have so many layers, dimensions, and qualities that resist facile interpretation and political service. And they work mostly at subconscious levels, which frustrates the utilitarian teacher.

American public schools have rarely resisted trends, markets, socio-political viruses, and student whims. The literary critic Roger Shattuck (1999) argued that teachers should not teach living authors. Students won't know to look for the dead, worthwhile authors on their own but will know about the living ones. In the meantime, time and culture will have sorted out the good from the bad authors (although the debates will continue). The school is obliged to teach, in part, what transcends time and happenstance, especially when the times are likely to ignore its cultural endowments. Classic stories are each child's cultural endowments. So, with Trueman in mind, children can imbibe the spirit of their ancestors from other ages as well as from their own: from the Political, e.g., *Gilgamesh* (Kovacs, 1998) and *The Odyssey* (Homer, 1997), the Religious, e.g., *Divine Comedy* (Alighieri, 1948), *Canterbury Tales* (Chaucer, 2013), and *Pilgrim's Progress* (Bunyan, 1999), and the Economic, e.g., *Pinocchio* (Collodi, 1995) and *Peter Pan* (Disney, 2007).

The late literary critic George Steiner (2008) acknowledges this challenge of teaching in limiting times. "No culture has a pact with eternity... The conditions which made possible the giants of the western poetic, aesthetic, philosophic tradition no longer really obtain." Steiner doesn't believe "there can be a Hamlet without a ghost, a Missa Solemnis without a missa, and if you say that the questions addressed by religion are 'nonsense or baby talk or trivial' ... [then] ... certain dimensions will be unavailable to you. Particularly today, when the atheist case is being put, if I may say so, with such vulgarity of mind." Adolescents need more dimensions and sensibilities, not fewer. As teachers, we must be older than the times we live in.

Among the hallmarks of adolescence are the keen perception of those "vulgarities of mind," the hypocrisies in adult culture, and a rising desire for something greater, more authentic, and vital. So, the third reason to match classic stories and adolescent development is to address their *natural ecstasies*, their organic breaking out-and-up period. Joan of Arc and Saint Teresa of Avila are archetypes of the grand opening of the sexual/spiritual realm in adolescence, but that opening is evident too in the frenzies, raves, edgy and profound music, mind-bending and nerve-knocking thrill-seeking horror movies, and the stunning, "what-were-you-thinking?" stunts so commonplace in the age. Adolescents burst with erotic power; they feel so alive! They are more easily fascinated, frightened, aroused, and charmed. And they have new obsessions and compulsions: with sex and love and others; with dark themes, especially about horror, death, and the supernatural; and with the bizarre, uncanny, and mysterious. They are given to emotional extremes and they live at a pitch barely contained in a short spread of years and carefully ignored when adulthood arrives. Far from ignoring emotions, classic stories (and harrowing rituals) for adolescents were created to match emotional intensity, volt for volt.

However, in modern, psychological times, we often tell children the wrong types of stories, ones that affirm and encourage self-authentication over transformation. Bruno Bettelheim (1976) says, "There is a widespread refusal to let children know that the source of much that goes wrong in life is due to our very own natures—the propensity of all men for acting aggressively, a-socially, selfishly, out of anger and anxiety" (p. 7). Classic stories challenge readers to change themselves rather than blame others. The difference between the two is exemplified by the two *Jungle Books,* produced by Disney (Taylor, 2016; Disney, 1967). The earlier version is a classic story, because young Mowgli must face archetypal predicaments and transform himself; he must grow up properly to fulfill his calling and to do his part in human society. In the live-action version, from 2016, Mowgli *stays* in the jungle in the end (confusing means and ends), untransformed, to hang out with his friends—none of which are human—which severs generational lines and makes him essentially *anti-cultural*. Similarly, in Disney's *Frozen* (2014) and the live-action *Mulan* (2020), there is no growth, *no transformation*, only a solipsistic stasis: *You are great just being you and everyone here is merely here to approve of you*. "Frozen" is an apt description of the modern, psychological story that favors affirmation over transformation. Frozen as in *static*. By contrast, Wendy ultimately learns to reject her erotic fantasy of "the boy who never grows up," embodied in Peter Pan, recognizing that he is stuck; he refuses to change. He cannot envision adulthood as a "grand adventure," as she does. Modern, bad stories cannot help adolescents in their excitement to change; they offer dull platitudes and a morbid sense of authenticity. True classic stories must deal with, in Bettelheim's words, the "problematic nature of life without being defeated by it, or giving into escapism" (p. 8).

Themes of Adolescence

Childhood is about *potentiality*: exploring and experimenting. *Adolescence* is about commitment: choosing, defining, focusing, and dedicating (Gopnik, 2016). This, not that, renouncing other options and potentials and getting to work. Childhood themes in stories are therefore distinct from those in adolescence. *Hansel & Gretel* teaches children that they can be resourceful enough to overcome parental failings. But adolescent themes are more about encouraging adolescents to remake themselves, hearing a call and rising to it. Below, we will identify four themes common to classic stories for adolescents: Erotics & Ecstasy; Power & Responsibility; Seeking Truth and Proper Authorities; and Transformation & Transcendence.

Erotics & Ecstasy

Change is coming, inside and out. Order is threatened, inside and out. Virility fires like a dragon, re-forming everything. You are surging with new life and new powers. Sexuality and spirituality are twins overtaking you. The Shire cannot contain you, and it is threatened.

You flee, or must flee, this order and venture into the Wilderness, the Great Unknown, the place of titanic forces of life and death where old rules and customs do not apply. Exodus! *Panic*! According to the poet Gary Snyder (1999), our opportunities in the wild are about getting in touch with our deeper—and more connected—spiritual sides, embracing the creative, imaginative, and feeling aspects of ourselves. And also a more creative, more imaginative and feeling side of ourselves. It is about life and death. Wilderness is uncontrolled Nature: the sacred mountain, the deep river. You are lost and wandering, uncertain how things work and how to succeed. It is mysterious and seemingly inscrutable. It is the place of the spiritual forces, "the force that through the green fuse drives the flower" (Thomas, 1971, p. 90), a place of reckoning, e.g., the Elephant Graveyard in *The Lion King* (Allers & Minkoff, 1994), in the vision quest, beyond the shire, e.g., *The Hobbit* and *Lord of the Rings*, and into the wilderness for Hansel & Gretel, Mowgli in *Jungle Book*, and the Biblical characters Moses and Jesus.

It is also the place of sexual forces. It animates Wendy and her stories of pirates, and crocodiles, and mermaids, and Indians, and a boy who never grows up, in *Peter Pan* (Barrie & Unwin, 1950). It is the Little Mermaid's opening to the wider world. It is the dangerous wilderness and its enticements—both flowers and wolves—that Little Red is told to avoid ("stay on the path"), if she wants to get to grandmotherhood. It is what Belle must take on to get out of her head and into her body (and with the third Masculine, the Beast who has learned to control his power and love) in *Beauty and the Beast*. It is what the queens and witches and stepmothers wish to stop when they lock Rapunzels into towers, enslave Cinderellas in service, and lull Beauties and Snow Whites into sleep. There are many jealous forces trying to blunt adolescence, keeping boys and girls on "Pleasure Islands," frightened, as they are, of the consequences of full-fledged adults in control of their sexual powers. And it is what Nala wishes to start when she cajoles Simba to take his place in the "Circle of Life" (*The Lion King*), and *Moana*, when she commits to leaving the island and breaching the security of the reef.

All children must reckon with their new sexual power in adolescence. Their changing bodies—curves and muscles—and new energies and desires unwittingly enroll them in a higher-level, complicated social game, something they have largely missed as children. Though recently children, these new adolescents must recognize that they will have a new standing in society and in the bigger game of life. They can sponsor new life. Earth-based cultures use rites of passage—including key stories told only at those moments—to help adolescents discipline their sexual energies in productive ways. Classic stories are replete with subconscious symbols about sexual ecstasies, responsibilities, and roles (especially as lovers, protectors, parents, and grandparents).

Power & Responsibility

You are gaining power; can you use it responsibly? You must discipline it, for reckless power endangers everyone. Simba, from *The Lion King* "can't wait to be king," but he, like Damocles, imagines only the benefits, including control over others. He does not see that he must accept the burden of leadership, *beginning with leadership over himself.* Are your new powers (eroticism, beauty, strength, intelligence, stamina) used to control others or to serve something greater? Are relationships based on love, respect, and dignity, or fear?

Young ones can identify with Snow White's or Cinderella's or Simba's or Nemo's innocence and naïveté about the adult world, and therefore can be warned about its perils. But they can also be warned about *their* future roles as parents and "kings" or "queens" of their adult realms and the ways that they can spoil their reigns. They can see what can go wrong in the kingdom when the rulers are wicked, feckless, or negligent: with Scar versus Mufasa in *The Lion King*; Snow White's and Cinderella's stepmothers, in the Queen of Hearts, in *Alice in Wonderland*; with the Beast in *Beauty and the Beast*; and with Edmund, Reagan, and Goneril, and King Lear himself in *King Lear*; and in the sultan in *Aladdin*. What will you do as an adult to ensure your proper kingdom is made and maintained? What is your place and will you take on the discipline that it demands? Sexuality is foundational power. Is it constructive?

Seeking Truth & Proper Authorities/Order

Your childhood, low-resolution schemes (Piaget, 1952) cannot accommodate all of this information. You need a bigger and more detailed map for a much bigger territory, one that will naturally contain mysterious, undiscovered, and potentially hazardous places. Part of becoming an adolescent means turning away from primary attachments and looking for secondary ones, including older mentors (classically embodied in apprenticeships). But whom to trust? Classic adolescent adventure stories present this dilemma for the hero in terms of false and genuine authorities. False authorities are those who exploit, flatter, or indulge: The Wizard of Oz; Jabar in *Aladdin*; Pinocchio's Fox, Cat, and Lampwick/Candlewick (wordplay on "Lucifer"); and the Python mesmerizing Mowgli. Other false authorities include hapless helpers: Scuttle and Flounder for Ariel in the *Little Mermaid*; Pumba and Timon leading Simba to hedonism in *Lion King*; Jiminy Cricket as the bungling apprentice authority in *Pinocchio*; and the Seven Dwarves (neither paternal nor sexual candidates; they only eat and work) in *Snow White*. There are wrong gender roles: the thief-husband in Rapunzel; Belle's three masculine roles to consider (her feckless father, the blowhard Gascon, and the Beast); and Laius, Oedipus's father. There are wrong rulers, led by appetite, greed, lust, and selfishness.

In these classic stories, disaster looms (the Wilderness in *Jungle Book*, etc.; the hyenas & Elephant Graveyard in *The Lion King*). The old order is crumbling, and without proper action chaos will reign. So, you must seek *new authorities*: wizards, ladies in lakes, and hermits with keys. And you must rise to the challenge to create a new order where many can flourish. But you need help. Genuine authorities are those who see the potential in you and seek to coax it from you. They will not flatter or simply affirm you; they challenge you to get over your limited sense of self, to take responsibility, and to dedicate yourself to a higher cause: Gandalf, from *Lord of the Rings*; Obi-Wan Kenobi in *Star Wars*; the fairy godmothers in *Cinderella, Sleeping Beauty* (Carruthers, 2015), and *Snow White*; the stars for Simba in *The Lion King*.

Transformation & Transcendence

How comfortable are you with change? It is inevitable. Do you embrace it or run from it, frantically keeping everything in place, as it was, so that you can feel safe? Or, could you expect it and use it to transform and transcend your older, inadequate self? Could it transform your community into something better? Disaster (the stars falling out of place) challenges all to adapt and transcend, or die. Can you rise to the challenge? Classic stories teach that

Chaos is the close relative of Order—Dionysius/Apollo; Seth/Osiris; Night/Day; T'Challa/Erik Killmonger; Cain/Abel; Loki/Thor; Edmund/Edward (*King Lear*); Scar/Mufasa (*The Lion King*)—so it cannot be just an enemy to vanquish. It must be part of life. Incorporate it.

The allure of transformation appears in several guises in classic stories. The thing you *could* become is the real goal, but it takes the form of the gold in the cave, the sacred ring, the sword in the stone, the treasure in the lair guarded by the dragon. It's Hercules's seven tasks, Dorothy's "Somewhere over the rainbow," and of course the obstacles: what you fear most (the West Wing in *Bluebeard/Beauty & the Beast*; Voldemort in *Harry Potter*; the whale in *Pinocchio*, the Huns in *Mulan*, the open ocean in *Moana* and *Nemo*; and the many dragons princes must defeat. Furthermore, the thing you could become can't be gained without an all-out struggle, even unto death (Joseph and the angel in the *Bible*; Osiris; Orpheus; Black Panther; the Evil Empire in *Star Wars*).

Many classic stories are written to excite the imagination and the will of young ones to prepare them for the challenges ahead, both inside and out. They hint that much of what is seen outside—as a danger or an opportunity—mirrors to a great extent what is happening on the inside, and it's growing. Four adolescent themes have been identified here with connections made to actual classic stories. Now we must show more explicitly how these classic stories can be dealt with in the classroom by students of teacher education and by their future students, to better understand their own adolescence.

Classics in the College Classroom

Development is normally taught in the foundations sections of teacher education programs and typically divided into physical, neural/cognitive, emotional, social, and sometimes moral segments. All are ripe for classic stories to illustrate the potential and consequences of a child's development into adolescence. Further, the stories add richness and dimension to understanding, allowing the student chances to supersede the usual clinical, de-spirited approach to the subject in formal schooling. The child will often resist the stiff moralism of the school or church lesson, and yet flee to the screen or the page for the same lesson, this time involving goblins, sorcerers, and magical deaths and resurrections. The teacher or the parent can give "the talk" to a child about to enter adolescence or, as an alternative, utilize stories like *Little Red*

Riding Hood, The Little Mermaid, Snow White, Sleeping Beauty, Cinderella, Jack and the Beanstalk (Malaspina, 2013), or *Jungle Book*.

Lessons using classic stories can go at least two layers deep: first, to inform the future teacher about adolescent development in a more holistic way (and, of course, to locate her own adolescent development in that frame); and second, for that future teacher's students, to better inform themselves about the issues and choices they are or will be facing. They are good for students *and* teachers, to give *both* a sense of direction, purpose, and meaning. Expressing it in a formula, we might say, Facts − context = nonsense. To make sense, teachers should add classic stories about growing, especially about the ecstatic, erotic, and spiritual qualities of growing up.

At base, they can be classic stories such as *Huckleberry Finn, A Separate Peace, Of Mice and Men*, and *To Kill a Mockingbird*—the kinds of stories the renowned educator Rafe Esquith (2007) uses in his fifth-grade class to help burgeoning adolescents move from heteronomy to autonomy, that is, from simple obedience to the rules of family and society, to the beginning of a more independent mind and greater moral responsibility. He uses the stories to put kids imaginatively in moral and emotional dilemmas to anticipate future challenges to their integrity. Will they just go along with what society and their peers want or do they stand on their own, on principle?

While Esquith's choices of novels are powerful and affecting, they are too realistic and straightforward, and therefore insufficient for our purposes here. At a higher level are the myths, with the archetypes and themes of transformation and transcendence. They should be transformation-centered and involve significant, threshold experiences (see the list and themes above). But some qualifications are necessary before making classroom recommendations.

First, there is no one-to-one correspondence between classic story and result (which frustrates equally the administrator and the didact). This can neither be taught nor taken in a direct way, as a kind of vaccination. Similarly, in spite of what is suggested here, these stories cannot be too precisely defined or delineated, for several reasons:

1. The older, more classic tales are multi-dimensional, with multiple entry points, and full of mystery, both literally and figuratively, which is why children and adults return to them and find *something else* in the story or a different perspective, given their current predicament.

2. We often do not know why we are attracted to some tales and not to others, why some resonate and others do not. The attractive ones seem to "speak to us" at deeper, subconscious levels, which means we really cannot explain it to ourselves.
3. The more didactic the tale, the less likely it will effect transformation.
4. Finally, it leaves out the important role of the reader/listener, in constituting the meaning, often in subconscious ways. After all, the story does not stand on its own.

As explained in an earlier section, development encompasses much more than the discrete, clinically approved changes. Yes, the traditional segments of development in terms of physical, cognitive, emotional, moral, and social must be understood, but they are insufficient, and they lack integration at higher levels, connected to meaning and purpose. Piaget's constructivist theory (1952), especially scheme theory, and the fourth level of cognitive reasoning, hypothetico-deductive; Lev Vygotsky's (1978) social constructivism, especially the role of the more knowledgeable other in learning; Alison Gopnik's (2016) evolutionary psychology; Bandura's (1997) theory of self-efficacy; and Kohlberg's (1981) six levels of moral development can be mapped onto the stories and vice versa. The recommendation would be to continue with the usual content of adolescent development but use one or two classic stories to provide greater meaning, purpose, and context for this development. Below is a list of possible assignments and activities to make the adolescent development content more obvious and practicable to the students.

Suggested Assignments and Activities

1. Update a classic story with contemporary content. For example, take *Pinocchio*. Keep the essential spirit, trials, and twists, but change the content to make it a story about growing up today. If you were in Collodi's shoes, trying to teach children about the hazards, challenges, and necessities of growing up in today's world—while preserving the archetypal/timeless issues—how would you tell the story? Argue for your changes. For instance, could Pinocchio be a robot instead of a puppet? What would today's versions be of "Pleasure Island/Island of Blockheads," of hedonism? What are today's versions of donkeys and salt mines? What is equivalent to the whale? What are today's versions of shortcuts to power,

fame, status, and wealth instead of true dedication to and sacrifice for one's true development (would, for instance, YouTube Influencer be a similar shortcut on the real work of development)? What is authentic (taking responsibility, serving something greater) vs. inauthentic (gaining power without responsibility) development in today's modes?

2. Take Pinocchio and make a version explicitly for girls. How could "Pinocchia" be changed to reach today's girls facing significant obstacles to growing up? And especially, what might have to be changed completely to better reflect the existential issues not addressed in *Pinocchio*? (Of course, this assignment could apply to any classic story that seems to be pitched more to one gender than to another.)

The above two assignments are especially stimulating when assigned to mixed groups. Structure places where they must discuss and debate their perspectives, to air their opinions. The younger they are, the more that you will have to structure the assignment to ensure that proper discussions and debates take place and that roles are assigned and well understood.

3. Students create an Adolescent Development Game: This would be a culminating activity, preferably announced at the beginning of the unit with drafts submitted throughout. Students, alone or in groups, would design a game called "Adolescence" (a board or video game, for instance), where they have to create goals/objectives, incentives, hazards, costs, and benefits, similar to what you find in adventure stories and games. Pattern it after successful games, such as Monopoly. What does it mean to "win" at Adolescence? What could cause you to lose points or regress in the game? Can Adolescence be "won" without defeating or undermining others? If so, how?

4. Design a Team Competition: This is a version of the above but with teams competing for the best designs for adolescent flourishing. That is, each team would have to design the best conditions for adolescents to grow and flourish and then to persuade the judges through promotional materials and presentations that theirs is the best design. Perhaps the team designs a theme park exclusively for adolescents but involving the full range of needed experiences (e.g., a simulation, like Westworld).

5. Myths of Growing Up Assignment: Students choose a favorite myth or fairy tale from childhood about growing up and then analyze it in terms

of its messages to youth. What made it so compelling to you? What makes it mythological? What one element would you change to change the message most (e.g., the protagonist's background; her mission, etc.)? Present to the class a couple of key scenes and run a discussion on its messages to adolescents.

6. Gender Lines and Parameters Questions: Take a classic, such as *Beauty and the Beast*, and analyze its messages to adolescents about the roles presented and the opportunities and hazards therein. For instance, the story presents to Belle at least four types of masculinity, none of which can match her: the sweet but feckless one (her father); the braggart/egotist who wants a trophy wife (Gascon); the cowardly, overly domesticated, and servile ones (the village men); and the powerful but heartless one (the Beast). A key part of growing up is figuring out the proper relationship with the other sex and its roles. What messages do you take from this story about these roles and Belle's ultimate match?

7. Similarly, classic stories often show the risks of males and females failing to integrate. For instance, in *Pinocchio*, the boys are on Pleasure Island/Island of Blockheads, by themselves, away from females. Alone in their pleasures, they turn into braying jackasses, incapable of speech. When you replace your voice with stupid braying, when you lose independent speech, there is a high probability that you'll become enslaved to a tyrant and his/her ideological speech. Solzhenitsyn (1973/2007) noted that the Stalinists thrown in the gulag couldn't be reached or helped until they repented, and began to line up language to reality, once again regaining the power of independent speech. What do students see in their lives that are versions of braying/ideological speech, turning adolescent boys and girls into jackasses in service to tyrants?

There are rich opportunities for discussion and investigation into the ecstasies of adolescent development. This is just a sample. Teachers should reinvest in classic stories, to enrich their students' education, using parables, symbols, and analogies to teach the imagination to support creativity and resilience over anxiety about the present and future.

References

Allers, R., & Minkoff, R. (Directors). (1994). *The lion king*. [Film; DVD]. Buena Vista Home Entertainment.

Alighieri, D. (1948). *The divine comedy*. New York: Pantheon. (Original work published 1742)
Anderson, H. (2013). *The little mermaid: The classic edition*. Applesauce. (Original work published 1837)
Bandura, A. (1997). *Self-efficacy: The exercise of control*. Worth.
Barrie, J. M., & Unwin, N. S. (1950). *Peter Pan*. Scribner. (Original work published 1902)
Baum, F. (2021). *The wonderful wizard of Oz*. East India Publishing Company. (Original work published 1900)
Bettelheim, B. (1976). *The uses of enchantment: The meaning and importance of fairy tales*. Vintage.
Buck, C. (Director). (2014). *Frozen*. [Film; DVD]. Buena Vista Home Entertainment.
Bunyan, J. (1999). *Pilgrim's progress*. Wordsworth Editions. (Original work published 1678)
Caro, N. (Director). (2020). *Mulan*. [Film; DVD]. Buena Vista Home Entertainment.
Carroll, L. (1993). *Alice's adventures in Wonderland*. Dover Thrift. (Original work published 1865)
Carruthers, A. (2015). *Sleeping Beauty and other tales of sleeping princesses (Origins of Fairy Tales from Around the World)*. Pook.
Chaucer, G. (2013). *The complete Canterbury Tales*. Arcturus. (Original work published 1387)
Crichton, M. (Director). (2000). *Westworld*. [Film; DVD]. Warner Brothers Home Entertainment.
Clements, R., & Musker, J. (Directors). (2017). *Moana*. [Film; DVD]. Buena Vista Home Entertainment.
Collodi, C. (1995). *Pinocchio*. Grolier. (Original work published 1883)
Coogler, R. (Director). (2018). *Black Panther*. [Film; DVD]. Buena Vista Home Entertainment.
Disney, W. (Producer). (2007). *Peter Pan*. [Film; DVD]. Buena Vista Home Entertainment. (Original film produced 1953)
Disney, W. (Producer). (1967). *The jungle book*. [Film; DVD]. Buena Vista Home Entertainment.
Erikson, E. H. (1980). *Identity and the life cycle*. Norton.
Esquith, R. (2007). *Teach like your hair's on fire: The methods and madness inside room 56*. Penguin.
Favreau, J. (Director). (2016). *Jungle book*. [Film; DVD]. Buena Vista Home Entertainment.
Fletcher, A. (2021). *Wonderworks: The 25 most powerful inventions in the history of literature*. Simon & Schuster.
Gennep, A. (1960). *The rites of passage*. University of Chicago Press. (Original work published 1909)
Gopnik, A. (2016). *The gardener and the carpenter: What the new science of child development tells us about the relationship between parents and children*. Farrar, Strauss, and Giroux.
Grimm, J., & Grimm, W. (2019). *Snow White: The classic edition*. Applesauce. (Original work published 1812)
Grimm, J., & Grimm, W. (1997). *Rapunzel*. Dutton. (Original work published 1812)
Grimm, J., & Grimm, W. (1916). *Hansel and Gretel: Full 1916 uncensored color reproduction*. Chump Change. (Original work published 1812)
Homer. (1997). *The odyssey*. New York: Viking. (Original work published 1488)
Houseman, L. (2019). *Aladdin and the wonderful lamp*. Dover. (Original work published 1704)
Jones, G. (2003). *Killing monsters: Why children need fantasy, superheroes, and make-believe violence*. Basic.
Kendrick, W. M. (1991). *The thrill of fear: 250 years of scary entertainment*. Grove Weidenfeld.

Knowles, J. (2003). *A separate peace*. Scribner.
Kohlberg, L. (1981). *The philosophy of moral development*. Harper & Row.
Kovacs, M. G. (1998). *The Epic of Gilgamesh*. https://archive.org/details/epic-of-gilgamesh (Original translation published 1880)
Lee, H. (1983). *To kill a mockingbird*. Mass Paperback.
Lewis, C. S. (2017). *The C. S. Lewis signature classics*. HarperOne. (Original work published 1943)
Lucas, G. (2004). *Star Wars trilogy: Collector's edition, episodes IV-VI*. Scholastic.
Malaspina, A. (2013). *Jack and the beanstalk: An English folktale*. Child's World.
Perrault, C. (1996). *Little Red Riding Hood and other stories: Illustrated by W. Heath Robinson* (Everyman's Library Children's Classics Series). Everyman's Library.
Perrault, C. (1954). *Cinderella: Or the little glass slipper*. Charles Scribner's Sons. (Original work published 1697)
Piaget, J. (1952). *The origins of intelligence in children*. International Universities.
Rowling, J. (2009). *Harry Potter paperback set*. Arthur Levine.
Shakespeare, W. (1994). *King Lear*. Dover Thrift.
Shattuck, R. (1999). *Candor and perversion: Literature, education, and the arts*. Norton.
Snyder, G., & Thoms, M. (1999). *Deep ecology series*. New Dimensions Foundations.
Solzhenitsyn, A. (2007). *The Gulag Archipelago - An experiment in literary investigation*. Harper. (Original work published 1973)
Sophocles. (2005). *Oedipus the king (Enriched Classics)*. Simon & Schuster. (Original work published ca. 425 BCE)
Steinbeck, J. (1993). *Of mice and men*. Penguin. (Original work published 1937)
Steiner, G., & Taylor, C. (2008, April 18). "Il postino." *The Guardian*.
Swift, J. (1997). *Gulliver's travels*. Wordsworth Editions. (Original work published 1726)
Thomas, D. (1971). *The poems of Dylan Thomas*. D. Jones (Ed.). New Directions. (Original work published 1934)
Tolkien, J. (2020). *Lord of the rings: 3-book paperback box set*. Clarion. (Original work published 1954)
Trueman, C. R., & Dreher, R. (2020a). *The rise and triumph of the modern self: Cultural amnesia, expressive individualism, and the road to sexual revolution*. Crossway.
Trueman, C. (2020b, November 9). The rise of psychological man. *Public Discourse*. https://www.thepublicdiscourse.com/2020/11/72156/.
Turner, V. W. (1969). *The ritual process: Structure and anti-structure*. Aldine Publishing Company.
Twain, M. (1996). *The adventures of Huckleberry Finn*. Random House. (Original work published 1885)
Villeneuve, M. (2017). *Madame de Villeneuve's original Beauty and the Beast – Illustrated by Edward Corbould and Brothers Dalziel*. Pook. (Original work published 1740)
Von Franz, M.-L. (1995). *Shadow and evil in fairy tales*. Shambhala.
Vygotsky, L. (1978). *Mind in society; the development of higher psychological processes*. Harvard Press.
Warner, M. (2014). *Once upon a time: A short history of fairy tale*. Oxford University Press.
Yeats, W. B. (1957). *The variorum edition of the poems of W. B. Yeats* (P. Allt & R. K. Alspach, Eds.). Macmillan. (Original work published 1920)

TWO

 Teacher Resilience and the Lessons of *Great Expectations*

Frank Giuseffi

JOHN CHARLES HUFFAM DICKENS (1812–1870) was a Victorian author of well-known novels such as *A Christmas Carol, A Tale of Two Cities*, and *Hard Times*. Dickens was known by many of his contemporaries as the writer of his time; he is arguably responsible for the modern English language novel (Pykett, 2002). Besides writing 14 extensive novels, Dickens wrote several nonfiction books, speeches, and plays; he also spent time as a journalist, owned his own literary magazines, and even dabbled in the theater (Slater, 2011). Dickens' themes and characters in his novels called attention to the crime, poverty, child labor, and other social ills that existed in his day (Himmelfarb, 2006). Dickens' social criticism also included issues with education. The novels *Hard Times, Oliver Twist, David Copperfield*, and *Great Expectations* explore the topic of education on several levels. Placing education as paramount in many of his works may indicate Dickens' own disappointment with his lack of formal education (McIntosh & Schweizer, 2012). In *Great Expectations* the theme of education is presented both in specific scenes of schooling and more broadly in the overall education of the main protagonist, Pip. Pip's education consists of formal yet ineffectual schooling common at the time among the lower classes of England. Readers will discover, however, that Pip has a far more wide-ranging education in the challenges he encounters as a young man of "great expectations." The ways Pip reacts to these challenges in light of the expectations he sets for himself instructs us on the importance of resiliency. For this reason, we turn to *Great Expectations*[1] and Richardson's Resiliency Model (1990) as a wellspring for teachers to develop their resiliency as they enter their professions. Teachers will have their own "great expectations"; however, as Pip struggles to do, they must be ready to adjust their expectations to build resiliency and flourish in their careers.[2]

To fully explore this thesis, this chapter first presents the importance of resiliency in the teaching profession. Second, it discusses a particular resiliency framework known as Richardson's Resiliency Model. Third, it summarizes and analyzes the major events in Pip's life through Richardson's Resiliency Model. Lastly, the chapter discusses how teachers can build their own resiliency through Richardson's Resiliency Model and from Pip's experiences.

The Importance of Resiliency in Teaching

Teachers must be resilient to the stressful situations that will invariably occur in their profession. To be resilient means to remain optimistic and to recover from and improve through challenges (Mullen et al., 2021). Resiliency is connected to the way individuals respond to challenges and difficulties; it is an active process that includes the person and the contexts they find themselves in (Mansfield et al., 2012). Resiliency has also been associated with personal attributes such as self-confidence and a belief in oneself (Beltman et al., 2011).

There are several positive outcomes that result from teacher resiliency. Being resilient has been associated with improved well-being, job satisfaction, and teacher retention (Fernandes et al., 2020; Mullen et al., 2021). Teacher resiliency is also a key quality in improving instruction and engaging and motivating students (Crosswell & Beutel, 2016). Teacher resiliency can develop through learned strategies and also acting from core values and personal beliefs (Mullen et al., 2021). For the purposes of this chapter, we look to Richardson's (1990) Resiliency Model as the framework to explore Pip's resiliency. Through that analysis, teachers can reflect on and enhance their own resiliency, which in turn can lead to important educational outcomes for both them and their students.

Richardson's Resiliency Model

Richardson's (1990) Resiliency Model was originally a framework to develop protective factors in health education (Figure 2.1). Upon closer examination, however, the model applies well to those involved in pedagogical pursuits. Richardson (1990) posits that resiliency develops from the interactions between individuals and their environments as opposed to it being fundamentally an attribute in the individual. According to Richardson (1990), resiliency is the:

process of coping with disruptive, stressful or challenging life events in a way that provides the individual with additional protective and coping skills than prior to the disruption that results from the event. When a person is faced with a challenge, a new experience, a major stressor or life event, the resilient person may temporarily experience change, sense some personal doubt, and experience some disorganization of his/her[their] worldview. In time however, he/she[they] will use reintegrative and coping skills that allow the individual to learn, develop new skills, and effectively deal with the life events. (p. 34)

Richardson's (1990) model works from the assertion that to develop resiliency the individual must accept and endure challenges and stressors, experience disorganization, reorganize their life, gain new knowledge from the challenging experience, and then emerge with new coping strategies known as protective factors. The essential elements of the framework include biopsychospiritual homeostasis, life events, biopsychospiritual protective factors, interaction, disruption, disorganization, and reintegration, which consists of four different kinds.

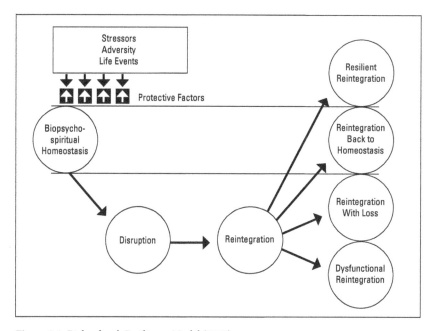

Figure 2.1. Richardson's Resiliency Model (1990).
Note: From "Reaching Resilience: Research Made Readable," by Denis Thomas. https://denisannthomas.wordpress.com/2011/04/08/the-resilience-model/richardsons-resilience-model-3/

According to Richardson (1990), biopsychospiritual homeostasis is the general state of stability and comfortability with one's biological and physical state. Biological homeostasis is when the individual's body physically reacts to any biological or physical instability. An example would be the individual perspiring as a response to increased body temperature. Psychological homeostasis strives to attain a desired psychological state. A positive strategy when experiencing a psychological imbalance would be exercising, while an unproductive one would be showing a fit of anger by committing acts of violence. Spiritual homeostasis occurs when there is congruency between the individual's belief system and behaviors. Spiritual homeostasis is disrupted when the individual's belief system and behaviors are incongruent. The result will be the person feeling guilty and revert back to the belief system. The intention is for the individual to always return to a balanced and stable homeostatic state.

> In essence, the individual in homeostasis is most comfortable with an intact worldview much like a puzzle. When the pieces fit and are in place, then there is a tendency to fight to maintain that worldview and the addition or subtraction of any additional pieces is resisted because it necessitates change. (p. 35)

Richardson (1990) defines "life events" by drawing from the psychosocial stressors as discussed by Erikson (1963), the stages of cognitive development developed by Piaget (1952), and the theories on moral development by Kohlberg (1976). Broadly speaking, however, Richardson (1990) notes how life events include "the barrage of positive and negative influences in a person's life that may cause disruption or changes" (p. 35). This becomes apparent with Pip; he encounters several positive and negative life events. Likewise, teachers will experience both life-affirming events such as efficacious lessons, improved student achievement, and professional knowledge. Teachers, however, will also confront troublesome events that impede self-efficacy and confidence in their pedagogical abilities. These events may include classroom management issues, little or no professional development, or lack of administrative support.

To Richardson (1990), there are protective factors that help the individual navigate through life events and build resiliency. These factors can be biological and psychospiritual. Biological factors can be genetic, such as fitness level, medical condition, pain tolerance, and duration of recovery. Many biological factors can be controlled through physical activity, workout routines, regular rest, and healthy nutrition. There are many psychospiritual protective factors that can be implemented when dealing with stressful situations; these include healthy self-esteem, purpose in life, self-control, effective decision-making skills, and a positive outlook on the future.

Interaction is when the individual applies the coping strategies (protective factors) to the life event. According to Richardson (1990), the particular life event should guide the individual in choosing the best suited strategy. Richardson (1990) goes on to argue, "The individual will either negotiate easily or have some difficulty which will lead him/her[them] into the next vital stage of the resiliency enhancing process, disruption" (p. 36). *Disruption* can be a positive state for the individual. While it may be an unsettling experience to move past the biopsychospiritual state, the disruptive stage is an opportunity for the individual to grow in self-reflection and develop the competencies to confront life events. The momentary state of *Disorganization* occurs when the biopsychospiritual "pieces" of an individual's life become disrupted, "such as with a new challenge and the person has to implement a plan to attack the challenge without having previous related experiences" (p. 36). There may be a complete disintegration of the individual's previous experiences, skills, and worldview when dealing with the life event. But this opens up an opportunity for the creation of new supports and new pieces that can be added to the individual's life experiences that deal with the new life event. During *Reintegration*, the individual attempts to "recover by creatively putting the pieces back together or by systematically problem solving and rebuilding" (p. 37). Reintegration can occur in four ways: resilient reintegration, homeostatic reintegration, maladaptive reintegration, and dysfunctional reintegration. Resilient reintegration is the highest, most productive level in adapting to a new life event. The individual enhances their original protective factors or develops new protective factors such as being more self-aware and self-motivated, being able to learn new skills, becoming task oriented, and possessing a clearer understanding of needed coping skills. Homeostatic reintegration is the individual's attempt to return to the original state of dealing with life events, using the same skills and protective factors. There is a strong possibility that the individual will continually experience the same stress based on the event unless there is an effort to develop new coping skills. Continually reverting to the original protective factors will not effectively address the new challenge. Maladaptive reintegration is when the individual actually loses their original coping skills due to the force and influence of the life event. The life event is so traumatic and impactful that the individual resigns themself to a less effective state of functioning. Lastly, dysfunctional reintegration occurs when the individual uses destructive measure to cope. They, in effect, need counseling. These individuals will reintegrate through harmful means: substance abuse, psychopathic behavior, suicide, and other dysfunctional coping skills.

Pip's Biopsychospiritual Homeostasis and Life Events

In *Great Expectations*, the main character Pip experiences several life events and stressors that force him to confront his own motivations, values, and "great expectations." Pip's "great expectation," which is to be a gentleman, is so strong that it eclipses any ability to adapt, adjust, or modify his life goals, thereby making it difficult for him to contend with difficult circumstances. It is not until the closing of the novel that Pip exhibits some coping skills and capacity to build resiliency in order to reintegrate and improve. Teachers may possess the same stubbornness as Pip in that they have their own persistent views about their expectations concerning teaching. Yet those expectations often do not comport with the realities of the profession.

Generally, we do not receive a clear picture of Pip's biopsychospiritual homeostasis or his attempt to find ways biologically, psychologically, or spiritually to curb his emotions and return to his original state. Yet it is clear that Pip's many life events influence his emotional state. Pip begins his life in sorrowful circumstances. The novel opens with him viewing his parents' and five young siblings' gravestones. It can be surmised that Pip has undergone some sort of trauma; he informs the reader that he is on the verge of tears as he views the graves in a dark and grim environment. But one unpleasant event is met with another as an escaped prisoner, Abel Magwitch, violently leaps upon him. On physical threat from the prisoner, Pip returns with food and a healthy fear of the prisoner. Although Magwitch, along with another prisoner named Compeyson, will be caught and sent back to prison, the forbidding character will emerge again as a major influence in Pip's life. Pip's distressing life event with Magwitch is balanced by the mundane life with his guardians, the humble and decent Joe Gargery, Pip's brother-in-law who he refers to as "Uncle Joe," and his high-strung and authoritarian sister, "Mrs. Joe." Pip learns to be a blacksmith from his uncle. To Pip the work of a blacksmith is unsatisfying. Indeed, Pip admits to Biddy, a good-natured and caring housemaid who assists Joe and Mrs. Joe, that he is miserable and wishes to go beyond his current station in life. Nonetheless, Pip finds some enjoyment as a companion to Dickens' colorful yet foreboding character, Miss Havisham, who still wears her wedding dress as an apparent sign of an earlier time being left at the altar on her wedding day. It is a different sort of life event that Pip has when he meets Estella, Miss Havisham's adopted daughter. Pip falls in love with Estella and commits to improving himself to be worthy of her. Another life event occurs when Pip receives an unannounced visit from Mr. Jaggers, a sly lawyer from London. Jaggers articulates the great opportunity for Pip to Joe Gargery:

> "that he [Pip] will come into a handsome property. Further, that it is the desire of the present possessor of that property that he be immediately removed from his present sphere of life and from this place, and be brought up as a gentleman—in a word, as a young fellow of great expectations." (p. 154)

It is this last life event that throws Pip into a world of excitement, competition, and status in London. This life event will also set in motion a number of other challenges that Pip will find difficult to navigate through. In the same way, as teachers enter the exhilarating world of teaching and learning, they will also be confronted with various challenging situations that they, like Pip, will struggle to respond to effectively. These challenges may include being able to meet children's academic needs, knowing the most effective instructional strategies to implement in diverse classrooms, or offering appropriate and helpful feedback to students' assignments.

Pip's Experiences with Disruption and Disorganization

The disruptive state and the disorganization that soon follows emerges as Pip becomes a resident of London. Initially, one could argue Pip follows Richardson's (1990) claim that disruption can be a positive move for individuals. As Richardson (1990) writes:

> Many people take on challenges or stressors because they know of the growth opportunities. The disruption may not be of a depressing nature but rather an excitement to master or accomplish. The disruption still occurs in that the experience is new and pieces of previous experiences must be taken to form a new perspective to face the challenge at hand. (p. 36)

Richardson's assertion reflects what teachers may experience. Teachers will undoubtedly realize instructing students is challenging, but it is those difficulties and stressful situations that make it a valuable learning opportunity. Pip fails to realize this during his time in London.

Referring back to Pip's earlier conversation with Biddy, he desires self-improvement and is excited about the prospects he may encounter moving to London, especially the possibility of being a gentleman as articulated by Mr. Jaggers. Therefore, we may credit Pip as being willing to venture into new territory and embrace disruption. The disruptive experiences in London, however, prove to be problematic. When Pip arrives, he meets Herbert Pockett. Pip first met Herbert as a competitor in a puerile boxing match at Miss Havisham's home. A well-mannered, refined person, Herbert, like Pip, wishes to seek his own fortune. Pip depends on Herbert to teach him the manners and behaviors of a gentleman. This convivial first meeting and eventual bond with Herbert is balanced by his troublesome encounter with Bentley Drummle, someone "who was so sulky a fellow that he even took up a book as if its writer had done him an injury" (p. 221). Drummle will be an annoyance for Pip throughout the novel. While in London, Pip receives a visit from his Uncle Joe. Different emotions and feelings run through both individuals during their visit. Joe has dressed as a person of means and refers to Pip as "sir." Pip recognizes Joe's "good honest face all glowing and shining . . ." (p. 239). As they sit down to eat, Pip informs readers of his observations about Joe; his uncomfortable clothes, his foibles during the meal, and how he felt "impatient of him and out of temper with him; in which condition he heaped coals of fire on my head" (p. 242). Joe informs Pip that Estella would like to see him again. During their visit, Joe has a serious epiphany about who he is as a person. Joe tells Pip that he cannot pretend to be something he is not; this is manifested in Joe's clothes, which he realizes he should not have worn.

> I'm wrong in these clothes. I'm wrong out of the forge, the kitchen, or off th' meshes. You won't find half so much fault in me if, you think of me in my forge dress, with my hammer in my hand, or even my pipe. (p. 244)

With these words, Pip recognizes his uncle's "simple dignity" and begins to understand the honorable person his Uncle Joe is. We may surmise that the only reason Pip can come to this conclusion is because he is able to contrast it with his own goals and expectations. Pip does not seem to change for the better after recognizing his uncle's character. When teachers ultimately enter the profession and encounter such honesty from others, whether that be from a colleague, former teacher, mentor, or friend, they should learn from those experiences and use them to ponder, develop, and adjust their expectations.

On seeing Estella again, Pip marvels at her beauty but also recognizes her pride and strength of will. We notice a moment of clarity and honesty in Pip's own flawed expectations. To Pip, Estella personifies the temporal and fleeting wants and desires he developed after being told of having a benefactor. Pip states: "Truly it was impossible to dissociate her presence from all those wretched hankerings after money and gentility that had disturbed my boyhood—from all those ill-regulated aspirations that had first made me ashamed of home and Joe" (p. 256). We may argue it is unfair of Pip to implicitly blame Estella for his inordinate desires. We can, however, understand how her personage represents a kind of world Pip chose to pursue. Ironically, teachers may formulate their expectations based on past teachers whom they considered models of excellent teaching. An overemphasis, however, on emulating another highly respected teacher may add to unrealistic expectations. In other words, the admiration a new teacher has for a former teacher creates an idealistic worldview about the profession and misplaced expectations.

In regard to his professional life in London, Pip erroneously considers himself "a first-rate man of business—prompt, decisive, energetic, clear, cool-headed" (p. 299). Yet this does not translate into reality. Pip runs up debts and irresponsibly spends the money given to him from his anonymous benefactor. Pip also expresses a nagging anxiety about the possibilities of his so-called expectations. But things change when on a stormy and windy evening, another important life event happens. Pip notices a stranger speaking to him from the shadows down the staircase of his abode. Pip invites him in and shockingly realizes the figure is Magwitch, the prisoner we were introduced to at the beginning of the story. From this moment on, surprises abound through the rest of the novel. Pip discovers that it was Magwitch who was the anonymous benefactor. We learn the reasons for Magwitch's financial support of Pip, "I've made a gentleman on you!" (p. 345), Magwitch exclaims to Pip. Magwitch proudly tells Pip that as a shepherd, every guinea he earned went to Pip. Magwitch is elated to see the comfortable lodgings, the elegant clothes, and the many books stacked around Pip's room. For Magwitch, the superficial material objects reflect Pip's success. Although we may conclude Magwitch's criteria for Pip's success is low, we also sympathize with the convict in his sincere desire to help Pip. All of this, of course, leads Pip to a moment of crisis but also lucidity; his thought that Miss Havisham was the benefactor was mistaken and his belief in how his journey toward becoming a gentleman began was destroyed.

> For an hour or more, I remained too stunned to think; and it was not until I began to think that I began fully to know how wrecked I was, and how the ship in which I had sailed was gone to pieces. (p. 348)

To reference Richardson (1990), during these disruptive events, Pip is in a disorganizing state of affairs. Pip's excitement about living in London and desire to be successful and achieve status collides with unforeseen events. But out of the stressful events emerges a conscience that reminds him of how he treated Joe and Biddy: "I suppose because my sense of my own worthless conduct to them was greater than every consideration. No wisdom on earth could have given me the comfort that I should have derived from their simplicity and fidelity..." (p. 349).

As mentioned earlier, a variety of life events occur in the teaching profession. If the teacher cannot negotiate the issue with their current coping skills, then disruption can occur. This can consequently lead to disorganization and elicit feelings of despair in their pedagogical abilities. But as argued by Richardson, the disruptive event can be an opportunity for growth and self-knowledge for teachers as they figure out how to navigate through the challenge. For instance, one can imagine the self-reflection a new teacher may go through as they consider their ineffective response to a student's misbehavior. While this disruptive stage may be unpleasant, the teacher leverages the experience as a time for professional and even personal growth.

Pip's meeting with Magwitch results in two important outcomes: Magwitch's joy in Pip's ostensibly great success and Pip's knowledge about his own behavior. While this is a positive turn in the story, trouble still lies ahead. Magwitch tells Pip that, as a deported prisoner, he cannot be seen by authorities in London; therefore, Pip, with Herbert's help, assists in Magwitch's escape to Hamburg. Before the escape plan is set in motion, Pip visits Miss Havisham to tell her what he learned about who was the true benefactor. Pip discovers Miss Havisham already knew who the benefactor was but allowed Pip to believe it was her. During this same visit, Pip discovers that Estella is to marry, of all people, Bentley Drummle.

During the process of helping Magwitch flee to Hamburg, law enforcement and Magwitch's former partner in crime, Compeyson, intercept the boat Pip had arranged for Magwitch to use for his escape. During the interception, Magwitch and Compeyson fight in the murky water. Magwitch is the sole survivor after the physical altercation and becomes ill after the ordeal. We are informed of Pip's innermost thoughts as he watches over a sickly Magwitch:

> It was a good thing that he had touched this point, for it put into my mind what I might not otherwise have thought until too late: that he need never know how his hopes of enriching me had perished. (p. 480)

We understand that it was not the material objects Magwitch financially provided for Pip that resulted in Pip's demise, but Pip's own single focus on status as a gentleman.

Pip's disorganization is unique. We do not notice the protective factors Pip uses when confronted with stressors. He seems to have no regard for the support and values Joe and Biddy taught him. Indeed, it seems his desire for success and status obscures the values these two people modeled and the world they gave him. As we have seen, Richardson (1990) asserts that *Disorganization* is a "temporary state wherein the biopsychospiritual 'pieces' of an individual's life become disrupted" (p. 36). Indeed, Pip's "great expectations" to be a gentleman and a man of means failed and any protective factors he tried to leverage also failed. This aligns with Richardson's (1990) claim in the *Disorganization* phase that "In a serious sense, there may be a complete falling apart of an individual's world view" (p. 36). Pip must now find a way to take the previous experiences, for instance, appreciating Joe and Biddy's values and support, and bring them into his new worldview. It is certainly the case that difficult situations challenge teachers' worldview and call into question their ideas on teaching and reasons for choosing the profession. And similar to Pip's actions toward the end of the novel, they must be ready to find strategies and coping mechanisms to recover from those negative events.

Pip's Reintegration

Pip comes to realize that he embraced selfish, unrealistic, and wrong expectations and goals. Interestingly, Pip's promising yet immature self-understanding hastily leads him to propose to Biddy. As one may ask: Is Pip's attempt to marry Biddy a way to associate with goodness and decency? If he cannot will those things for himself, then he can at least be with someone who possesses those qualities. As he travels back to the town near Kent, Pip begins to envision a better life for himself.

> But it was only the pleasanter to turn to Biddy and to Joe, whose great forbearance shone more brightly than before, if that could be, contrasted with this brazen pretender. I went towards them slowly, for my limbs were weak, but with a sense of increasing relief as I drew nearer to them, and a sense of leaving arrogance and untruthfulness further and further behind. (p. 512)

Pip dreams of how Joe and Biddy's "guiding spirit" and "home-wisdom" (p. 512) can be his salvation. Pip, however, discovers that Biddy has married Joe. To his credit, Pip congratulates both of them and again realizes his poor behavior and debt of gratitude to the both of them: "receive my humble thanks for all you have done for me, and all I have so ill-repaid" (p. 514). In a sign of familial and parental support, Joe and Biddy forgive Pip.

A new sense of responsibility takes hold of Pip. He decides to work with Herbert, learns how to manage money, and pays back debts he accrued while in London. After 11 years pass, Pip returns to visit Joe and Biddy. He discovers they have two young children, a daughter and a son they call "Little Pip." Biddy asks Pip if he has forgotten about Estella. Pip responds that "poor dream, as I once used to call it, has all gone by, Biddy, all gone by!" (p. 518). At a later time in London, Pip encounters Estella while he is walking with "Little Pip." We are told that Estella had suffered a great deal in her life. She separated from Drummle, who showed himself to be a harsh husband. Estella then married a doctor; they lived together on her small fortune. As they meet each other, Estella wishes to kiss Little Pip, who she thinks is Pip's son. Pip informs the reader that he was delighted to have met with Estella; he understood that the suffering she endured gave her an understanding of the feelings Pip once possessed for her.[3]

How then does Pip reintegrate? As we have already discussed, Richardson's (1990) reintegration stage indicates the individual reorganizes "affected biopsychospiritual pieces into a new world perspective" (p. 37). For Pip, putting the pieces back together means identifying the goodness of people in one's life; focusing on real-world issues such as working positively with people; and reassessing one's expectations and goals. Similarly, teachers who will face stressors and difficult life events can reintegrate by following the same actions as Pip does, especially reviewing their expectations for themselves as educators.

We are not convinced that Pip arrives at a complete epiphany in regard to the noblest things in life. Indeed, the reader will expect Pip's reintegration process to take some time. Yet Pip does reflect Richardson's (1990) *Resilient Reintegration*, where "the individual learns new skills, has more self-understanding, and has a better comprehension of personal envirosocial influences" (p, 37). Referring back to the attributes of *Resilient Reintegration*, Pip exhibits self-motivation and the ability to perform tasks by securing a position and paying off his debts; reflects self-awareness and introspection by making amends with Joe and Biddy; and displays effective social problem-solving skills by engaging positively with Estella again. We may cautiously argue that in general, given these positive reintegrative protective factors, Pip is also able to recover from adversity. Lastly, these actions that Pip sees as important quite late in the novel, also implies the "great expectations" Pip should have worked toward throughout his stay in London. Instead of being selfish in his pursuit of becoming a gentleman, Pip should have conceived of expectations more in line with the protective factors he used during reintegration. Then he would have had a more pleasurable and beneficial experience striving for his goal without ignoring those who cared for him, namely Joe and Biddy, models of simplicity and fidelity.

Teacher Resiliency, Pip's Exploits, and the Resiliency Model

Referring back to Richardson's (1990) definition of life events, teachers will encounter positive and negative experiences in their profession. To deal with these life events, they will attempt to reach homeostasis through various protective factors. Drawing from Richardson (1990), the protective factors teachers can apply include, but are not limited to, possessing self-esteem, using solid skills for making decisions, developing self-control, having a positive view of the future, and pursuing a cause or purpose in life greater than themselves.

More broadly, returning to these biological, psychological, and spiritual protective factors when experiencing stressors is vital to surviving and growing in the education profession. These stressors, as mentioned earlier, will include struggles with students' academic and behavioral issues, circumspection about meaningful subject matter and effective instructional strategies, and external forces such as having limited resources, negative school culture and morale, and mandated tests. But if teachers' expectations are too idealistic, then the stress from the impending challenges will be heightened; they will have difficulties coping as Pip did. Moreover, when they fail to recognize the need to adjust expectations, as Pip did not, an emptiness can follow in that their hopes and dreams have not come true. An attitude of surprise or shock sets in and their ideas about pedagogical goals, classroom management, assessment, and more generally, their chosen profession will be perceived as difficult and off the mark as it was for Pip. Teachers' unrealistic expectations can also produce an overblown sense of uprightness as Pip's expectations did with him. We remember Pip's seemingly haughty attitude toward Biddy before he left for London and toward Joe when they dined together. In other words, the mere fact that teachers' expectations deal, for instance, with high quality instruction and student achievement precludes them from thinking there might be times when expectations must be adjusted. Consequently, teachers must guard against developing impractical expectations, as noble as they may be, to help navigate through life events and confront, as Richardson (1990) notes, disruption. Once disruption happens for a teacher, then as the Resiliency Model (1990) indicates, disorganization occurs. The teacher's previous worldview is shaken by the event. Now the teacher must reintegrate by reconciling their original worldview, in this case, their expectations about teaching and their original protective factors, with the new adjusted expectations and more applicable protective factors. These new protective factors may include a renewal of previous ones, but as has already been noted, Richardson (1990) also details others that may be helpful as well.

Conclusion

Teachers can learn about resiliency from the character Pip in *Great Expectations*. By analyzing Pip's behavior through Richardson's Resiliency Model (1990), teachers understand the importance of adjusting expectations throughout the course of their teaching career and commit to developing new protective factors during the state of disorganization. In this way, teachers will reintegrate the new protective factors to build more resiliency. The unique marriage of the classic novel *Great Expectations* and Richardson's Resiliency Model (1990) presents, for those already in the profession, those ready to enter the profession in the future, or those new to the profession, opportunities to creatively explore how to build resiliency when challenges emerge. More broadly, the fusion of disciplines can offer those in the education field unique and creative ways to navigate through the complexities of teaching and rediscover how laudable the profession truly is.

Discussion Questions

As a future teacher, do you see how your own expectations about teaching can be a source for problems like they were for Pip? If so, how?

In what ways, if any, do Pip's experiences inform you about developing expectations about teaching and building resiliency?

Describe the current protective factors you use when dealing with difficulties?

Do your current protective factors help you deal with disruption? Explain whether they do or not.

Have you ever successfully reintegrated after a stressful experience? If so, how?

What protective factors do you plan on using when you begin your teaching career?

What protective factors would you use to help you adjust your expectations about teaching?

Discuss a difficulty or challenge you might encounter as a new teacher that would require you to apply the Resiliency Model and also adjust your expectations?

Notes

1. I have used the 1963 New American Library version of *Great Expectations*. It comes from the "Charles Dickens" Edition of 1867 that Dickens revised for the press at the time.

2. I am grateful to Professor McLaughlin for sharing ideas with me about how teacher resiliency can be the educational subject for this chapter.

3. Dickens' original ending was later reworked because the original was not well-received from the public. Unlike the reworked ending, Dickens' original ending does not make the reader think there is the possibility of Pip and Estella developing a romantic relationship; however, it indicates the mutual understanding of the suffering they both endured. I have chosen to stay with the original ending.

References

Beltman, S., Mansfield, C., & Price, A. (2011) Thriving not just surviving: A review of research on teacher resilience. *Educational Research Review, 6*(3), 185–207. http://dx.doi.org/10.1080/02643944.2015.1074265

Crosswell, L., & Beutel, D. (2016). 21st century teachers: How nontraditional pre-service teachers navigate their initial experiences of contemporary classrooms. *Asia Pacific Journal of Teacher Education. 45*(4), 416–431. https://doi.org/10.1080/1359866X.2017.1312281

Dickens, C. (1963). *Great expectations.* The New American Library. (Original work published 1867).

Erikson, E. (1963). *Childhood and society.* (2nd ed). Norton.

Fernandes, L., Peixoto, F., Gouveia, M. J., & Silva, J. C. (2020). Positive education: A professional learning programme to foster teachers' resilience and well-being. In C.F. Mansfield (Ed.). *Cultivating Teacher Resilience* (pp. 103–124). Springer. doi:10.1007/978-981-15-5963-1_7 ResearchGate.

Himmelfarb, G. (2006). *The moral imagination.* Ivan R. Dee.

Kohlberg, L. (1976). Moral stages and moralization: The cognitive/developmental approach. In T. Lickona. (Ed.). *Moral development and behavior.* (pp. 31–53). Holt, Rinehart & Winston.

Mansfield, C. F., Beltman, S., Price, A. E., & McConney, A. (2012). "Don't sweat the small stuff": Understanding teacher resilience at the chalk face. *Teaching and Teacher Education, 28*(3), 357–367. https://doi.org/10.1016/j.tate.2011.11.001

McIntosh, N., & Schweizer, F. (2012). Great expectations: Charles Dickens and education – A bicentenary perspective. *Use of English. 64*(1), 47–56. https://search-ebscohost-com.wwu.idm.oclc.org/login.aspx?direct+true&AN+84332764&site=eds-live

Mullen, C. A., Shields, L. B., & Tienken, C. H. (2021). Developing teacher resilience and resilient school cultures. *AASA Journal of Scholarship & Practice. 18*(1) p. 8–24. https://search-ebscohost-com.wwu.idm.oclc.org/login.aspx?direct=true&db=eue&AN=149897553&site=eds-live

Piaget, J. (1952). *The origins of intelligence in children* (M. Cook, Trans.). International Universities Press.

Pykett, L. (2002). *Critical issues: Charles Dickens.* Red Globe Press.

Richardson, G. E., Neiger, B. L., Jenson, S., & Kumpfer, K. L. (1990). The resiliency model. *Health Education. 21*(6), 33–39. https://doi.org/10.1080/00970050.1990.10614589

Slater, M. (2011). *Charles Dickens.* Yale University Press.

THREE

"A Mighty, Mighty Thing": Jason Reynolds' Poem *For Every One* as a Framework for Examining Adolescent Identity Development and Teacher Identity Development

Erin Hill

IN 2018, JASON REYNOLDS PUBLISHED *For Every One*, what he calls "A poem. A nod. A nothing to lose." While he wrote and performed the work in 2011 for the unveiling of the Dr. Martin Luther King Jr. memorial at the Kennedy Center, Reynolds explains in the book's opening note that when he "started writing this, I didn't know what it was. A poem in form only, a letter written in parts, an offering that I've now been working on for years. A thing" (2018a, p. 2). He was 28 at the time.

Over 10 years later, Mr. Reynolds is a prolific author, highly decorated—a recipient of Newbery, Printz, Edgar, NAACP Image, Coretta Scott King, and Carnegie awards. In 2020, he was named the Library of Congress' National Ambassador for Young People's Literature. If readers visit his Wikipedia page, they will find lengthy paragraphs detailing the plots of his young adult and middle grade novels and the many accolades they have earned. Readers will find just three short sentences about *For Every One*—perhaps because it resists categorization or description.

On the dedication page, we see that Mr. Reynolds wrote *For Every One* "For You. For Me." He writes in his introductory note that the process of finding his place in the world ". . . was basically just the undoing of . . . me—a twenty-something clinging tight to the nugget of thin air I referred to as my dream" (2018a, p. 2). At the same time, he met "quite a few teenagers who carried with them an unfortunate practicality . . . as if their imaginations had been seat belted, kept safe from accidents . . . they could admit their dreams were real and that there were things they wanted to do, say, see, and make, but they couldn't get past how foolish it is to be foolish" (2018a, p. 3). Mr. Reynolds was not unacquainted with challenges as a young person; while inspired by poetry and a deep love of music in his early years, he admits to not having read a novel until he was 17. He earned poor grades in his English classes at the University of Maryland. Today, he describes himself as "Crazy. About stories" and on his personal website, he vows two things:

1. "Here is what I know: I know there are a lot—A LOT—of young people who hate reading. I know that many of these book haters are boys. I know that many of these book-hating boys, don't actually hate books, they hate boredom . . . know that I feel you. I REALLY do. Because even though I'm a writer, I hate boring books too" (Reynolds, 2016, para. 6).
2. "Here's what I plan to do: not write boring books" (Reynolds, 2016, para. 1).

By the end of *For Every One*'s introductory note, Mr. Reynolds calls the poem an "offering, that I've now been working on for years . . ." that which has evolved from "a thing" to "a *mighty, mighty* thing [italics mine]" (2018a, p. 3).

In this space between his teens and his offering lies an interesting intersection for those of us working with adolescents, young adults, and preservice teachers: when we consider the massive identity development that happens between the ages of 16 and 28, the age range Mr. Reynolds covers in this short work, there is thrilling potential for curiosity, growth, and learning. A mighty, mighty thing, indeed.

How fitting, then, that *For Every One* lives in the ambiguous middle space of genre. This text, so much about figuring out who we are and where we fit and how we honor our dreams while doing so, speaks to the ambiguous space students and teachers navigate every day. Identity construction is tricky business: fluid and frustrating, bumpy and beautiful. Helping young people and young educators navigate that process is the work so many of us in teacher preparation are called to and passionate about.

What follows is a brief overview of how the poem connects to both adolescent identity development and teacher identity development. For the poetry purists, note that the approach below is neither a complete nor chronological line-by-line explication but rather a broad stroke, thematic connection to theories of development. The chapter concludes with a set of general lesson plans for a 50-minute (never enough!) MWF 200-level adolescent development and education class, a sample assessment, and sample student responses. My hope is that these are scalable for your purposes and your students in teacher education.

For Every One and Adolescent Identity Development

Mr. Reynolds begins his poem-letter by directly addressing the readers: "Dear Dreamer/ This letter is being written/from a place of raw honesty and love/ but not at all/a place of expertise/on how to make/your dreams come true" (2018a, p. 5). Readers of any age are likely to recognize and relate to Reynolds' description of the fluid and nonlinear aspects of identity development over time: "At sixteen I thought/I would've made it by now/At eighteen I said twenty-five/is when I'd make my first million/At twenty-five I moved back in/with my mother/ bill collectors/breathing on me like/Brooklyn summer . . . Dreams don't have timelines/ deadlines/and aren't always in straight lines" (2018a, pp. 14, 76). For adolescents, a sensitivity to what they presume as a "timeline" of development is particularly acute as they are quick to compare themselves to one another. As adults, we have the lived experience to know "identity is clearly not stable, but is instead an ongoing process of self-reflection and change as one moves through life" (Dolgin, 2011, p. 157). Because of our lived experience and our confidence in our ability to navigate change, those changes are perhaps less seismic than they feel for the adolescent.

Adolescents often associate social milestones and rites of passage with particular numbers: 10 and finally double digits; 13 and finally a teenager; 16 and finally eligible to drive; 18 and finally an "adult"; 21 and finally able to purchase alcohol, and so on. Anything over 25 is officially old and the implication is then that one must have life figured out at that point . . . and beyond. Adolescents are also highly aware that "Society expects young people to decide on a college and/or a job, to become romantically involved, and to make choices regarding political philosophies and religious practices . . ." (Dolgin, 2011, p. 157). They internalize all of these expectations—their own, their peers', their parents'/guardians', and society's. Mr. Reynolds speaks to the weight of those expectations: ". . . experts and/dream catchers/who swear that I/can one plus one/and right foot/left foot/my way into fulfillment/never taking into/considering/all this mess I got/strapped to my/back and my head/ and my legs and/my heart" (2018a, pp. 20–21).

When undergraduate students begin studying theories of identity development, often in their late teens or early twenties, there is sometimes a collective moment of discovery in class, and a brave student will raise a hand to say, "Oh, okay, so what we went through was—is—normal?" We all laugh together at the recognition. The veil has been pulled back on the social and emotional tumult of adolescence, and they have a keen interest in learning more. Our class discussions on those days are usually lively and filled with organic self-reflection, engagement, and commiseration. Mr. Reynolds' poem is an ideal entry point for discussing traditional theories of adolescent development; he tells readers, "This letter/is being written/from the inside/From the front line/and the fault line/From the uncertain thick of it all" (Reynolds, 2018a, pp. 10–11). Students relate to "the uncertain thick of it all," and the phrase "the fault line" is a useful starting point for discussing the shifts adolescents make during identity exploration, particularly those delineated in Erik Erikson's seven conflicts and Marcia's four-status crisis and commitments scheme (Dolgin, 2011).

Adolescence is a period of identity expansion and exploration. As an educator, it is a privilege to witness and to walk alongside young people as they try on different roles. It is fulfilling work, especially if we can encourage and support without judgment or our own agenda, reminding students that "As one moves through adolescence, if these values, beliefs, goals, and practices are no longer appropriate, one can engage in a task of identity redefinition and refinement" (Dolgin, 2011, p. 157).

For Every One and Teacher Identity Development

Many undergraduate students, especially those enrolled in 100-level or 200-level education classes, are exploring interests and are not yet admitted to a formal teacher preparation program. Even for those students who declare education as a major or minor early in their undergraduate career, it is likely many have not yet begun the reflective practice of considering their identity as professional educators. In the 200-level Adolescent Development and Education course for which this study and series of lessons is proposed, Mr. Reynolds' poem can serve as a low-stakes introduction to the concept of teacher identity. It can be a tool for exploration and inquiry—as all great literature can.

Some researchers suggest that our attention to teacher identity development in educator preparation programs could be improved, particularly by addressing it more explicitly and earlier in the program. According to Zur and Ravid (2018), "the teacher training phase is a critical stage for teacher identity formation" (p. 121). According to Villegas et al. (2020), "Teacher education programs require overt attention to the importance of this issue in order to instill an awareness of the need to develop teacher identity" (p. 9); they suggest further research into this intentional attention to teacher identity development "particularly prior to the completion of the practicum period" (p. 9). Drawing on research from the '90s, Castañeda (2011) provides a useful infographic with three threads for focus: community, knowledge systems and beliefs, and goals (see Figure 3.1).

What we might do, then, for students at this level—long before they student teach—is invite them to begin thinking about the kind of educator they aspire to be and to consider that in the context of what they are learning about identity construction at all ages.

One way to orient this thinking is to invite reflection on why they chose (or are considering) a teaching career, the experiences and/or people who led them to this choice, and what they expect their work as a professional educator

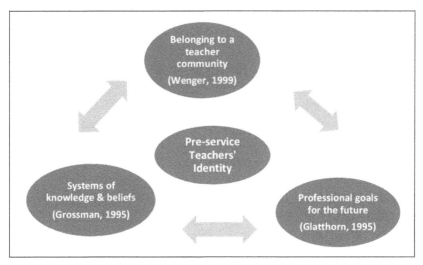

Figure 3.1. Castañeda's three components contributing to pre-service teacher identity development.
Note: From Castañeda, J.A.F. (2011). *Teacher identity construction: Exploring the nature of becoming a primary school language teacher.* [Doctoral Dissertation, Newcastle University]. Academic Search Complete.

might entail. According to Newburgh (2019), "upon entering the profession new teachers carry with them an image of the role they believe a teacher should play. When they begin enacting that role, they realize that being an educator is very different from enacting the preconceived role of an educator" (p. 1239). As faculty members, advisors, and professional mentors, we have an opportunity to engage students in ongoing conversations about this tension between students' perceived roles as educators and their roles as they play out in practicum classrooms each semester leading up to their student teaching semester.

Regardless of when students make the choice to commit to education as a profession, it is an important moment. According to Castañeda (2014),

> When a student makes the decision to choose teaching, this early act of belonging is the beginning of a long journey of constructing, sustaining and transforming a professional identity. Choosing teaching is argued in this study to be the first foundational act of belonging to a teacher community. Although the meaning of being a teacher evolves as a trajectory that is shaped and transformed as teachers gain experience and professional recognition, the *story* of how teaching first attracted them is believed to provide some key notions about how professional identities are constructed. More importantly, it can be claimed that it is an early act of professional affiliation, as it signifies the beginning of a professional and personal development journey [italics mine]. (p. 51)

Using Mr. Reynolds' poem as a mentor text for students to write about their own journey toward teaching is a way to help them begin claiming the power of their voice, their choices, their professional identity, and their story. We know that narratives can be a highly effective tool for this kind of reflection; according to Villegas et al. (2020), "narratives seek to restore remarkable memories and experiences that may reveal how [students] see themselves as teachers and how they construct their professional identity" (p. 3). Izadinia's (2013) research affirms journal writing and biographical narrative as useful tools for teacher identity development (as cited in Zur & Ravid, 2018). A primary goal in this work is to prompt students to articulate their goals, values, and beliefs as they work toward a deeply considered sense of self and teaching philosophy that will anchor them when they are on what Mr. Reynolds refers to as "the front line" (2018, p. 10). Narratives are a powerful way to do this.

We want students to leave our programs not with every "answer" to every pedagogical challenge they will face but rather with confidence that they have the personal and professional tools to reflect, adapt, and make choices in line with their values and identity—and that they are a part of a teaching community who are also on the front lines with them: "This letter is for us all/to remind us/that we are many/That we are right/for trying/That purpose is real/That making it is possible" (Reynolds, 2018a, p. 85). While Mr. Reynolds doesn't address educators specifically, he does address the courageous—and we know it takes courage to teach: "This letter isn't/for any specific/kind of dream/It isn't intended/for a certain genre/medium/trade, or/denomination/It is only intended/for the courageous" (Reynolds, 2018a, pp. 67–68).

Conclusion

In December of 2023, the same year this anthology was published, Mr. Reynolds turned 40. As many of us know—or will come to find out—it's another rite of passage that can spur reflection on one's identity. No longer young, but not necessarily old, our forties can be as murky a middle space as adolescence. We may find ourselves uncertain of where we fit, heavy with responsibility on all sides—with children, with aging family members, with the demands of mid-career goals and aspirations. It is an ever-shifting negotiation of and with the self—and I try to be honest about this with the mostly early-twenties crowd I teach. I hope they see this as a comfort; "Oh, okay, we're all just navigating these 'fault lines' and figuring it out as we go," as opposed to, "Wait, what?!? No one knows what's going on?? Not even my professors?"

Honesty seems the way. Mr. Reynolds refers to one of his moments of truth as "the meltdown," when our dreams run up against reality, for him as "a twenty-something clinging tight to the nugget of thin air I referred to as my dream" (2018, p. 1). Honesty seems the way—especially given how perceptive and attuned young people can be to the hints of thwarted ambition they see in us. We think we're hiding it; often we're not. "People in my family, the 'responsibles,' whom I argued and disagreed with, never knew that I could see that the remnants of this same kind of meltdown that may have happened forty years prior were still there, hiding beneath their tongues" (2018a, p. 1).

I try to be honest about the dreaming, too. When I was young, I (myopically) thought dreaming was a young person's game; now, nearing 50, I know differently. We keep evolving, we keep learning, we keep reaching. The most interesting people I know have lived many disparate lives and are still figuring out who they are and what they want to be when they grow up. They "live the questions," as Rilke encouraged us to do in *Letters to a Young Poet* (1934, p. 35). If we are still listening, our dreams may evolve but they never die: "If you are/anything like me/you hope/it never stops/You hope the/bubbling never/ dies down/and the yearning to/break out and/and break through/never simmers./You hope/the voice that/delivers the/loudest whispers/of what you envision never silences/That it never cowers behind fear/and expectations that other people/strap to your life/like a backpack full of bricks/(or books written by experts)" (Reynolds, 2018, pp. 42–43).

Mr. Reynolds quotes James Baldwin in the epigraph of *For Every One*: "Though we do not wholly believe it yet, the interior life is a real life, and the intangible dreams of people have a tangible effect on the world" (2018a, p. 4). Our work as educators—and as educators of the future educators—is to develop a keen sensitivity to our young people's interior lives (and our own, for that matter), to help them understand the ongoing complexity of identity development both personally and professionally, and to encourage the inspired pursuit of their dreams. Teaching is a long game, of course, but like Mr. Reynolds, we carry on "the only way/he knows how/splitting his cries/and his smiles/right down the middle/ swallowing his moonshine mistakes/while in the sunlight his sweat/irrigates his life and that life he—/like you—/has been tilling, hoping there's a harvest coming" (2018a, pp. 12–13).

Sample Plan, Class Session One

Pre-Reading

Students arrive to class having reviewed instructor-selected course text on adolescent development, specifically Erikson's and Marcia's theories of identity development (covered in depth in the prior class, including critiques of both theories).

Pre-Assessment/Warm Up (~10 mins)

At the beginning of class, students generate a list of all the roles they played/ hats they wore/identities they fulfilled as early adolescents (I use 4x6 note cards for this task). I tend to frame this as a "Who were you in high school?" kind of brainstorm. Students can list roles such as sibling, cousin, child, grandchild, soccer player, striver, slacker, friend, volunteer, band member, employee, office aide, and so on. I push them to create a list that is as specific and as comprehensive as possible. After a few minutes, I ask students to circle the roles that were most important to them when they were in high school. Students then reflect/discuss with each other in small groups; time permitting, there may be some whole group sharing out.

Key Question(s)

Which of Erikson's or Marcia's stages of development do we see reflected in part one of Jason Reynolds' poem *For Every One*? Why is it important for educators to understand these stages? Time permitting: Should we explicitly teach adolescents about their own development?

Body of Lesson (~30 mins)

1. Quick student-led review of Erikson's stages of identity development (assign to two students ahead of time).
2. Quick student-led review of Marcia's stages of identity development (assign to two students ahead of time).
3. Read Part One of Jason Reynolds' *For Every One* (pp. 4–35); instructor decides reading process.
4. In small groups, students identify and discuss potential stage(s) of development and "fault lines" present in this first section of the poem; if needed, instructor will direct students to lines such as "At sixteen I thought/I would have made it by now" (Reynolds, 2018, p. 14) and "At eighteen I said twenty-five/is when I'd make my first million" (Reynolds, 2018, p. 14), and "Now/I'm making up/what making it/means/as I go" (Reynolds, 2018, pp. 33–34). Students may connect to one or more of Erikson's seven stages or one of Marcia's four stages of crisis and commitment.
5. Small groups share out.

Post-Assessment (~ 5 mins)

Students answer the key questions on the back of the 4x6 note card, using the class session's reading and discussion as a basis for their explanation. For next session: Read Parts Two through Four of *For Every One* (pp. 38–101).

Sample Plan, Class Session Two

Pre-Reading

Students arrive to class having read Parts Two through Four of *For Every One* (pp. 38–101).

Pre-Assessment (~10 mins)

On a new 4x6 note card, students generate a list of all the roles they play as current undergraduate students. I ask them to circle the roles that are most important to them now. I then distribute the cards from class session one and ask them to identify areas of consistency and areas of change. Students then reflect/discuss with each other in small groups; time permitting, there may be some whole group sharing out.

Key Questions

How has your identity shifted over time? How did Mr. Reynolds' identity shift over time? What are three contributing factors to preservice teacher identity development? Why is each factor important?

Body of Lesson (~30 minutes)

1. Small group review and share out: What additional "fault lines" of adolescent development did you identify with in Parts Two through Four of *For Every One*? How are those fault lines connected to Erikson's seven stages of development or Marcia's four stages of crisis and commitment? Instructor can orchestrate/modify this review process as needed.
2. Instructor delivers short mini-lecture (no more than 10 minutes) on factors influencing teacher identity development (see Figure 1).

A Mighty, Mighty Thing

3. Small group work and share out: Which elements of Mr. Reynolds' development as an artist overlap with the three factors influencing teacher identity development? Is that overlap important?

Post-Assessment (~10 minutes)

Students answer the key questions on the back of the 4x6 note card, using the class session's reading and discussion as a basis for their explanation.

For next session: Read Thomas Armstrong's chapter on the benefits of expressive arts activities for adolescents (2016, pp. 121–133).

Sample Plan, Class Session Three

Pre-Reading

Students arrive to class having read Thomas Armstrong's chapter on the benefits of expressive arts activities for adolescents (2016, pp. 121–133).

Pre-Assessment (~ 5 minutes)

According to Armstrong, what are two or three benefits of using expressive arts activities with adolescent students?

Key Question

How does telling a story help us clarify and communicate our own values and identities?

Body of Lesson (~ 30 minutes)

1. Instructor shows the 826 Digital video of Mr. Reynolds (2018b) reciting *For Every One* (approximately 20-minute video linked in references).
2. On the back of note cards, students will respond to the following questions: Describe your experience hearing and seeing Jason Reynolds' "performance" of his poem. Did this embodied recitation change your understanding in any way? How so? Did you notice different elements of the poem? Did it reinforce or detract from any of our content discussions of identity development this week?
3. Time permitting, students may share out.

Post-Assessment

Explanation with Student Samples (~15 minutes): In the introductory note to his poem, Mr. Reynolds says "So, I started writing this. A letter to myself to keep from quitting. It was written while I was afraid. Unsure. Doubtful. And at first, I wasn't sure what it was. A poem in form only, a letter written in parts, an offering, that I've been working on for years. For me, a mighty, mighty thing" (Reynolds, 2018a, p. 2).

We know that expressive arts activities are valuable for all learners, not just adolescents, of course, so your assignment is to write a letter to yourself using Mr. Reynolds' work as your model. The format and structure are up to you. If you want to experiment with poetic lines, great. If "POEM" is going to get in the way of your thinking, then a standard letter (or email) to yourself works too. Food for thought questions (these do not need to be answered entirely or in order or even at all; these are just options to prompt your thinking): Where are you now on your journey as a learner and perhaps a preservice educator? Where do you hope or expect to be in 5, 10, or 15 years from now? What are you afraid of? What obstacles do you anticipate? What, if anything, are you certain of? What do you need to put down on paper as a reminder to yourself? What do you want to accomplish? What dreams are on your mind and heart? Will you remind yourself that "dreams don't have timelines/deadlines/and aren't always in/straight lines"? Like Mr. Reynolds, will you "jump anyway"?

Read student samples together (included below).

Please submit your poem or letter to (insert LMS here) no later than (insert deadline here). You will not be required to share your work with your peers next class session, but time will be provided if you would like to share.

[Note for instructors: the use of post-writing reflection questions is encouraged, particularly in this case: "As narrative inquiry requires going beyond the use of narratives as a rhetorical structure, that is, beyond simply telling stories, to an analytical examination of the underlying insights and assumptions that the story reveals" (Bell, 2002, as cited in Villegas et al., 2020).]

After you have written your poem or letter, please answer the following reflection questions and submit as a separate document on (insert LMS here) no later than (insert deadline here).

1. Describe your process for this assignment. Did you start right away? Did you procrastinate? Did the work feel accessible? Was your process for this kind of writing different than for other academic writing assignments? How so/why/why not?

A Mighty, Mighty Thing

2. There was no rubric provided for this assignment. Describe how that helped or hindered your process.
3. How did you decide or know the piece was "completed"? How did you decide or know you were "satisfied" with your piece?
4. As you thought and wrote, did anything surprise you? Why/why not?
5. Reread your submission. What underlying insights or assumptions does your poem or letter reveal?

Sample Student Responses

> Dear Younger, Present, Future Self
> Much like this letter,
> You'll always be a work in progress.
> I know we thought you were a
> In the line, follow the rules type of guy,
> Man with the four-year plan, hello, goodbye,
> On a straight path with a straight line,
> But what we've come to find is
> Life doesn't work out that way sometimes.
>
> That's neither here
>   nor
>   there
> Sometimes you have to go somewhere
> To find out where you truly belong.
> You're still a teacher like your mother
> And so is your brother
> It's funny; there must be something in the blood or water
> Full of wonder like a child's face when
> A book takes him to a place for the first time:
>
> I wonder if she knew what she was doing
> When she brought me to her classroom at the age of four
> Spending all day laughing, reading on the floor;
> Did my father understand the weight of his words
> When he told me that authors get paid the same as ball players?
>
> A seed of generational teaching was planted within me
> And the tree has grown strong and happy.
> Just like happiness is contagious
> When you're faced with a crowd of smiling faces,
> I've been taught that teaching can spread the most powerful message.
>
> Yes, you're still a work in progress
> Like the moments you write,
> The lessons you teach,
> Or the things you do,
> But they're all part of the winding path
> That makes your dreams come true.

Figure 3.2. Student Work Sample #1 (Lambert, 2021).
Note: From Anonymous (2022). Used with permission.

> It's crazy that I'm even here
> Because I was sent home 49 times from school
> In one year!
> Teachers sat my desk outside the classroom
> What am I supposed to learn here?
> But if they could look at me now they'd say
> Daaaaaaaaamn
> How'd you get here?!!!!!!!!
> I'd tell 'em
> I took the road less traveled paved with bruises, bumps, and tears
> Had to get a steamroller to straighten out my fears
> I was 32 trying on new shoes
> Anxiety lived here
> Only heightened when I realized *what am I doing here?*
> In five years' time I'll be looking for a new career
> I gotta find something I can put my heart into
> Tear my heart in two
> Get back what I put in times two
> Too few teachers I would call and say *Look how much I grew*
> I'd sure run out of digits if I added *in spite of you*
> I've seen graduation streamers turn into crime scene tape
> Had to come to Hill's class and try to think straight
> When I cruise around my city I'm reminded you gotta keep your foot on the gas
> Trees saran wrapped trying to immortalized dreams that perished
> A car circles the block constantly
> It's a parent looking for answers where questions can be threatening and put your life in danger
> I'm in a constant state of being a student of these harsh life lessons
> I'm trying to teach teachers that student's tone is pain
> NOT AGGRESSION
> I've seen few with the same hue as me in these educational courses
> I'd live horse if it'd have my brothers and sisters sign up for these courses in droves
> So much so there's now a waitlist
> Can it be a burden if it's weightless?
> It's not an obligation but a callin
> And just so you know I'm ALL-IN!

Figure 3.3. Student Work Sample #2 (Marshall II, 2021).
Note: From Anonymous (2022). Used with permission.

References

Armstrong, T. (2016). *The power of the adolescent brain: Strategies for teaching middle and high school students*. ASCD.

Castañeda, J. A. F. (2011). Teacher identity construction: Exploring the nature of becoming a primary school language teacher. [Doctoral Dissertation, Newcastle University]. Academic Search Complete.

Castañeda, J. A. F. (2014). Learning to teach and professional identity: Images of personal and professional recognition. *PROFILE Issues in Teachers' Professional Development, 16*(2), 49–65. http://dx.doi.org/10.154446/profile.v16n2.38075

Dolgin, K. G. (2011). *The Adolescent: Development, relationships, and culture*. Pearson.

Izadinia, M. (2013). A review of research on student teachers' professional identity. *British Educational Research Journal, 39*(4), 694–713.

Jason Reynolds. In *Wikipedia*. https://en.wikipedia.org/wiki/Jason_Reynolds

Lambert, L. (2021). *Dear younger, present, future self* [Unpublished course assignment]. Wittenberg University.

Marshall II, K. (2021). *It's crazy that I'm even here* [Unpublished course assignment]. Wittenberg University.

Newburgh, K. (2019). Teaching in good faith: Towards a framework for defining the deep supports that grow and retain first-year teachers. *Educational Philosophy and Theory, 51*(12), 1237–1251. http://doi.org/10.1080/00131857.2018.1537878

Reynolds, J. (2018a). *For Every One*. Atheneum Press.

Reynolds, J. (2018b). *For Every One* [Video]. 826Digital. https://826digital.com/for-every-one/

Reynolds, J. (2016). *About Jason Reynolds*. JasonWritesBooks. https://www.jasonwritesbooks.com/about

Rilke, R. M. (1934). *Letters to a young poet*. Norton.

Villegas, D. F. M., Varona, W. H., & Sanchez, A. G. (2020). Student teachers' identity construction: A socially-constructed narrative in a second-language teacher education program. *Teaching and Teacher Education* 91, 1–10.

Zur, A. & Ravid, R. (2018). Designing the ideal school as transformative process: an approach to promoting teacher identity in pre-service teachers. *Teaching in Higher Education, 23*(1), 121–136. DOI: 10.1080/13562517.2017.1360271.

FOUR

 John Milton's *Paradise Lost*: Eve's Construction of Knowledge, Identity, and Morality

Anna Gallagher

PARADISE LOST (MILTON, 1667/2021B), BASED on the Bible's Book of Genesis, is essentially a story about our first education. So, it has a particularly fitting spot in a book aimed at encouraging use of literature in support of pedagogical studies. My focus will be on Eve's construction of knowledge, identity, and morality over the course of Milton's great epic; but, as a bonus, this study can offer education students a second level of knowledge construction—their own, as readers vulnerable to cultural snares and preconceived notions so common with diversity issues. This is surely something important to be aware of while standing in front of a classroom. I found myself vulnerable to these snares, and it was only with close reading and the support of feminist scholarship that I began to see Eve's growth. I believe that as Eve—and readers—progress along a developmental journey, a host of education concepts will be illuminated: growth theory, memory modeling, cognition-constructivism, and general critical thinking, among others. The epic excerpts used throughout this chapter can be found online in their full context at the John Milton Reading Room, edited by Thomas Luxon and hosted by Dartmouth College trustees (2021). Note also that these excerpts retain the poetic spelling shown in Luxon.

Knowledge and Identity Development

Over the course of *Paradise Lost*, Eve's identity develops from nascent, newly created woman to self-constructed empowered woman ready to leave Eden as a full partner to Adam—far beyond the role assigned to her by all the males of the epic. Unfortunately, I have found that this growth is often invisible to readers. Her journey offers many opportunities to delve into educational psychology topics—from broad concepts of cognition and psychosocial development to the tools of education pedagogy like Bronfenbrenner's ecology modeling (Bronfenbrenner, 1999; Mapping the ecology of identity, n.d.), memory system modeling, feminist textual analysis, and growth stage theory. All these will be part of the discussion that follows.

To begin, Bronfenbrenner's Ecology model (see Figure 4.1) can provide teachers with a quick summary of advantages and disadvantages that a given student might bring to the classroom (Slavin, 2018; Woolfolk, 2019). The same model can be applied to Eve for similar information. Figure 4.1 is an example model for a student. With each expanding ring, influences on the student, from most pointed (at center) to most diffuse (outer ring) can be easily seen—the bullseye might include age, gender, race, while the outer ring might describe influences of community traditions, history, and laws. A similar model for Eve is shown in Figure 4.2. Students can use Figure 4.2 to discuss what sort of information this aerial view offers about Eve's situation. Two things seem significant to me: first, Eve is the only female (except for the allegorical daughter of Satan—half female, half monster); second, Eve lives in an extremely hierarchical society where she is assigned a subordinate position.

With this preliminary information, students can be introduced to the first passages about Eve. Interestingly, it is Satan, recently arrived in Eden with fell intent, who introduces her to us. He sees Eve as she and Adam appear in a clearing, and we hear his impressions:

Satan:
Not equal, as thir sex not equal seemd;
For contemplation hee and valour formd,
For softness shee and sweet attractive Grace,
Hee for God only, shee for God in him ... (IV.296–99)

A few lines later, Eve speaks to Adam:

Eve:
... O thou for whom
And from whom I was formd flesh of thy flesh,
And without whom am to no end, my Guide
And Head, ... (IV.440–43)

John Milton's Paradise Lost

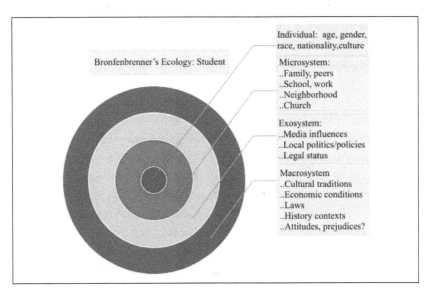

Figure 4.1. Bronfenbrenner's Ecology Model for a typical student.
Note: From Bronfenbrenner, U. (1999). Environments in development perspective: Theoretical and operational models. In *Measuring environment across the lifespan: Emerging models and concepts* (1st ed., pp. 3–28). American Psychological Association.

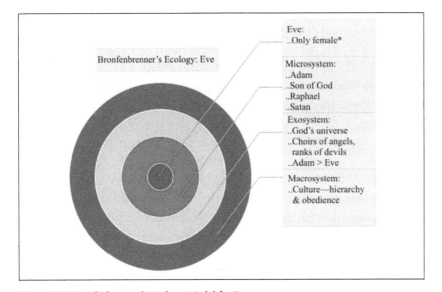

Figure 4.2. Bronfenbrenner's Ecology Model for Eve.
Note: Based on Bronfenbrenner, U. (1999). Environments in development perspective: Theoretical and operational models. In *Measuring environment across the lifespan: Emerging models and concepts* (1st ed., pp. 3–28). American Psychological Association.

With these first lines of introduction to Eve, students might be asked for impressions of our first mother. I suspect she will seem submissive and uninspiring. While pondering these lines, another cornerstone concept of education can be introduced, the memory and information system model. This model depicts how information is curated critically before being accepted as fact. Considering today's concern for misinformation—from classroom to newsroom to living room—this is a timely issue. One version of this information model is the Atkinson-Shiffrin 3-Stage Model (Noushad & Khurshid, 2019), shown in Figure 4.3. The importance of this memory schematic is that it describes how sensory stimuli arriving at our five senses are vast and must be winnowed before passing to the limited dimensions of short- and long-term memory. This filtering process is mediated by our preferences, cultural expectations, biases—and by knowledge already sitting in our long-term memory. In light of this last consideration, education students—and readers—might want to ensure the proper training of memory filters so that faulty information is not sent to long-term archives and recursively brought to bear in future situations. This is important so that teachers interact fairly with diverse students, and so that they can teach students to do the same. To drive home this point, consider the introductory epic passages above. How might students challenge first impressions of docility for Eve? Perhaps by recognizing that the speaker is Satan! Surely his perceptions and motives must be weighed carefully, not uncritically accepted. Yet, even if teachers are trained to be aware of diversity effects, their students may already have internalized damage from such effects. Similarly, Eve seems to have internalized subordination—as seen in the second passage.

At the character level, Eve, of course, has not been privy to Satan's views, so why does she accept a submissive role? To help answer this, students can be introduced to new passages that compare creation stories that Adam and Eve share with each other. This is information that neither Satan nor readers are aware of during those introductory lines above, but Eve is probably responding to them. First, there is Eve's creation story: she describes awakening in the shade not knowing who or where she was before wandering to a stream and spying her reflection, which captivated her until God's voice leads her to Adam, to "hee / Whose image thou art [and for whom she would] beare / Multitudes like thy self" (IV.471–74). Eve follows the voice, but seeing Adam, she turns away finding him "less faire / Less winning soft, less amiablie

John Milton's Paradise Lost

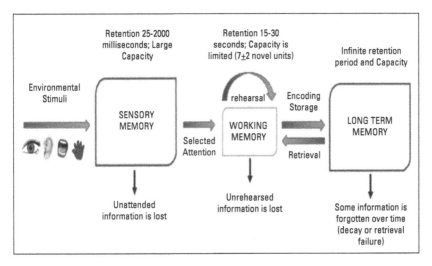

Figure 4.3. Atkinson-Shiffrin 3-Stage Model.
Note: From Noushad, B. & Khurshid, F. (2019). Facilitating student learning: An instructional design perspective for health professions educators. *Research and Development in Medical Education, 8*(2):69–74, from https://rdme.tbzmed.ac.ir/Article/rdme-31764

milde, / Then that smooth watry image" (IV.478–80). Now, compare Adam's creation story: he awakens in the sun, receives a "shape Divine [who says] thy Mansion wants thee, Adam, rise, / First Man . . . / call'd by thee I come thy Guide" (VIII.295-98). After this God bestows upon Adam dominion over all the beasts of Eden. But Adam is not merely grateful for these gifts, he "presum'[s]" (VIII.356) to ask for a mate. And now, students can be invited to ponder why Eve seems to behave submissively. Students can be asked what sort of information is likely to have passed to Eve's long-term memory so far? I suspect they will note the preferential treatment of Adam by the all-important Creator, whom Adam sees, speaks with, and asks favors of, while Eve neither sees nor speaks with Him. Surely Eve responds to this power imbalance. And, of course, God's relegation of her to mere image of Adam made for the purpose of bearing children might have slighting effects. In addition, Adam is the first created, which psychologically supports his dominance. So, Eve's memory filters may be overwhelmed by the many patriarchal messages. Again, readers will also be affected by these stories. What impressions might be passing to their own long-term memory? They might, as I did at first, accept the pat message of power asymmetry, so similar to those we ourselves may have internalized over a lifetime. But, in spite of this avalanche of gendered messaging, readers may spot a nugget of identity expression on Eve's part. Students can be asked whether they picked out this nugget: her instinctive partiality to her own image.

Moving on, if the Bronfenbrenner model can reveal advantages and disadvantages, and if the memory system can explain how misinformation passes to long-term memory, a knowledge of growth stage theory can help to identify age-appropriate expectations of a student—or Eve. Without this understanding, preliminary judgments might be harsh and unfair, which may explain the very trap that readers and Eve fall into—at least, initially—by accepting Eve as a subordinate. This too will be important awareness for future teachers. Growth stage theory describes the expected psychosocial trajectory as well as the potential pitfalls of each stage. Erik Erikson's model tracks growth from childhood through old age (Cherry, 2021). The stages are listed below:

Stage 1: Infancy period—Trust vs. Mistrust. Child is dependent. Security is key to proper growth.

Stage 2: Early Childhood period—Autonomy vs. Shame, doubt. Child should be gaining personal control.

Stage 3: Play Age period—Initiative vs. Guilt. Child should be encouraged when exhibiting choice, power, skill.

Stage 4: School Age period—Industry vs. Inferiority. Child should be developing pride in accomplishments.

Stage 5: Adolescence period—Identity vs. Identity confusion. Teenager needs to be individuating successfully, developing a sense of self and morals.

Stage 6: Young Adulthood period—Intimacy vs. Isolation. Young adult should be forming intimate, loving, strong relationships based on a healthy sense of self.

Stage 7: Adulthood period—Generativity vs. Stagnation/Self-absorption. Adult should become a productive family and community member.

Stage 8: Old Age period—Integrity vs. Despair: Adult should be able to reflect proudly on a life filled with accomplishments. (Orenstein & Lewis, 2021)

With these stages as reference, what do students think about Eve? What stage would they assign to her so far? For me, she is a newly minted human being, very dependent—Stage 1. But, as stage theory holds, there is no expectation that she will remain there—first impressions should not be fixed too firmly, even though we humans tend to invest these first impressions with outsized weight. Let's take a look at Eve a little further into the story. In this scene, God, having seen Satan's arrival in Eden, sends the angel Raphael to gird Adam with protective knowledge against Satan's malign intent—yes, he sends Raphael to "converse with Adam" (V.230)—not Eve. Here is the scene as it unfolds:

Adam:
Adam discernd [the angel], as in the dore he sat.
Of his coole Bowre,
. . .
And *Eve* within, due at her hour prepar'd
For dinner savourie fruits . . .
Adam to Eve:
. . . goe with speed
And what thy stores contain, bring forth and poure
Abundance, fit to honour and receive
Our Heav'nly stranger . . . (V.299–300, 303–04, 313–16)
Eve (responds to Adam's request above):
I will haste and from each bough and break,
. . . juiciest Gourd will pluck
. . . so contriv'd as not to mix
Tastes, not well joynd . . . but bring
Taste after taste upheld with kindliest change,
[Then we're told]. . . for drink the Grape
She crushes, inoffensive moust, and meathes
From many a berrie, and from sweet kernels prest
She tempers dulcet creams . . . (V.326–27, 334–36, 344–47)

Students can be asked to respond to these passages. Is the dynamic between Adam and Eve similar to earlier passages? A couple of interesting details that students may see include the personal pronouns used by Adam when he refers to "*his* coole Bower" and when he sends Eve to prepare lunch from "*thy* stores." There is a clear alignment with commonly held gender roles here, which feminist teaching helps to expose. Where would students place Eve on the growth stage arc? For me, knowledge construction is clear and may reveal Stage 2 to 4 development where Erikson describes the sense of pride in accomplishment. I think Eve is clearly demonstrating this. Positive feedback from others would support this growth, though I don't think she receives this from Adam or Raphael. Nevertheless, Adam's dependence on her knowledge is, at least, oblique positive feedback. And, of course, her own feelings of accomplishment certainly figure importantly. Here is where I begin to see more and more disconnect between what the males say about Eve and Eve's increasingly empowered behavior. But, now let's move on as Raphael arrives at the bower and greets both Adam and Eve:

> Raphael (to Adam):
> Adam, I therefore came, . . .
> To visit thee . . . (V.372, 375)
> Raphael (to Eve):
> Haile Mother of Mankind, whose fruitful Womb
> Shall fill the World more numerous with thy Sons
> Then with these various fruits the Trees of God
> Have heap'd this Table. (V.388–91)

What do students think of these greetings by the angel? How might Eve feel about them? Is there importance attached to Adam being greeted by name while Eve is greeted with respect to her functional role? Is there importance attached to Raphael's clear statement that he is here to see Adam, not Eve? Students should know that Eve is never invited to join the males for lunch; although, she does largely remain nearby listening. Can students recall similar gender-insensitive situations in their own lives? How might such situations arise in the classroom? To encourage discussion, recent research on diversity issues can be shared with a class. Jones and Dindia (2004) showed that teachers tend to interact more with males than females and that they tend to punish aggressiveness in females more than males. Herbert and Stipek (2005) revealed that high school males tend to overestimate their skills while females underestimate them. Research by Okagaki and Luster (2005) revealed that stereotyping diminishes student performance. Finally, Brannon (2002) noted that overrepresentation of males both in and out of classrooms, as voices of authority, diminish female performance. Surely a correlation can be drawn between this research and Eve's situation in *Paradise Lost*—and perhaps in the experience of today's students.

Returning to the epic, Raphael and Adam converse over lunch. When Raphael finishes relating the lessons he came to give, Adam is eager to prevent the angel from leaving and distracts him with a question.

> Adam:
> When I behold this goodly Frame, this World
> of Heav'n and Earth . . .
> And all her numberd Starrs, that seem to rowle
> Spaces incomprehensible . . .
> . . . merely to officiate light
> Round this opacous Earth, . . .
> I oft admire . . . (VIII.15–16, 19–20, 22–23, 25)

Adam finishes by asking the angel to explain the workings of the night sky. Students should know that this question is an echo of an earlier one spoken by Eve as she and Adam pondered the night sky ahead of Raphael's arrival:

> Eve:
> But wherefore all night long shine these, for whom
> This glorious sight, when sleep hath shut all eyes? (IV.657–58)

With these companion passages in mind, consider Eve's behavior after Adam asks his question of Raphael.

> So spake our Sire, and by his count'nance seemd
> Entring on studious thoughts abstruse, which *Eve*
> Perceaving where she sat retir'd in sight,
> With lowliness Majestic from her seat,
> And Grace that won who saw to wish her stay,
> Rose, and went forth among her Fruits and Flours,
> . . .
> Yet went she not, as not with such discourse
> Delighted, or not capable her eare
> Of what was high: such pleasure she reserv'd,
> *Adam* relating, she sole Auditress;
> Her Husband the Relater she preferr'd
> Before the Angel, and of him to ask
> Chose rather: hee, she knew would intermix

> Grateful digressions, and solve high dispute
> With conjugal Caresses, from his Lip
> Not Words alone pleas'd her. (VIII.39–44, 48–56)

Do students see evidence of feminine marginalization in these lines? Modern diversity research may help to reveal this diminishment. Let's look more closely at this research below.

Robin Lakoff (2004) provides research on how gendered linguistics entrench gendered power dynamics. One of these linguistic tools is silencing—in the form of trivialization, speech prevention, usurpation, misunderstanding, or invalidation. The purpose of silencing is to lock a woman into a subordinate position. Students can be asked whether they see any silencing in the above passages. For me there is the trivializing of Eve in Raphael's greeting that reinforces her role as breeder. There is explicit silencing when Eve is not invited to join the lunch conversation. And there is a usurpation by Adam of Eve's own "abstruse" question about the starry skies. But Milton is not done with silencing, for, as noted above, our narrator then mutters a paean to Eve's intelligence while emphasizing her sexuality. Students can be asked for their responses. What if such a scene played out in a modern setting? How would a woman of today respond to similar treatment? What might modern interpretations be for her leaving? I would suspect some irritation on Eve's part. We will soon find out how she responds, but the males are not quite done talking.

As the Adam–Raphael lunch scene winds down, Adam is still eager to delay the angel's departure; and he shares the pair's creation stories, his request for a fit mate, and his delight in Eve. It is in this passage that Adam describes that moment during Eve's creation story when she turns away from his "less amiablie milde" (IV.479) appearance. Let's see how Adam relates this moment to Raphael:

> Adam:
> ... seeing me, she turn'd;
> I follow'd her, she what was Honour knew,
> And with obsequious Majestie approv'd
> My pleaded reason. To the Nuptial Bowre
> I led her blushing like the Morn ... (VIII.507–11)

After students ponder this passage they can be asked for responses. Is Adam's revision of Eve's words more of Lakoff's silencing—via misunderstanding or invalidation? And consider this combination of modifiers: "obsequious Majestie" (VIII.509), which echoes the previously mentioned "lowliness Majestic" (VIII.42). Even the fused modifiers are in tension. Milton cannot give to Eve without also taking away immediately. How might students expect to see this tension in their own classrooms?

Adam's final words with Raphael are a continuation of Eve's creation story. After sharing the details, Adam is effusive in his passion for Eve, although he prefaces this with awareness of her inferiority—more of that tug of war between censure and compliment.

> Adam (to Raphael):
> ... [God] on her bestow'd
> Too much of Ornament, in outward shew
> Elaborate, of inward less exact.
> For well I understand in the prime end
> Of Nature her th' inferiour, in the mind
> And inward Faculties, ...
> In outward also her resembling less
> His Image who made both,
> ... yet when I approach
> Her loveliness, so absolute she seems
> And in her self compleat, so well to know
> Her own, that what she wills to do or say,
> Seems wisest, vertuouest, discreetest, best;
> ...
> As one intended first, not after made.
> (VIII.537–42, 546–50, 555)

Raphael is quick to admonish Adam for "attributing overmuch to things / Less excellent" (VIII.565–66). But Adam's intuitive admission that Eve's worth seems greater than convention permits is striking; even though it is nearly swamped by the conventional words of male dominance. For me, first reads of these minor notes—the admissions of appreciation for Eve—seemed like token generosities—easily dismissed as mere social lubricant. The overwhelming diminishment was what struck major notes. And I believe this has been true for Eve, as well. But things are about to change. There will be evidence that she has not strayed far from the lunch table, that she has heard this conversation about her, and dynamics between the pair will change.

Following this lunch scene, feminist theory and growth stage theory will reveal major change in Eve's development. The feminist scholar Jean Baker Miller (1986) has written that patriarchy damages both sexes and that conflict always attends inequality. We will also soon see how growth stage theory is operating to demand confrontation by Eve of the power imbalance. She surely knows that she has developed many skills. And with the many diminishments to her worth by Raphael and Adam over the lunch scene, I think she is ready to exert her identity. Have students read the following lines, the first words we hear between the couple following Raphael's departure.

> Eve:
> Adam, well may we labour still to dress
> This Garden, still to tend Plant, Herb and Flour,
> Our pleasant task enjoyn'd, but till more hands
> Aid us, the work under our labour grows
> ... hear what to my minde first thoughts present,
> Let us divide our labours (IX.205–08 213–14)
> Adam:
> ... mild answer *Adam* thus return'd.
> Sole *Eve*, Associate sole, to me beyond
> Compare above all living Creatures deare,
> ...
> nothing lovelier can be found
> In Woman, then to studie houshold good,
> And good workes in her Husband to promote. (IX.226–28, 232–34)
> [Eve is silent. Adam continues ...]
> But if much converse perhaps
> Thee satiate, to short absence I could yield.
> For solitude somtimes is best societie ... (IX.247–49)
> [Eve is still silent. And again, Adam continues ...]
> But other doubt possesses me, least harm
> Befall thee sever'd from me; for thou knowst
> What hath bin warn'd us, [about a] malicious Foe
> ...
> The Wife, where danger or dishonour lurks,

Safest and seemliest by her Husband staies,
Who guards her ... (IX.251-53, 267-69)

What do students think of this exchange? Have dynamics shifted? Eve's language is no longer docile. She is trenchant. Adam is now more docile—almost cajoling. Interestingly, as far as communication goes, both fail to be explicit about what might be going on under the surface. Is Adam perhaps sheepishly aware that Eve has some reasons for dudgeon? If this is true, he rather flatfootedly reinforces the injury to Eve with his various themes on womanly virtue. Conflict is in the air—just as Miller (1986) and growth stage theory predict. The exchange continues:

Eve:
That such an Enemie we have, who seeks
Our ruin, both by thee informd I learne,
And from the parting Angel over-heard
As in a shadie nook I stood
...
that thou shouldst my firmness therfore doubt
To God or thee, because we have a foe
May tempt it, I expected not to hear. (IX.274-77, 279-81)

First, I would note, from these lines, that Eve *confirms* she did not stray far from the lunch scene, so she probably did overhear the angel's diminishment of her. Again, students can be asked for responses. They may see continued direct (nondocile) language from Eve. Adam is surely on the back foot— guessing at her motives and spinning them to fit patriarchal dimensions. But it is the next remark that underscores another of Miller's feminist perceptions: dominant groups often "militate against stirring of greater rationality or greater humanity in their own members," i.e., men who "allow their women" more power than is proper get ridiculed (1986, pp. 7-8). We are told: "So spake domestick Adam" (IX.318). First Raphael admonishes Adam's uxoriousness, now Milton does the same.

Adam continues to warn Eve about the danger in Eden should she set out on her own. Eve is not dissuaded. Her valedictory response before leaving the clearing alone is especially powerful:

> Eve (to Adam):
> If this be our condition, thus to dwell
> In narrow circuit strait'nd by a Foe ...
> How are we happie ...
> ... what is Faith, Love, Vertue unassaid
> Alone, without exterior help sustaind? (IX.322–23, 326, 335–36)

Not only is this line powerful on its own merits, but it is powerful, as well, for being an echo of exhortations on freedom of speech from *Areopagitica* (Milton, 1644/2021a), another of Milton's works, where he argued at length for the end of licensing in Britain. His is a hauntingly similar line to Eve's; he wrote "I cannot praise a fugitive and cloister'd virtue, unexercised and unbreathed, that never sallies out and sees her adversary."

So, Eve wins the debate and leaves to work alone. Her reasoning has been elegant and compelling. If we have caught Milton's rhythm throughout the epic, however, we will probably expect a token sexualization, or some diminishment of Eve's worth after an example of empowerment; and if so, we will be rewarded for the insight. As Eve walks away from Adam, Milton delivers an epic simile based on the Roman myth of Pamona and Vertumnous.

This myth tells of Pamona, a wood nymph, guardian of fruit trees, who is pursued by the Vertumnus, the god of changing seasons. The beautiful Pamona, who has rejected romance out of devotion to her gardens, is eventually won over—after much trickery—by Vertumnus. Is this a presage of what is to come: that Eve will be tricked by Satan? Probably. But it is also a sly nod to the superiority of males who always triumph over females. Milton, it seems, must keep Eve subordinate. For students, this venture into mythology may not be of much interest, but I would argue that in any classroom—with students living out diverse customs—cultural stories are important.

As we all know, Eve succumbs to Satan's trickery as shown in the following passage. Students can be invited to respond after reading. As background to these lines, Satan is delighted to espy Eve approaching on her own. He makes a show of dazzling her in the guise of serpent, coils undulating seductively before her. Then he speaks, which truly takes her aback. He shares that he has become more elevated than is proper to his kind (serpent) through eating of the Tree of Knowledge of Good and Evil. Then, demonstrating a piercing awareness of Eve's great psychic wound based on her subordination, he advances a suggestion that she too can advance her station. Thus begins the scene of the Fall.

> Satan (to Eve):
> ... what are Gods that Man may not become
> As they, participating God-like food?
> The Gods are first, and that advantage use ...
> Why then was this forbid? ...
> Why but to keep ye low and ignorant ... (IX.716–18, 703–04)
> Narrator:
> He ended, and his words replete with guile
> Into her heart too easie entrance won ... (IX.733–34)

Eve eats the fruit, and "such delight til then, ... she never tasted" (IX.787–88). Within a few lines she exclaims "Inferior who is free" (IX.825). Students may have many responses to this epic climax. Which of Erikson's stages does Eve represent at this point? What do students think of Eve at this moment? What do students think about her reason for eating? For me there is an almost fatalistic expectation that she will eat. She will be trapped in Stage 5—the teenage, rebellious stage—unless she pushes through it. Until gender inequality is reconciled, there will be no peace for her—or Adam, if Miller (1986) is right. The great instability created by gender inequality is perhaps the pre-original sin in Eden. We tend to see the Fall as a fully negative event, but is it? Or is it a necessary part of growth and identity construction? Can students relate the lessons of this passage to their experiences in classrooms? Can they see any importance for their future in teaching?

Eve returns to Adam laden with the doomful fruit. He is horrified, but he eats—more horrified by thoughts of being separated from her through promised death than by dying himself. After an orgy-filled session of indulging, the pair awaken confounded by their trespass. They begin to cast blame back and forth until the Son arrives and challenges them both. Adam continues to rail at Eve, laying full blame upon her. But Eve makes a major transition at this very significant point in the story. When the Son asks her for an explanation she replies simply: "The Serpent me beguil'd and I did eate" (X.162). She never again casts blame on Adam.

Moral Development

Before we continue with the epic storyline, a review of Carol Gilligan's (1982) gender social theory is important. Gilligan describes the unfolding of her theory as a response to Lawrence Kohlberg's (McLeod, 2013) moral development theory—a theory rooted in a cognitive (i.e., based on reasoning) process that tracks moral development based on response to rightness or wrongness of behavior measured against an abstract system of logic and law. When Gilligan noticed that females often scored lower than males on the Kohlberg scale, she was compelled to uncover reasons for this. She discovered two things: first, that Kolhberg's experimental cohorts were all males, and second, that the two genders seemed, empirically, to approach moral issues differently. Both observations led Gilligan to further research. Using mixed-gender experimental cohorts, Gilligan's research revealed differences between the way males and females tend to view social situations: men see danger in personal connection, women in personal disconnection. Based on her findings, she went on to describe an ethic of care that seemed to guide women's sense of morality. In short, women tend to be less content in social hierarchies, more content in social patterns that emphasize interconnectedness. This information was key for my discernment of a more vital and effective Eve. With this information, let's look at the passage following the Son's departure from the pair. Adam continues to give voice to a deluge of derision:

> Adam:
> O why did God,
> Creator wise, that peopl'd highest Heav'n
> With Spirits Masculine, create at last
> This noveltie on Earth, this fair defect
> Of Nature, and not fill the World at once
> With Men as Angels without Feminine,
> Or find some other way to generate
> Mankind? (X.888–95)

While Adam rants, Eve, with that simple admission of guilt to the Son, transitions away from anger to something that looks very much like Gilligan's ethic of care.

Eve:
Forsake me not thus, *Adam*, witness Heav'n
What love sincere, and reverence in my heart
I beare thee, . . . (X.914–16)

Her words have a profound effect on Adam:

Adam responds:
. . . soon his heart relented
Towards her . . .
As one disarm'd his anger all he lost . . . (X.940–41, 945)

Students can be asked to respond with their own thoughts after reading these lines. What growth stage from Erikson's list does Eve seem to be exhibiting with this final exchange of conversation? I would place her at Stage 7 (Generativity vs. Stagnation/Self-absorption), a productive member of her community. How do students rate Eve's moral development? Is there any likelihood that her humility might be misread as docility or perhaps insufficiently rigorous in a moral sense—i.e., not sufficiently emphasizing abstract, impersonal laws of morality—as Kohlberg's scale emphasized? Or do students see Gilligan's ethic of care in action here? Can students recall personal classroom examples where Kohlberg or Gilligan interpretations were operating? Do students prefer Kohlberg or Gilligan's moral framework—or something different?

At this point, students can be asked if they find value in feminist insights with regard to the epic and, beyond that, with regard to teaching in future diverse classrooms? How does knowledge and identity development relate to moral development—for Eve and by extension for teachers and students? Students can also be asked if any of the above experiences in gender communication rang a familiar note with respect to their own lives. Can they see any value in using *Paradise Lost* to support their education lessons in a classroom?

Additional Passages from Paradise Lost for Discussion

Additional passages for use in class, along with discussion ideas, are shown below.

Reading 1: Have students read Adam's first words of the epic. He is talking with Eve about the one rule God has set for them in Eden:

> From us no other service then to keep
> This one, this easie charge, of all the Trees
> In Paradise that bear delicious fruit
> So various, not to taste that onely Tree
> Of knowledge, planted by the Tree of Life,
> So neer grows Death to Life, what ere Death is . . . (IV.411–25)

Discussion ideas:
1. Ask for general impressions of the covenant between God and humans: Life in exchange for not eating of the Tree of Knowledge.
2. Is it a problem that Adam and Eve do not understand what is meant by "death"?
3. Is there a rational reason for obedience? Is the reason obvious to Adam and Eve?
4. What education issues come to mind when reading this introductory passage of Adam's first words?
    a. What place does obedience have in a classroom?
    b. What growth stage is operating under the conditions of the covenant?
    c. What sort of messages are being routed to long-term memory?
    d. What questions would you raise if you were Adam or Eve given the terms of the covenant?
    e. Is it important that no reason is given for the prohibition of eating from the Tree of Knowledge? How would such an arbitrary rule feel to students in a classroom today?

Reading 2 (comparison passages): Having left Hell in search of God's new creatures (man), a disguised Satan asks for directions from the angel Uriel.

> Satan (to Uriel):
> . . . Brightest Seraph tell
> In which of all these shining Orbes hath Man
> His fixed seat . . .
> That I may find him, and with secret gaze,
> Or open admiration him behold [him. . . and] . . .

> The Universal Maker we may praise ... (III.667–69, 671–72, 677)
> Narrator:
> So spake the false dissembler unperceivd;
> For neither Man nor Angel can discern
> Hypocrisie, the onely evil that walks
> Invisible, except to God alone ... (III.681–84)

Ask students to consider the above passages with the following companion passage where Satan again disguises himself by inhabiting the body of a serpent to beguile and trick Eve.

> Narrator (of Satan):
> ... the Enemie of Mankind, enclos'd
> In Serpent ...
> Address'd his way,
> ... pleasing was his shape,
> And lovely, never since of Serpent kind
> Lovelier, ...
> ... of his tortuous Traine
> Curld many a wanton wreath in sight of *Eve*,
> To lure her Eye ...
> His fraudulent temptation thus began. (IX.494–96, 503–05, 516–18, 531)

As we know, Eve succumbs to Satan's guile. His words "too easie entrance won" (IX.734). So, both Uriel and Eve are duped by Satan. However, Uriel is given a pass—for only God could see past Satan's guile; but Eve is soundly rebuked and ejected from Eden.

Discussion ideas:

1. Ask for general thoughts on these companion passages—Satan's trickery of Uriel versus Satan's trickery of Eve's.

Are there similarities in fault? Are there differences? Is Eve more severely punished for being tricked by the "false dissembler" whose hypocrisy is the "onely evil that walks / Invisible, except to God alone" (III.683–84)? And does some of the research cited in the chapter seem relevant here (that females are more harshly punished than males for "aggressive" behavior)?

Epilogue

Robin Lakoff famously wrote that "language uses us as much as we use language" (2004, p. 39). This is perhaps one of the most powerful perceptions to internalize as one stands in front of a classroom. It is also intricately linked to critical thinking. *Paradise Lost*, a bravura piece of literature, offers a host of opportunities to inspire and strengthen these capabilities and the many tools of pedagogy that depend upon language use. Picking out the right words for the Bronfenbrenner model, accurately describing a student's growth stage with fairness for social-cultural-individual impediments and strengths, sending correct information through memory filters that sidesteps snares of bias all depend upon perceptive use of language—seeing beyond our automatic, enculturated, and often unfair interpretation of information. As there are few places like classical literature for ennobling, enlarging, and fine-tuning our language and social skills, these are indispensably and delightfully useful for empowering future teachers.

References

Brannon, L. (2009). *Gender: Psychological perspectives*. Allyn and Bacon.

Bronfenbrenner, U. (1999). Environments in development perspective: Theoretical and operational models. In *Measuring environment across the lifespan: Emerging models and concepts* (1st ed., pp. 3–28). American Psychological Association.

Cherry, K. (2021). Erik Erikson's stages of psychosocial development. *Verywell Mind*. Retrieved June 14, 2022, from https://www.verywellmind.com/about-us-5184564

Gilligan, C. (1982). *In a different voice*. Harvard University Press.

Herbert, J., & Stipek, D. (2005). The emergence of gender differences in children's perceptions of their academic competence. *Applied Developmental Psychology, 26*, 276–295.

Jones, S., & Dindia, K. (2004). A meta-analytic perspective on sex equity in the classroom. *Review of Educational Research, 74*(4), 443–472.

Lakoff, R. (2004). *Language and woman's place*. Oxford University Press.

Mapping the ecology of identity. (n.d.). *Re-imagining Migration*. Retrieved February 22, 2022, from https://reimaginingmigration.org/ecology-of-identity/

McLeod, S. (2013). Kohlberg's theory of moral development. *Simply Psychology*. Retrieved July 5, 2022, from https://www.simplypsychology.org/kohlberg.html.

Miller, J. B. (1986). *Toward a new psychology of women*. Beacon Press.

Milton, J. (2021a). *Areopagitica*. (T. Luxon, Ed.). The John Milton Reading Room: Dartmouth College Trustees. https://milton.host.dartmouth.edu/reading_room/areopagitica/text.shtml (Original work published 1644).

Milton, J. (2021b). *Paradise lost*. (T. Luxon, Ed). The John Milton Reading Room. Dartmouth College Trustees. https://milton.host.dartmouth.edu/reading_room/pl/book_1/text.shtml (Originally work published 1667).

Noushad, B., & Khurshid, F. (2019). Facilitating student learning: An instructional design perspective for health professions educators. *Research and Development in Medical Education, 8*(2), 69–74, from https://rdme.tbzmed.ac.ir/Article/rdme-31764

Okagaki, L., & Luster, T. (2005). Research on parental socialization of child outcomes: Current controversies and future directions. In T. Luster & L. Okagaki (Eds.), *Ecological perspective on parenting* (2nd ed., pp. 377–401). Lawrence Erlbaum Associates.

Orenstein, G. A., & Lewis, L. (2021). Erikson's stages of psychosocial development. *National Library of Medicine: National Center for Biotechnology Information*. Retrieved May 27, 2022, from https://www.ncbi.nlm.nih.gov/books/NBK556096/.

Slavin, R. E. (2018). *Educational psychology: Theory and practice* (12th ed.). Pearson.

Woolfolk, A. (2019). *Educational psychology*. (14th ed.). Pearson.

FIVE

 The Crooked Roads of Genius: William Blake and Educational Psychology

Jeff McLaughlin

WILLIAM BLAKE (1757–1827) WAS A poet, painter, printmaker, engraver, and visionary who remained largely unrecognized during his own lifetime. His body of work includes poetry, prose, illustration, and painting. Blake's most recognized work is *Songs of Innocence and Experience*, a series of poems and accompanying engraved illustrations (Erdman, 1982). (As Blake's writings remained unpublished during his lifetime, all references herein will be to Erdman's definitive 1982 volume of Blake's complete poetry and prose.) Other well-known works include *The Marriage of Heaven and Hell*, *Jerusalem*, *The Four Zoas*, *Milton*, and *The Book of Urizen* (Erdman, 1982).

The writings of William Blake contain many examples of poetry and prose that could be connected to concepts of educational psychology. These topics include cognition, identity development, moral reasoning, intelligence, and motivation. In this chapter, two of these areas—cognition and identity—will be reviewed in the context of Blake's writings.

Cognition and Cognitive Development

Throughout William Blake's extensive poetry and prose, there are numerous and varied references to cognition and to specific elements and processes comprising cognitive activity. An appropriate place to begin is with the work entitled *The Marriage of Heaven and Hell*, one of Blake's earlier illuminated (illustrated) books (Erdman, 1982). The original manuscript of *The Marriage of Heaven and Hell* includes both poetry and narrative in a series of 27 engraved color plates. In this work, Blake presented a philosophical and psychological vision of reality that encompasses physical, mental, moral, and spiritual planes. As the following examples will clarify, Blake believed human intelligence and imagination to be a reflection of a divine element within humans. In this view, development of one's unique and individual imagination is preferred over the acceptance of unexamined rationalist "truths" from external sources, such as school and church. As such, Blake has been variously labeled as a humanist (Keynes, 1975), as a mystic (White, 1964), and also—in some circles—as a heretic (Garnett, 2020). In more contemporary pedagogical terms, he might be labeled a visionary cognitive constructivist.

The term *constructivism* generally refers to theories of cognition based on the research of Piaget (1964), Vygotsky (1978), Bruner (1966), and others. While specific definitions vary widely, most constructivist theories emphasize the idea of a learner's active construction of meaning, a process that goes beyond information provided from an external source (Chi & Wylie, 2014; Schunk, 2020). This idea parallels Blake's idea of the imagination, as represented in the following line from *The Marriage of Heaven and Hell* (Erdman, 1982, p. 35): "A fool sees not the same tree that a wise man sees." (Note: In this and all following excerpts from Blake, original spellings, grammatical constructions, and punctuation are preserved, as reproduced in Erdman's definitive 1982 volume of Blake's complete poetry and prose.) Meaning-making, in the sense that Blake describes it here, is an individual and variable experience.

One of Blake's most widely recognized verses comes from *The Marriage of Heaven and Hell*: "If the doors of perception were cleansed everything would appear to man as it is, Infinite. For man has closed himself up, till he sees all things thro' narrow chinks in his cavern" (Erdman, 1982, p. 39). Again, the sense is that perception is most dependent upon individual cognitive interpretation, a process inevitably mediated with misunderstandings, limitations, and biases. This notion is one of the hallmarks of a constructivist view of cognition, and passages such as these could be used to frame an introductory classroom discussion of cognitive constructivism.

The "doors of perception" passage could also provide an opening to discuss the information-processing model of human memory (see Figure 5.1), an important theoretical conception of how perceptions are manipulated and managed in working (or short-term) memory prior to being encoded in long-term memory (Atkinson & Shiffrin, 1968; Radvansky & Ashcraft, 2018; Sternberg & Sternberg, 2016). For one thing, according to this model, the capacity of working memory is limited, with the respective roles of attention and perception being to select and then efficiently package sensory input, while also filtering irrelevant data (Anderson, 2015; Leppink et al., 2014; Sternberg & Sternberg, 2016). Also, it is at the perceptual stage of the process that preconceived

The Crooked Roads of Genius

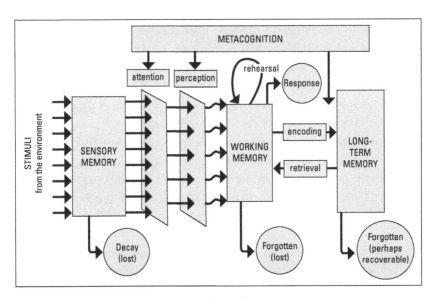

Figure 5.1. The information processing model of human memory.
Note: From Eggen, P., & Kauchak, D. (2016). *Educational psychology: Windows on classrooms* (10th ed.), p. 269. Pearson.

knowledge, implicit biases, and prior misconceptions (inaccurate knowledge) can form "narrow chinks" through which only a limited amount of new information can pass (diSessa, 2006; Vosniadou, 2007). Given this tendency, part of a teacher's role is to assist students in cleansing their perceptual doors to increase the likelihood that the world will be seen "as it is" and not as the learner has predetermined it to be. This brief passage from Blake could, given these connections, provide an illustrative introduction to the study of the information processing model of human memory. Upon reading this passage for themselves, students could be asked questions such as, "From this brief excerpt, what would you conclude is William Blake's concept of human memory?" and "How would cleansing one's doors of perception improve cognition?"

Another interpretive approach to the "doors of perception" passage would be to discuss what many educators and researchers have viewed as an overemphasis on rational-linguistic thinking in schools (Vassallo, 2017; Eggen & Kauchak, 2016). In other words, as teachers focus on specific (e.g., as represented on standardized tests) subject matter—particularly in language arts and math—they may contribute to a further blocking up of the doors of perception. This has the effect of limiting other (e.g., nontested) modes and styles of thought that might enhance perception (open the doors), including creative and imaginative thinking, collaborative learning, and physical, hands-on activity in the real world. Using Blake's words as a springboard, students could be asked to describe aspects of their own schooling that may have closed doors in their own perceptual experiences.

In another section of *The Marriage of Heaven and Hell*, Blake offers a description of alternate modes of perception, specifically perception that occurs beyond the senses. This passage recounts a scenario where Blake is dining with the Old Testament prophets Isaiah and Ezekiel. Blake uses the discussion with the prophets to illustrate his conviction that the imagination may provide a more truthful vision than is available through the five senses (or "finite organical perception" in Blake's words). An excerpt follows:

> The prophets Isaiah and Ezekiel dined with me, and I asked them how they dared so roundly to assert that God spake to them.; and whether they did not think at the time, that they would be misunderstood, & so be the cause of imposition. Isaiah answer'd. I saw no God, nor heard any, in a finite organical perception; but my senses discover'd the infinite in every thing. . . . Then I asked: does a firm perswasion that a thing is so, make it so? He replied. All poets believe that it does, & in ages of imagination, this firm perswasion removed mountains; but many are not capable of a firm perswasion of any thing. (Erdman, 1982, p. 38)

While the meaning of this passage is open to varied interpretations and critiques, the reality of perception beyond the five senses is worthy of consideration, as the information processing model does not appear to account for this possibility. Again, the excerpt could provide a springboard to classroom discussions about the possibilities and limitations of human perception.

In another passage from the same work, there is a rather detailed description of the transmission and expansion of knowledge, beginning with perception via the five senses and progressing to the permanent encoding of knowledge in long-term memory (and also, in this case, in books).

> I was in a Printing house in Hell & saw the method in which knowledge is transmitted from generation to generation.
> In the first chamber was a Dragon-Man, clearing away the rubbish from the caves mouth; within, a number of Dragons were hollowing the cave,
> In the second chamber was a Viper folding round the rock & cave, and others adorning it with gold silver and precious stones.

> In the third chamber was an Eagle with wings and feathers of air, he caused the inside of the cave to be infinite, around were numbers of Eagle like men, who built palaces in the immense cliffs.
> In the fourth chamber were Lions of flaming fire raging around & melting the metals into living fluids.
> In the fifth chamber were Unnam'd forms, which cast the metals into the expanse.
> There they were reciev'd by men who occupied the sixth chamber, and took the forms of books & were arranged in libraries. (Erdman, 1982, p. 40)

There are additional instances in *The Marriage of Heaven and Hell* (Erdman, 1982) that further illustrate phases of the memory process. Two examples follow, along with connections to information processing. In each instance, students could read the passage and infer (individually or in group discussions) the connection to memory and information processing. To provide further reinforcement of the concepts, students could also be asked to recount experiences from their own educational histories that illustrate the central ideas that Blake conveys. (1) "The man who never alters his opinion is like standing water & breeds reptiles of the mind" (p. 42). In working memory, via various cognitive strategies, information is processed for encoding into long-term memory. Often, the encoded information is at odds with the thinker's existing knowledge base and some accommodation (Piaget, 1955) must occur or thinking and knowledge become, to use Blake's imagery, stagnant. (2) "How do you know but ev'ry bird that cuts the airy way, is an immense world of delight clos'd by your senses five?" (p. 35). Once perception has been impaired, it becomes difficult to acquire deep knowledge of the world.

There are numerous other excerpts from Blake that could be naturally related to cognitive processing. Two examples are summarized below, along with the specific concepts they illustrate.

Attention and Perception (from *The Book of Urizen*)

> Then the Inhabitants of those Cities
> Felt their Nerves change into Marrow
> And hardening Bones began
> In swift diseases and torments,
> In throbbings & shootings & grindings

> Thro' all the coasts; till weaken'd
> The Senses inward rush'd shrinking,
> Beneath the dark net of infection.
> Till the shrunken eyes clouded over
> Discernd not the woven hipocracy
> But the streaky slime in their heavens
> Brought together by narrowing perceptions
> Appeard transparent air; for their eyes
> Grew small like the eyes of a man
> And in reptile forms shrinking together
> Of seven feet stature they remaind . . .
> No more could they rise at will
> In the infinite void, but bound down
> To earth by their narrowing perceptions. (Erdman, 1982, pp. 82–83)

While this passage may seem somewhat obscure, it could be a rich source for discussing stages of cognitive processing and, more specifically, the causes and consequences of failures to process information at those stages. For example, students could infer to what Blake was referring when he wrote, "The Senses inward rush'd shrinking, / Beneath the dark net of infection?" Also, students could be asked to connect the following phrases with cognition and information processing: "shrunken eyes clouded over," "No more could they rise at will in the infinite void, "bound down to earth by their narrowing perceptions."

The entirety of *The Book of Urizen* can actually be seen as a commentary on the role (and limitations) of sensory perception. Urizen (or "your reason," as many commentators interpret it) is an embodiment of the rational human tendency to mark boundaries in perception, to separate and divide, to see the details and overlook the whole. Urizen represents the primacy of rationality over passion and imagination (named Los). Perception that is limited in this way is perception reduced to particulars and lacking meaningful context. It is also perception that is egocentric and self-referenced, or in Blake's words (Erdman, 1982), "unprolific," "self-clos'd," a "soul-shuddering vacuum," and "petrific abominable chaos" (pp. 70–71).

The Book of Urizen is among the many manuscripts that were published as illuminated texts, usually in the form of engraved plates including both words and illustrations. In these cases, Blake's method of production and presentation actually serves as an additional instance of the limitations of rational perception and thought (Bigwood, 2001). In other words, the illuminated texts, with words and illustrations intertwined, facilitate—maybe even necessitate—a holistic reading (perceiving like Los) that results in a fuller perceptual experience than would be possible by reading printed words alone (perceiving like Urizen).

The Limitations of Perception (from *Milton*)

According to the information processing model, attention acts as a filter that selects, from the myriad of incoming sensory information, what is actually perceived and, ultimately, processed in short-term memory. Information that does not receive attention is, presumably, permanently lost. The action of the attention filter is a function of prior knowledge, past experience, and bias, among other factors. The filtering process can result in attention (and ultimately, perception) that is limited by prior experience or selective bias, focusing on some perceptual data at the expense of other information presented in the sensory field. The following two passages capture something of these attentional limitations and could be presented as an introduction to the topic.

> Ah weak & wide astray! Ah shut in narrow doleful form
> Creeping in reptile flesh upon the bosom of the ground
> The Eye of Man a little narrow orb closed up & dark
> Scarcely beholding the great light conversing with the Void.
> (from *Milton*, Erdman, 1982, p. 99)

> He who binds to himself a joy
> Does the winged life destroy
> But he who kisses the joy as it flies
> Lives in eternity's sun rise. (from *Eternity*, Erdman, 1982, p. 470)

Creative Thinking

The entirety of Blake's *Songs of Innocence and Songs of Experience* (Erdman, 1982, pp. 7–32) is essentially a testament to the possibility of contrary (and seemingly contradictory) concepts existing in tandem within the human mind. This ability is one of the hallmarks of creative thinking, according to numerous theorists in this area (Beghetto & Kaufman, 2017; Csikszentmihalyi, 2013; Kaufman & Gregoire, 2017; Kim & Lim, 2019; Sawyer, 2015). The following paired poems from *Songs of Innocence and Songs of Experience* (Erdman, 1982) illustrate the coexistence of such contraries from the perspective of an infant's view of the world:

> Infant Joy (Song 25)
> I have no name
> I am but two days old. –
> What shall I call thee?
> I happy am
> Joy is my name, –
> Sweet joy befall thee!
> Pretty joy!
> Sweet joy but two days old,
> Sweet joy I call thee;
> Thou dost smile.
> I sing the while
> Sweet joy befall thee. (Erdman, 1982, p. 16)

> Infant Sorrow (Song 48)
> My mother groand! My father wept.
> Into the dangerous world I leapt:
> Helpless, naked, piping loud;
> Like a fiend hid in a cloud.
> Struggling in my fathers hands:
> Striving against my swadling bands:
> Bound and weary I thought best
> To sulk upon my mothers breast. (Erdman, 1982, p. 28)

Additional paired poems from *Songs of Innocence and Songs of Experience* (Erdman, 1982) exemplify contrary perceptions of various phenomena. These include *Nurse's Song / Nurses Song* (pp. 15, 23), *The Chimney Sweeper / The Chimney Sweeper* (pp. 10, 22–23), and *The Divine Image / The Human Abstract* (pp. 12, 27). Students in the college classroom could discuss the issues raised in the poems from the diverse (contrary) perspectives and then relate their own cognitive processing to the constructs of creativity and critical thinking.

As a follow-up to the above discussion, *The Marriage of Heaven and Hell* (Erdman, 1982) contains a very specific reference to these creative thought processes:

> Without Contraries is no progression. Attraction and Repulsion, Reason and Energy, Love and Hate, are necessary to Human existence.
> From these contraries spring what the religious call Good & Evil. Good is the passive that obeys Reason. Evil is the active springing from Energy.
> Good is Heaven. Evil is Hell. (p. 34)

From the initial idea of contraries, classroom discussions could focus upon a range of cognitive phenomena related to creativity. For example: What do these passages suggest about the cognitive processing involved in creative thinking? What other aspects of creative thinking can you discern in these verses? Is anything in these passages reflective of your own creative process?

To conclude this section on cognition, the following selected lines from *Auguries of Innocence* (Erdman, 1982, pp. 490-493) could be used to facilitate a summary discussion of cognitive processing and cognitive development:

> To see a World in a Grain of Sand
> And a Heaven in a Wild Flower
> Hold Infinity in the palm of your hand
> And Eternity in an hour
> The Bat that flits at close of Eve
> Has left the Brain that wont Believe
> The Owl that calls upon the Night
> Speaks the Unbelievers fright
> He who mocks the Infants Faith
> Shall be mock'd in Age & Death
> He who shall teach the Child to Doubt
> The rotting Grave shall neer get out
> He who respects the Infants faith
> Triumphs over Hell & Death
> The Questioner who sits so sly
> Shall never know how to Reply
> He who replies to words of Doubt
> Doth put the Light of Knowledge out
> He who Doubts from what he sees
> Will neer Believe do what you Please
> If the Sun & Moon should Doubt
> Theyd immediately Go out
> We are led to Believe a Lie
> When we see not Thro the eye

Identity Development

In his writings, Blake had a great deal to say about the formation of human identity. For example, many of his poetic descriptions parallel Erik Erikson's stage theory of identity development (Erikson, 1980), which will be the focus of this section. For example, consider the following passage from *The Marriage of Heaven and Hell*:

> Once meek, and in a perilous path,
> The just man kept his course along
> The vale of death.
> Roses are planted where thorns grow.
> And on the barren heath sing the honey bees.
> Then the perilous path was planted:
> And a river, and a spring
> On every cliff and tomb;
> And on the bleached bones
> Red clay brought forth.
> Till the villain left the paths of ease,
> To walk in perilous paths, and drive
> The just man into barren climes.
> Now the sneaking serpent walks
> In mild humility.
> And the just man rages in the wilds
> Where lions roam.

In these verses, Blake essentially outlines the process—proposed by Erikson (1980)—whereby individuals who develop a sense of autonomy in early childhood are better equipped to succeed in healthy ego formation during adolescence and beyond. The "perilous path" represents the kind of identity crisis that Erikson describes at each stage of development across the lifespan. In early childhood, healthy guidance can result in a sense of autonomy and self-initiative while shame, guilt, and a sense of inferiority result from a lack of positive adult modeling and direction. In adolescence, a sense of personal identity is the goal, while role confusion and a weak sense of self can represent failure to constructively negotiate this stage of development. At each stage of Erikson's model, if the relevant crisis is negotiated adequately, the individual is prepared to weather the "barren heath." In this context (as is typical for Blake) the "villain" is actually the protagonist, the one who eschews conformity in order to establish an individual (and wholesome) identity. In the educational psychology classroom, students could be asked to interpret these lines and then relate them to the various stages and identity crises described by Erikson.

More specifically related to identity development in very young children, some lines (also quoted above in connection with cognition) from *Auguries of Innocence* (Erdman, 1982, p. 492) seem to describe Erikson's earliest stages of identity development, occurring from infancy through pre-kindergarten age.

> He who shall teach the Child to Doubt
> The rotting Grave shall ne'er get out
> He who respects the Infants faith
> Triumphs over Hell and death . . .
> If the Sun & Moon should Doubt
> They'd immediately Go out.

Infants develop a sense of trust when caregivers provide reliable support. Later, as children begin to assert control over their environments, they need support to develop a sense of purpose and initiative. These developmental requirements are succinctly summarized in the lines above. Then, in adolescence, individuals are faced with new challenges to the sense of self and personal identity. These challenges—or crises—are reinforced through social (peer) relationships and by an increased ability and interest in imagining the future.

The following two examples reinforce the notion that identity development involves a degree of risk, as individuals assert independence and thereby turn away from some of the securities of early childhood. The first excerpt is from a letter from Blake to Reverend Dr. Trusler, written in 1799:

> Every body does not see alike. To the Eyes of a Miser a Guinea is more beautiful than the Sun . . . The tree which moves some to tears of joy is in the Eyes of others only a Green thing that stands in the way . . . As a Man is So he Sees. (Erdman, 1982, p. 702)

The second excerpt is from The Book of Urizen (Erdman, 1982, p. 71):

> Hidden set apart in my stern counsels
> Reserv'd for the days of futurity,

> I have sought for a joy without pain,
> For a solid without fluctuation

The Book of Urizen (Erdman, 1982, pp. 70–83) was cited in the previous section as exemplary of the limitations of rational and reductionistic perception. There is also a connection to identity here, for as perceptions are "petrified," identity becomes—to use Erikson's term—"foreclosed." In other words, to the extent that our perception results in a "petrified" knowledge base, we are no longer constructing new meanings for ourselves; we have made our choices and thereby "foreclosed" upon any further development of knowledge or understanding. This idea of foreclosure suggests implications for a variety of college classroom discussions focusing on identity and knowledge development and, specifically, on issues such as stereotyping, political partisanship, racism, and climate change denial.

The individual who is able to move beyond identity foreclosure, to consider and even embrace new possibilities, enters a state the Erikson called identity achievement. That process of leaving one's comfort zone (foreclosure) can be fraught with anxiety and anguish, as suggested in the poem called *Mad Song* (Erdman, 1982, p. 415–416):

> Like a fiend in a cloud
> With howling woe,
> After night I do croud,
> And with night will go;
> I turn my back to the east,
> From whence comforts have increas'd;
> For light doth seize my brain
> With frantic pain.

Moving beyond Erikson's popular theory of identity development, Blake's writings contain many other glimpses at the nature of identity, of selfhood, and of individuation. In the varied cosmic scenarios depicted throughout Blake's writings, an eternal struggle rages among the separate dimensions of human identity. Blake often expressed his concern with the way individuals lose trust in their own experiences and instead substitute a defensive false self or alternate identity. In *America*, Blake advised,

The Crooked Roads of Genius 83

> Let the slave grinding at the mill, run out into the field:
> Let him look up into the heavens & laugh in the bright air;
> Let the inchained soul shut up in darkness and in sighing, . . .
> Rise and look out, his chains are loose, . . . (Erdman, 1982, p. 53).

This passage could become the basis for a wide-ranging discussion of identity development; students might be asked to interpret the line and also to cite illustrative examples from their own lived experience as students.

In a section of *The Marriage of Heaven and Hell* called "Proverbs of Hell" (Erdman, 1982, pp. 35–38), Blake provides the following axioms, each of which could be used to advance a classroom discussion of identity formation in children and adolescents.

> In seed time, learn, in harvest time, teach, in winter, enjoy.
> No bird soars too high, if he soars with his own wings.
> Always be ready to speak your mind, and a base man will avoid you.
> Every thing possible to be believ'd is an image of truth.
> The eagle never lost so much time as when he submitted to learn from the crow.
> The tygers of wrath are wiser than the horses of instruction.
> Expect poison from standing water.
> The crow wish'd every thing was black, the owl, that everything was white.
> Improvement makes strait roads, but the crooked roads without Improvement, are roads of Genius.

In several of Blake's longer poems, a character named Urizen represents the rational component of human identity. In Blake's worldview, much suffering and alienation results from this element becoming splintered off to gain dominance over the rest of the perceiving personality. In poems such as *America, The Book of Urizen, Milton,* and *The Four Zoas,* the result of Urizen's (reason's) domination is a weakening of other human faculties of perception such as imagination and passion. When the various components of personhood are disintegrated in this way, individuals cannot hope to realize their true selves. Blake assigned a variety of human institutions with responsibility for forming individuals thus limited in perception, including schools. (Of course, Blake also had much to say about the influence of the institutional church in this regard, but for present purposes, the impact of schooling will be the focus.) In his *Satiric Verses* (Erdman, 1982, p. 510), Blake announces, "Thank God I was never sent To School, / To be Flogged into following the Style of a Fool." In the college classroom, a range of discussions could revolve around this notion of the limitations imposed by schools that, while charged with the task of expanding students' intellectual horizons, may actually shrink them for the sake of narrowly specified gains in intellectual achievement. The following poem from *Songs of Experience* (Erdman, 1982, p. 31) illustrates this phenomenon from Blake's perspective.

> The School Boy
> I love to rise in a summer morn,
> When the birds sing on every tree;
> The distant huntsman winds his horn,
> And the sky-lark sings with me.
> O! what sweet company.
> But to go to school in a summer morn,
> O! it drives all joy away;
> Under a cruel eye outworn,
> The little ones spend the day,
> In sighing and dismay.
> Ah! then at times I drooping sit,
> And spend many an anxious hour.
> Nor in my book can I take delight,
> Nor sit in learnings bower,
> Worn thro' with the dreary shower.
> How can the bird that is born for joy,
> Sit in a cage and sing.
> How can a child when fears annoy,
> But droop his tender wing,
> And forget his youthful spring.
> O! father and mother, if buds are nipped,
> And blossoms blown away,
> And if the tender plants are strip'd
> Of their joy in the springing day,
> By sorrow and cares dismay,
> How shall the summer arise in joy.
> Or the summer fruits appear,
> Or how shall we gather what griefs destroy
> Or bless the mellowing year,
> When the blasts of winter appear.

The following excerpts deal specifically with Urizen's destructive influence on the developing identity. The language in these lines is rather esoteric and difficult to read (as in much of Blake's writing). However, the goal is not to arrive at a single endorsed interpretation, but rather to facilitate students' deep thinking about the impact of society and school on a child's emerging identity.

> O Urizen! Creator of men! mistaken Demon of heaven:
> Thy joys are tears! thy labor vain, to form men to thine image.
> (from *Visions of the Daughters of Albion*, Erdman, 1982, p. 48)

> Times on times [Urizen] divided, & measured
> Space by space in his ninefold darkness
> Unseen, unknown! changes appeard
> In his desolate mountains rifted furious
> By the black winds of perturbation.
> (from *The Book of Urizen*, Erdman, 1982, p. 70)

Again, the goal here is not literary interpretation but rather creative and thoughtful application of Blake's words to concepts related to the role of schools and teachers in personality and identity development. For example, with the second excerpt above, a discussion might begin with the simple question, "So, in what ways does that sound like your own high school experience?"

For Blake, once an individual succeeds in rejecting stifling systems of thought, identity becomes reintegrated, with all of its dimensions coexisting in harmonious activity. This is the process of becoming fully human, or in more pedagogical terms, of becoming educated.

Sample Lesson Plan: "Your Brain at School"
Introduction to Information Processing (75-minute class session)

Lesson Objectives

The three main objectives of this introductory lesson are:

1. to introduce the information processing model of human memory and learning;
2. to facilitate student understanding by connecting elements of the information processing model with selected passages from the writings of William Blake;

3. to encourage students to relate information processing theory to their own experiences as learners.

Materials / Resources

- Eggen and Kauchak (2016, p. 269): diagram of the information processing model.
- Excerpts from William Blake's *The Book of Urizen*, Spring, and others (Erdman, 1982).
- Online discussion forum. (My institution uses *D2L*, but any platform that allows for public posting and commenting will suffice.)
- Presentation software. (I use *Keynote* for Apple devices, but PowerPoint or similar tools will also suffice.)

Method

Begin with the presentation of the following passage from William Blake's poem entitled *The Book of Urizen* (Erdman, 1982):

> Then the Inhabitants of those Cities
> Felt their Nerves change into Marrow
> And hardening Bones began
> In swift diseases and torments,
> In throbbings & shootings & grindings
> Thro' all the coasts; till weaken'd
> The Senses inward rush'd shrinking,
> Beneath the dark net of infection.
> Till the shrunken eyes clouded over
> Discernd not the woven hipocracy
> But the streaky slime in their heavens
> Brought together by narrowing perceptions
> Appeard transparent air; for their eyes
> Grew small like the eyes of a man
> And in reptile forms shrinking together
> Of seven feet stature they remaind . . .
> No more could they rise at will
> In the infinite void, but bound down
> To earth by their narrowing perceptions. (pp. 82–83)

The Crooked Roads of Genius

Project the entire passage and/or distribute individual copies to students. Ask students to read the passage for themselves and then facilitate an initial discussion with questions such as:

What does this passage mean to you?

How does the passage relate to psychological concepts such as perception, memory, or learning?

Is there anything in this passage to which you can relate personally (for example, from your own school, family, or social background)?

Next, refer to the diagram of the information processing model (see Figure 5.2). Point out and elaborate briefly upon the three main elements: sensory memory, short-term (working) memory, and long-term memory. Ask: Which of these phases of the memory process is reflected in the passage from Blake? How? What does the Blake passage indicate about how our memories function? (Answers will vary.)

A more detailed overview of the model should now be presented. It is assumed that subsequent class sessions will focus in more detail upon the specific structure and function of the information processing model. For

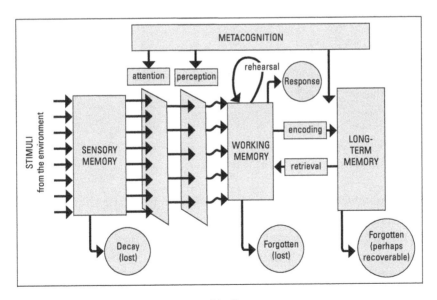

Figure 5.2. The information processing model of human memory.
Note: From Eggen, P., & Kauchak, D. (2016). *Educational psychology: Windows on classrooms* (10th ed.), Pearson. p. 269.

introductory purposes, each of the three phases should be defined with the following emphases:

Sensory memory is the initial stage, where incoming stimuli are sensed, then perceived, and then attended to, prior to being transferred to working memory. At this stage, prior knowledge, biases, and misconceptions can determine which bits of information receive further processing and which are lost and therefore unavailable for processing.

Working memory is where data are encoded for eventual transfer into long-term memory. Because working memory is limited, strategies such as rehearsal, automaticity, imagery, and chunking are used to reduce the memory load and enable numerous bits of knowledge to be processed efficiently.

Long-term memory is where information is stored permanently and made available for eventual retrieval. The form in which the information is initially stored (i.e., how it was processed in working memory) will determine the manner in which it is most effectively retrieved.

Memory activity: Read aloud the following passage from Blake's *Spring* (Erdman, 1982, pp. 14–15) after informing students that they will be asked to recite as much of the passage as they can remember.

> Sound the Flute!
> Now it's mute.
> Birds delight
> Day and Night.
> Nightingale
> In the dale
> Lark in Sky
> Merrily
> Merrily Merrily to welcome in the Year

As volunteers recite from memory, ask them to describe how they processed the passage while listening. Document the strategies used, specifically as they correspond with working memory processes such as rehearsal, automaticity, imagery, and chunking.

Culminating activity: Divide the class into discussion groups, with the number of groups and individual group sizes dependent upon the overall class size. Each group should receive one Blake excerpt from the following group:

1. "If the doors of perception were cleansed everything would appear to man as it is, Infinite. For man has closed himself up, till he sees all things thro' narrow chinks in his cavern" (Erdman, 1982, p. 39).
2. "The tree which moves some to tears of joy is in the eyes of others only a green thing which stands in the way" (Erdman, 1982, p. 702).
3. "The man who never alters his opinion is like standing water & breeds reptiles of the mind" (Erdman, 1982, p. 42).
4. "How do you know but ev'ry bird that cuts the airy way, is an immense world of delight clos'd by your senses five?" (Erdman, 1982, p. 35).
5. "The Eye of Man a little narrow orb closed up & dark / Scarcely beholding the great light conversing with the Void" (Erdman, 1982, p. 99).
6. "If the Sun & Moon should Doubt / Theyd immediately Go out" (Erdman, 1982, p. 492).
7. "We are led to Believe a Lie / When we see not Thro the eye" (Erdman, 1982, p. 492).

Instruct students to first read and reflect independently upon the assigned passage. Then, the groups should assemble to discuss (for approximately 10 minutes) the following questions:

To which part of the information processing model does your passage most closely relate? Based on this brief passage, what might you assume about William Blake's notion of memory? Is there any way that this passage connects with your own personal experience as a learner?

If time permits, bring the class back together and have groups summarize the connections between their assigned passages and the information processing model. Specific responses and ideas should be expected to vary among students. In other words, there is no single correct interpretation implied in these passages from Blake. The overriding purpose is to facilitate discussion and reflection upon possible connections between literature and the psychological concepts.

The presentation and discussion above should provide students with a foundational basis upon which to build further understanding of and insight into the information processing model. Again, it is assumed that subsequent class sessions will build upon this introductory framework, with additional discussion of relevant concepts from the information processing model.

Conclusion and Suggestions for Follow-up Research

The writings of William Blake provide a rich source of examples of and references to psychological concepts of the kind typically discussed in educational psychology courses. Both undergraduate and graduate students could enhance their understanding of these concepts through interpretive discussions of Blake's poetry and prose. I have focused on two of these conceptual areas (cognition and identity) and also suggested additional areas where Blake's writings would apply.

While I can personally attest to the efficacy of the approaches herein described, more intentional follow-up research should be designed to determine whether these strategies do, in fact, enhance student understanding and application of psychological concepts. A qualitative or mixed-methods approach would be appropriate for assessing student understanding of and engagement with psychological material represented in Blake's writings. It would also be feasible to design an investigation among multiple sections of a course in educational psychology to determine the relative efficacy of alternate approaches, including one based on literary material.

In addition to the research implications, a rationale has been established for the design and implementation of additional lessons incorporating the writings of William Blake in college classrooms. Perhaps the example of William Blake (along with others in this volume) could serve as motivation for others to design—and assess—college-level courses and lessons that integrate literature with teacher education curricula.

References

Anderson, J. R. (2015). *Cognitive psychology and its implications* (8th ed.). Worth.

Atkinson R. C., & Shiffrin, R. M. (1968). Human memory: A proposed system and its control processes. In K. Spence & J. Spence (Eds.), *The psychology of learning and motivation* (pp. 89–195). Academic Press.

Beghetto, R. A., & Kaufman, J. C. (Eds.). (2017). *Nurturing Creativity In The Classroom* (2nd Ed). Cambridge University Press.

Bigwood, C. (2001). Seeing Blake's illuminated texts. *The Journal of Aesthetics and Art Criticism, 49*, 4, 307–315. https://doi.org/10.2307/431031

Blake, W. (1975). *The marriage of Heaven and Hell*. Oxford.

Bruner, J. S. (1966). *Toward a theory of instruction*. Norton.

Chi, M. T. H., & Wylie, R. (2014). The ICAP Framework: Linking cognitive engagement to active learning outcomes. *Educational Psychologist, 49*, 219–243. https://doi.org/10.1080/00461520.2014.965823

Csikszentmihalyi, M. (2013). *Creativity: The psychology of discovery and invention.* Harper Perennial.

diSessa, A. (2006). A history of conceptual change research: Threads and fault lines. In R. K. Sawyer (Ed.). *Cambridge handbook of the learning sciences* (pp. 265–282). Cambridge University Press.

Eggen, P., & Kauchak, D. (2016). *Educational psychology: Windows on classrooms* (10th ed.). Pearson.

Erdman, D. V. (Ed.) (1982). *The complete poetry and prose of William Blake.* University of California Press.

Erikson, E. H. (1980). *Identity and the life cycle.* Norton.

Garnett, I. (2020). *William Blake: Painter and Poet* (Annotated). Castillo.

Kaufman, S. B., & Gregoire, C. (2017). *Wired to create: Unraveling the mysteries of the creative mind.* TarcherPerigee.

Kim, D., & Lim, H. (2019). Creativity and simultaneous interpretation - The two shall never meet? *International Journal of Bilingualism, 23*(6), 1316–1332. https://doi.org/10.1177/1367006918786472

Leppink, J., Paas, F., van Gog, T., van der Vleuten, C. P. M., & van Merriënboer, J. J. C. (2014). Effects of pairs of problems and examples on task performance and different types of cognitive load. *Learning and Instruction, 30*, 32–42. https://doi.org/10.1016/j.learninstruc.2013.12.001

Piaget, J. (1955). *The construction of reality in the child.* Routledge and Kegan Paul.

Piaget, J. (1964). *The moral judgment of the child.* Free Press.

Radvansky, G. A., & Ashcroft, M. H. (2018). *Cognition* (7th ed.). Pearson.

Sawyer, K. (2015). A call to action: The challenges of creative thinking and learning. *Teachers College Record, 117*, 1–34.

Schunk, D. H. (2020). *Learning theories: An educational perspective* (8th ed.). Allyn & Bacon/Pearson.

Sternberg, R. J., & Sternberg, K. (2016). *Cognitive psychology* (7th ed.). Wadsworth.

Vassallo, S. (2017). *Critical educational psychology.* Johns Hopkins University Press.

Vosniadou, S. (2007). The cognitive-situative divide and the problem of conceptual change. *Educational Psychologist, 42*(1), 55–66. https://doi.org/10.1080/00461520709336918

Vygotsky, L. S. (1978). *Mind in society.* Harvard University Press.

White, H. C. (1964). *The mysticism of William Blake.* Russell & Russell.

SIX

 Gilgamesh, Enkidu, and Ishtar: Lessons on Living for Incarnated Souls

Margarita García-Notario

EXPERIENCED TEACHERS KNOW WHAT IT is like to walk into a classroom where students can't wait to work on the material. It normally takes a while until one becomes a teacher who can make classes *truly* exciting and rewarding. While not all materials contain that potential, stories are naturally attractive. In this chapter, I will use a beautiful old story to offer future teachers some examples of how selected folktales and legends can be used as a valuable teaching tool for teacher education students.

Humans love stories; we seem naturally attuned to them. Myths, folktales, and legends have a special magic; they help us transcend bleakness and witness human resilience, effort, and commitment to intuitive values. Stories can invoke strength in the listener, rivet their attention, and encourage them to prepare to face the *next* challenge, which will inevitably emerge, much in the same way as in the story of Hercules combating the Hydra, a monster whose heads multiplied as Hercules cut them off. There will always pop up a new "threatening head" in our lives, so we need to be aware and prepare. Many stories also pose moral dilemmas such as justice vs. injustice, abuse vs. respect, or generosity vs. fraud. Classic myths illuminate many questions on moral and character development, a key issue for future teachers.

Inside the myths of ancient cultures, human nature and human experience reveal themselves as something much more stable and predictable than many current explanations and reasonings would have it. While getting to know old stories, we can recognize many of the everyday conflicts and difficulties that all humans face. In teacher education, these stories can be especially useful in helping future teachers to embrace multiple perspectives and, in turn, to promote thoughtful discussions with their own future students. For future teachers exploring old stories, other relevant topics include the quest for happiness and fulfillment, sex, taboos and censorship, freedom, and the fragility of life.

Gilgamesh works like the majority of classic myths: not everything works out the way most of us would hope for or prefer; but their stories connect with all of us, and especially with the youth at a deep level. In the Sumerian *Epic of Gilgamesh* (Kovacs, 1998), both male and female figures coexist in ways that enrich, expand, balance, and complete how we might understand and build better selves through their collaborative experiences and knowledge. The "message" of the story is more authentic and meaningful because the male and the female roles are compatible and mutual, instead of competitively destructive.

The Epic of Gilgamesh is the oldest written literary document unearthed by archeologists (George, 2017). Europeans recovered and revived this story, along with other ancient documents, in the middle of the 19th century. In the following sections, I offer suggestions for using Gilgamesh with future teachers. I will also propose some guiding questions for discussion about some of the epic's most relevant topics.

Wildness and The City: Gilgamesh and Enkidu

The Epic of Gilgamesh tells the story of a king who is part god and part human:

> [He is] supreme over other kings, lordly in appearance, he is the hero, born of Uruk, the goring wild bull. He walks out in front, the leader, and walks at the rear, trusted by his companions. Mighty net, protector of his people, raging flood wave who destroys even walls of stone. . . . Gilgamesh is . . . awesome to perfection. (Kovacs, 1998, Tablet I)

Gilgamesh is, however, a flawed king who does dishonorable things, such as taking the first night of every bride in his city of Uruk. The people of Uruk complain to the gods, and the goddess Ururu (to whom the story attributes the creation of humans) responds by creating an equal to Gilgamesh, called Enkidu, who can teach him a lesson or put him in his place.

> [Ururu] created valiant Enkidu, born of Silence, endowed with strength by Ninurta. His whole body was shaggy with hair, he had a full head of hair like a woman, his locks billowed in profusion like Ashnan. . . . He ate grasses with the gazelles and jostled at the watering hole with the animals. (Kovacs, 1998, Tablet I)

The Primitive Task of Womankind

Enkidu can teach many lessons to us, as he did to the people of Uruk for whom the epic was created. Enkidu reminds us of the times when humans lived nomadic lives. Enkidu has animal powers; his knowledge comes from basic instincts about what to eat, when to mate, and where to seek refuge. However, in order for him to correct and reform Gilgamesh's ways, he needs to be tamed or civilized. In the story, this is the role of the woman; a harlot called Shamat is sent to "de-wild" Enkidu and she does so through her irresistible sexual attraction:

> She spread out her robe and he lay upon her, she performed for the primitive the task of womankind. His lust groaned over her; for six days and seven nights Enkidu stayed aroused and had intercourse with the harlot until he was sated with her charms. (Kovacs, 1998, Tablet I)

This part of the story may make some students a bit squeamish, but it is a golden opportunity for the teacher to gently talk about sexual attraction, its importance in bringing men and women together, and its obvious role to guarantee that we don't perish as a species. In this moment in the story, sex takes place as an instinctual action. Enkidu is more animal than human and the attraction he experiences for Shamat is uncontrollable. Through her he loses his wildness. Once tamed, the animals don't recognize Enkidu. Shamat then takes him to Uruk to join the joys of ordinary life.

A One-Of-A-Kind Friendship

Enkidu arrives in Uruk and stops Gilgamesh from taking the first night of a new bride by fighting with him; from this fight, Enkidu and Gilgamesh become inseparable best friends. The epic becomes a tale about friendship, manhood, physical strength, valor, and human community. Their adventures include great and dangerous challenges through which wildness becomes civilization, roads are made, paths are discovered, monsters are killed, and resources are collected for the service of the people of Uruk.

Despite all the good that Gilgamesh and Enkidu perform, they overreach and thoughtlessly intrude in the territory of the gods. Myths always warn us about not testing or challenging the gods (or goddesses). Humans need to know their place; these stories clearly state the dire consequences of crossing the line. Gilgamesh intends to bring cedar wood to his people, but the Cedar Forest is guarded by Humbaba, a scary beast so terrifying that everybody, including Enkidu, tries to dissuade Gilgamesh from this plan.

Gilgamesh's behavior represents an extraordinary opportunity for future teachers to reflect upon and discuss the different ways that boys and girls mature, make mistakes, and learn. Future teachers can also consider how pedagogical methods will have different results when teaching boys and girls.

The elders of Uruk warn Gilgamesh about the enormous risk he will take but fail to change Gilgamesh's mind. In the end Gilgamesh and Enkidu kill Humbaba. Now they can cut the wood for their people, so they rejoice. This part of the story echoes today's global concern for the environment and creates an opportunity for a lovely discussion. The god Enlil is the protector of this special, sacred forest, and he has named a guardian. Enkidu, after cutting the trees, addresses the gravity of their actions: "My friend, we have cut down the towering Cedar whose top scrapes the sky" (Kovacs, 1998, Tablet V).

The author of this ancient epic makes a moral judgment in two ways: first, humans inhabit an environment and should not destroy it. Second, it is not acceptable to move to a foreign place, take the people's king by force, and steal their wealth. Some questions for a discussion on our relationship with the environment may be: Do we humans have the right to dominate our planet or should some areas be left alone and protected from us? How do we find the balance between meeting human needs and taking care of nature? Humans came out of the wild and slowly tamed nature to be able to settle and live more safely and comfortably. But should we establish some boundaries and promote an attitude of respect and protection for the nonhuman world?

Ishtar: A Daring Goddess and The Bull of Heaven

After killing Humbaba and taking the cedar wood to his people, Gilgamesh goes to the river to get clean and dressed. The goddess Ishtar sees him, falls in love with him, asks him to marry her, and promises all kinds of riches and pleasures. Gilgamesh refuses, for Ishtar has a terrible reputation; she has done terrible things to her many lovers. Gilgamesh recites the list of Ishtar's lovers and their appalling ends. The goddess throws a tantrum, like a conceited adolescent girl, and goes up to the heavens and to Anu, her father.

She asks for the Bull of Heaven to teach Gilgamesh a lesson. Her father reminds her that *she* is the one who provoked Gilgamesh and warns about the consequences for the people of Uruk, but nothing changes the goddess' mind. Anu, powerless in the hand of his daughter, releases the Bull of Heaven. Surprisingly, Gilgamesh and Enkidu kill the Bull. This further enrages Ishtar, who punishes them by killing Enkidu.

This part of the story is well-suited to discussing the ways in which young boys and girls might behave. There is plenty of blame for both Gilgamesh and Ishtar to share. Future teachers can help students recognize moments like this in their lives. Gilgamesh and Enkidu have used their gifts and powers foolishly and thoughtlessly, and so has the goddess. The consequences affect all of them; Enkidu dies and the people of Uruk will also suffer greatly. This narrative provides a means for future teachers to reflect on moments when adolescents abuse their powers and act in hurtful ways.

The Fate of Mankind Overtakes Enkidu

At this point, through the deep sorrow that Gilgamesh feels by the death of his very special friend, we learn about mortality, a human inevitability. Nearly every human has struggled with the realization of death. A productive and engaging discussion could revolve around these questions: Why do we die? Is death the end, or is there something afterwards? And, if so, what is that afterlife like? Does it resemble life as we know it? Is it a good or a bad place? If it is good, what are the conditions to make it there?

To this point, Gilgamesh has been a good king in service to his people. But Enkidu's death sparks a great internal crisis. Gilgamesh is in terrible pain; he fears his own death. He begins a long, lonesome, and arduous journey in search of immortality. Specifically, Gilgamesh intends to find a particular man who has escaped mortality and learn his secret.

Teachers at all grade levels are likely to confront students affected by deaths of pets, friends, and family members. There are appropriate ways to discuss death with students at every developmental stage. Since Gilgamesh is not a pessimistic story, it can be a useful vehicle for helping students understand death and can also remind them to live fully in the present and to enjoy life's pleasures. We can all benefit from this advice; young people understand it. Through his pursuit of immortality, Gilgamesh comes to accept his mortal condition and understands that the only immortality humans can truly achieve is through the legacies they leave.

Guiding Questions for Class Discussions

For future teachers, *The Epic of Gilgamesh* can facilitate the discussion of ethical behavior, gender identity and roles, environmental concerns, mortality, religious beliefs, leadership, resilience, acceptance of limits, and friendship. Each of these issues is likely to surface in K–12 classrooms. For this reason, it is important for future teachers to clarify their own beliefs and opinions. Some specific questions for discussion in the college classroom are described below.

On Gods, Ethics, and Mortality

Are gods and goddesses a human invention? Why do we need them or why would our ancestors create them? Would we need gods and goddesses if we did not die? What things or phenomena in the world do we, as humans, observe or experience that make us think of a transcendent or spiritual reality? What are the advantages of mortality? For instance, does knowledge of mortality force us to use our time more wisely and take better care of ourselves? Does this knowledge cause us to put more effort into making our living conditions better, e.g., by building roads, creating effective education systems, discovering cures for illnesses, or developing tools to make work more efficient? Is our awareness of death the reason for the existence of religion and the belief in an afterlife? Would we have morals and ethical rules if we were immortal? What is the reasoning behind a choice for polytheism by ancient cultures instead of monotheism? What advantages and disadvantages do you see in each of them?

On the Characteristics of Leaders

Gilgamesh is the leader of Uruk and the epic describes him as part god and part human. Do those who lead us or rule our societies need special qualities? Should they be stronger, more intelligent, humbler, kinder, more respectful, and/or more open minded?

Gilgamesh embarks on two different journeys. In the first, he feels powerful and positive that he will conquer the world and find everything that his people need with the help of Enkidu. How would you describe Gilgamesh in this part of the story? What other figures, real or fictional, can you compare to Gilgamesh in his arrogant, impetuous, conceited, and reckless state? If you criticize Gilgamesh and those like him for their risky single-mindedness, how do you reconcile that with the knowledge that great discoveries and accomplishments—the moon landing, skyscrapers and other massive works built, descents to the bottom of the oceans, etc.—required these same qualities?

In his second journey Gilgamesh's only goal is to find the secret to immortality. He has lost the person who meant the most to him and he is devastated and terrified of death. He goes to the end of the world hoping to become immortal, but he comes back having learned that immortality is not achievable. For the first time, Gilgamesh is humbler and more accepting. He then chooses to make himself useful, leave a legacy in the city of Uruk, and act as a leader. As adolescents are actively searching for identity and purpose, these are key concepts. In what ways does this story help you prepare for a possible future defeat? Which role models can teach resilience and persistence, especially given that things often don't go the way we want and yet we must keep going anyway?

In spite of Gilgamesh's exceptional physical qualities, he makes many mistakes. Does the story help you be more understanding and accepting of your mistakes? What do you find most inspirational and encouraging in protagonists like Gilgamesh? How would you use this story to encourage a friend who is going through a tough time? How can it inspire you to get along with others and to be willing to do things for them? We can connect these questions with the section below.

On Friendship, Trust, and Courage

The friendship between Enkidu and Gilgamesh is an example of true personal connection and of how we become attracted to people with similar interests, qualities, and talents. This friendship starts in a wrestling competition where both protagonists begin to admire one other through beating each other. Have you had or do you have a friend as good and special as Enkidu? What has made this relationship so good for you? Throughout the story there are moments when Gilgamesh and Enkidu don't agree about what to do. What does the epic teach you about how to resolve disagreements? Is it important to give up sometimes to preserve a friendship? Should we always stick to our principles and fight for them? How important is it to maintain a friendship in which we can be ourselves and, at the same time, count on others to help us correct our ways?

In the beginning Gilgamesh is a bully. He takes advantage of his power, his physical strength, and his family's position. Enkidu confronts him to stop Gilgamesh's abuse. They choose to use their incredible physical strength to fight each other, and then, the bully and the wild man develop a most beautiful friendship. Should we confront bullies? Should we use a physical fight if we have the necessary physical qualities? What else can we do if fighting is not the best idea? What happens when nobody confronts a bully? Are we better friends when we firmly discourage our friends from misbehaving?

On the Roles and Complementarity Between Men and Women

In Gilgamesh, goddesses and women have many different roles. One of them is to civilize or settle men through sexual attraction. How do men and society benefit from this enticement from women to settle down? Which is more beneficial for children, the settled lifestyle or the nomadic one? Could biological factors such as menstruation and pregnancy have influenced changes in the way humans transformed from nomadic ways to permanent settlements (villages and cities)? What effects do females' advice and guidance have in the Gilgamesh story? How does this guidance benefit the males in the epic? *The Epic of Gilgamesh* also offers a terrible example by the goddess Ishtar. What lessons do we take from the consequences of her behavior? What could young girls learn from Ishtar's behavior?

Stories are a treasured method for helping humans develop through their imaginations, to foresee opportunities and challenges, and to forestall inevitable obstacles and challenges. *The Epic of Gilgamesh* can help future teachers wrestle with these issues and thereby be better equipped to help their own students do the same.

References

George, A. (2017). *The Epic of Gilgamesh, a lecture at Harvard Museum of the Ancient Near East* [Video]. YouTube. https://youtu.be/Rd7MrGy_tEg

Kovacs, M. G. (1998). *The Epic of Gilgamesh*. https://uruk-warka.dk/Gilgamish/The%20Epic%20 of%20Gilgamesh.pdf (ca. 2000 B.C.E.)

SEVEN

O Brave New World, That Has Such People In't!

Cory Glenn

PRESERVICE TEACHER EDUCATION PROGRAMS—IN CONTRAST to the day-to-day operations of a school—are constant reminders of this truth from William Shakespeare's *Merchant of Venice*: "If to do were as easy as to know what were good to do, chapels had been churches and poor men's cottages princes' palaces" (Shakespeare, 1600/2007a, 1.2.11–13). One great challenge in teaching future teachers is providing them with actionable understandings about the systems they will soon inhabit. What seems obvious within the safety of the academic walls of higher education can quickly become preposterous in the context of an elementary and secondary school classroom. How can teacher educators address this disconnect? In this chapter, I will pose one possibility as I share my experience using literature to connect future teachers with the complicated landscape of modern education.

As I was growing up, school seemed like a game to be beaten on the way to a separate, unrelated goal. I found no intrinsic motivation in the classroom; my passion was in the arts and, indeed, that is where I spent around a decade and a half of my adult life. I am a lover of the arts. There are things I know for certain about life and the universe; these are all things I have learned through artistic pursuit and appreciation. School was a necessary evil where empowered elites required young, inspired minds to repeat useless information in order to gain admission into adult life. Fortunately, my perceptions were greatly altered by an inspiring teacher who helped me connect the growth I experienced from the arts to the growth I might be able to provide for my own students in a classroom. This epiphany changed the type of educator I was becoming. It pushed me towards developing a new understanding about education, one that can be easy to neglect in teacher preparation programs full of new technological tools, new lesson plan structures, innovative methods, educational flavors of the month, best practices, commitments to equity, and of course, tools for assessment. In an overcrowded curriculum, the politics, philosophies, and history of education can easily get pushed aside by the elements of required coursework for certification.

This chapter will focus on my experience with using Aldous Huxley's *Brave New World* (1932/2013) in the college classroom, specifically in the area of educational foundations. I will describe some of my strategies for exploring the subject matter, along with some specific areas in the book that apply to that strategy. I will also suggest driving questions that might help fuel the conversation in the reader's own classroom.

Education reflects the society in which it takes place. Who are the people engaging in the educational system? What are the objectives of teachers and what can the system offer the students? One cannot look at any educational system without also looking at the culture in which that system is taking place. In recognizing this truth, most preservice teacher education programs require a course discussing societal influences on their country's education system. I teach one such course, entitled *School and Society*, a broadly named course with broad expectations. It can be generally stated that a course investigating societal influences on American education would discuss cultural norms and expectations, assessment of desired outcomes, and systematic implementation of procedures within a school. In other words: what, why, and how should a school teach? In order to investigate these questions, I believe that a perspective of comparison is helpful. Students benefit from a focused lens through which to look in order to test their understandings and assumptions. To provide my students with such a lens, I find help in a piece of artistic expression. I use a novel written in response to concerns about American culture, first published in 1932. Using a near-century-old novel to investigate modern societal challenges might at first seem outmoded, but I've found that Aldous Huxley's (1932/2013) perspective on American society has grown more prescient as time goes on and civilization creeps ever closer to the culture he creates in his novel *Brave New World*.

Why *Brave New World*?

"O Wonder! How many goodly creatures are there here!" (*The Tempest*, Act V, Scene 1. This and all subsequent references to *The Tempest* are from Shakespeare, 2007b.)

Aldous Huxley spent his entire adult life writing novels, fiction, and nonfiction books, as well as numerous essays. His life has been recorded in various biographies, essays, and websites; while it might provide a deeper insight into the ideas presented in this chapter, Huxley's biography is not central to the understanding of these concepts. For that reason, I'll leave the details of his life, which include multiple marriages, religious connections to mysticism, Buddhism, and Hinduism, and time spent experimenting with LSD in the company of Timothy Leary, up to the further interest of the reader. The important quality about Huxley for this chapter is his infinite fascination with society and the probable future that might exist for humanity. Huxley wrote extensively about his concerns with the state of society, but more specifically about what he thought might become of a society that continued in the manner of western civilization as he saw it. His greatest depiction of these concerns comes in what is widely considered his masterpiece, the novel, *Brave New World* (Huxley, 1932/2013).

This revolutionary text accurately provides access to the moral and ethical debate surrounding the school and society. Its inquiry into the realization of utopia bridges Plato's *Republic* with modern conversations around essentialism, equality, and tracking. Huxley places his focus directly on the development of the human being. He asks questions about the morality and effectiveness of practices involved in the growth of the individual human, as well as the individual human's relationship to the greater society. His future world where people are decanted and conditioned seems all too familiar when compared to the modern American education system where students are taught through standardized litany.

Using *Brave New World* as a text can allow future teachers to take Huxley's dilemmas about a society built on comfort, efficiency, lust, and the pursuit of happiness and connect them to the modern arguments about intrinsic motivation, productivity, and the purpose of education. Marshall McLuhan is famous for creating the aphorism: "The medium is the message," a sentiment that Neil Postman (1969) wisely connected to education and its practices both positively through John Dewey's (1900/1990) desire to actively involve students in an environment and negatively by identifying the unfortunate themes in the hidden curriculum. Aldous Huxley's *Brave New World* gives educators an incredible vehicle with which to discuss *the medium* in which we educate and to question whether or not we are satisfied with the message.

Educational Themes in *Brave New World*

"Do not for one repulse forego the purpose that you resolved to effect."
(*The Tempest*, Act III, Scene III)

Educational Purpose

What is the purpose of education? If there is one primary question to be addressed in my *School and Society* class, this is it. This is a question often reserved for graduate students to discuss in theoretical absolutes. It pervades the academic conversations of elite thinkers as they share quotations from great philosophers in the persistent pursuit of the great truth about education. It also lives in the carefully constructed paragraphs assembled by preservice teachers as they attempt to explain their understanding of their pedagogical role to potential employers. Anyone who has spent time in a classroom also knows that this question is of great importance to young minds trying to come to terms with the mandated dissemination of information. It is often communicated through the age-old question, "Why do we need to know this?" While the importance of the question is obvious, the answer seems to be considerably more elusive. Educational purpose is clearly important, but how can we help aspiring teachers access the deep debate surrounding this meaningful topic?

I generally begin with my students by thinking about the basic big ideas that society has used to frame education. It is easy and common to see education as the preparation of children for participation in society. Indeed, this might be the most widely accepted understanding of what education is about. John Dewey (1900/1990), one of the greatest American educational philosophers, is famous for refuting that very idea. He rejected the notion that teachers could serve as fortune-tellers, determining the knowledge and skills students would need at some future date. Beginning with this juxtaposition of foundational ideas, I frame my teaching about the purpose of education around five popularly recognized philosophies of education, based on the framework provided by David E. Diehl (2006).

First, Perennialism aims to help students understand the intrinsic truths of life through the expanse of cultural literacy, focusing mainly on western civilization. It asks big questions about the nature of humanity and the universe in pursuit of transcendent knowledge. Second, Essentialism, which is the current foundation of the American educational system, seeks to provide students with the necessary ideas of a society in pursuit of cultural literacy. It removes the extraneous pursuits of wonder in favor of societally agreed upon fundamentals. Third, Progressivism is the belief that education is the authentic solving of problems. Progressivism focuses on the active participation of students in projects, experiments, and hands-on activities in order to meaningfully connect knowledge to life. Fourth, Reconstructionism seeks to teach students about the real-world issues of society, how they came about, and what can be done to solve them. This idea focuses on equity in education in society and the belief that students should be equipped with the skills and knowledge to move humankind to become more fair and equitable. Fifth, Educational Existentialism is a school of thought that places its focus solely on the student. This philosophy does not believe in the pursuit of ultimate truths, but rather personal truths. Educational Existentialism uses play, exploration, and student-directed interest to help students develop individual understandings of themselves and their world.

In my class, after discussing these philosophies, I find it important to identify three elements they all share. First, they all desire in some way to transmit knowledge or culture to students. Second, they all share a belief that education has something to do with the growth or personal understanding of individuals. Finally, all five contain some kind of social or political expectation of students.

These initial understandings about the purpose of education are important for preservice educators to consider. However, it can be difficult for prospective teachers to easily connect them to the real experiences they expect in real classrooms. It can be even more difficult to attempt to foresee the implications of classroom decisions made on the basis of one or another of these philosophies. This is where the use of great fiction can become so important. So much of preservice teacher training is about absolutes and replicable processes. I want students in my *School and Society* class to question the things they take for granted and ask themselves—and eventually their own students—"Why?"

Educational Purpose in *Brave New World*

> "We are such stuff as dreams are made on, and our little life is rounded with sleep." (*The Tempest*, Act IV, Scene 1)

What is the purpose of life? This question rests at the center of Aldous Huxley's *Brave New World* and at the center of the discussions about education taking place in my classroom. It is a question present in every corner of education. No great novel, formula, discovery, or idea, no economic theory or philosophical argument is created except by motivation to know or understand more clearly the human situation. As Kieran Egan (2005) puts it: "All knowledge is human knowledge and all knowledge is a product of human hopes, fears, and passions" (p. 96). *Brave New World* is a novel that delves into the depths of human hopes, fears, and passions and thereby asks how humans should be developed, grown, taught, and influenced. I provide an introduction with this paragraph from the beginning of the novel:

> A squat grey building only thirty-four storeys. Over the main entrance the words, CENTRAL LONDON HATCHERY AND CONDITIONING CENTRE, and a shield, the World State's motto, COMMUNITY, IDENTITY, STABILITY. (Huxley, 1932/2013, p. 5)

This opening passage provides an excellent opportunity to help students begin the discussion. I like to discuss just this sentence in class before sending the students home to read more. This sentence sounds very much like a typical description of a modern school: a generally unimpressive building, owned and operated by the government, built for function not beauty, and notably displaying some broad statement of purpose. In particular, there are three words that associate directly with the three shared ideas of educational philosophy. COMMUNITY fulfills the societal or political expectation of educational purpose; the individual will participate properly in the community. IDENTITY is the individual growth or understanding of a human being's role and STABILITY would relate to the transmission of knowledge or culture, more specifically the continuance of shared knowledge within a culture. What does the brave new world expect of humans as they develop? What does it expect of the institution being described? What can we know about the type of education taking place here from just this passage? There is an implied expectation that citizens will be a nondisruptive part of the community, that they will accept their identity or occupation as defined by society, and that they will participate in the stability of the established norms. Good or bad, this appears to me to be very similar to the expectations of the modern education system. Do my students agree?

In the first chapter of the novel, there is also this quotation from the director of hatcheries, who is the person in charge of the development of human beings from fetus to adult:

> For of course some sort of general idea they must have, if they were to do their work intelligently—though as little of one, if they were to be good and happy members of society, as possible. For particulars, as everyone knows, make for virtue and happiness; generalities are intellectually necessary evils. Not philosophers, but fret-sawyers and stamp collectors compose the backbone of society. (Huxley, 1932/2013, p. 6)

This passage indicates that the goal of human development or education in *Brave New World* is a happy person who participates. It is not important that a person become a learner, a wanderer, or as the director states, a philosopher, but rather that a person take on an occupation, a hobby, and a disposition for enjoying both. What similar traits are recognizable in our own society? What do parents expect their children to learn in school? What do legislators expect of graduates?

Later in Chapter Two, the director states, "that is the secret of happiness and virtue—liking what you've got to do" (p. 16).

Is this correct? Is our ultimate goal happiness? Should the role of the school be to help students discover the tasks for which they show dispositions and to provide them strategies for tolerating those parts of participation in society which they find unenjoyable? I find that when this question is proposed to preservice teachers, the answer is generally yes. Aldous Huxley, though, asks the reader to question that understanding of development, or at least to take it to its inevitable ends and see how it stacks up. If the greatest thing education can offer humanity is access to happiness, then education really has two priorities. Education should reward students in some way for behavior that, while not necessarily desirable for the student, is desirable for society, and education should stratify students in such a way as to provide for all necessary roles within its society. Does this currently happen in schools? How is it happening? Are the techniques used to condition children in *Brave New World* monstrous? And if so, are they only monstrous to a modern American perspective?

The themes around purpose from the first chapter continue to appear chapter after chapter and they provide access to rich conversations about education. I have found it helpful to also provide corresponding readings, such as short essays or excerpts from educational texts, to provide varying perspectives on this subject. This technique also allows the class to discuss the five major educational philosophies in relation to the novel, while connecting modern events and supplemental reading to discovered themes. However, since my purpose here is only to show the opportunity in this text rather than describe every detail of my teaching, I'll skip ahead to chapter eleven.

In this chapter, our main characters are visiting a school. To this point in the novel, Huxley has given us detailed descriptions of the kind of conditioning involved in his future society and the way it ensures that each human becomes exactly who the society needs them to be. He has described a civilization based on a caste system, where each caste is programmed to prefer itself and its role within the society. This programming has led to a utopian civilization where the people happily occupy their time with pursuits that have little to do with important or inquisitive thought but everything to do with comfort and pleasant distraction. This of course looks very much like the perfect city in *The Republic of Plato* (375 BCE/2016). As the characters begin to tour the school, Huxley hints at a possible truth that is being ignored by this utopia.

> "Oh no," the Provost answered. "Eton is reserved exclusively for upper-caste boys and girls. One egg, one adult. It makes education more difficult, of course. But as they'll be called upon to take responsibilities and deal with unexpected emergencies, it can't be helped." (p. 136)

This passage is so important to the conversation of purpose. First, there is a recognition that a standardized conditioning is not acceptable for the most important students because they are expected to do great things. On the other hand, memorization and testing are acceptable for the lower castes who have no need for understanding, analysis, or synthesis. Lower caste students are merely expected to repeat processes or regurgitate facts. Does this seem like modern education, where we see schools implementing educational techniques based on individualized exploration of subject matter? What about the techniques in the public school system where standardized repetition of process is prioritized? Huxley shows us the end version of the current system, where the affluent higher caste is provided an education for understanding conceptual truths and the lower castes are given an education of repeatable skills. Is the current American education system stratified? Should it be? Is stratification the result of student interest, or something else? Is there a different definition of education for the rich than for the poor? What could a teacher do to provide access to greater understanding in a system built around rote memorization?

Brave New World provides opportunities for discussion of the purpose of education on nearly every page, but the center of Huxley's argument about purpose comes in Chapter 11. Here the character of Mustapha Mond, a powerful World Controller, considers the impact of a new scientific theory, one that he thinks is correct, but ultimately censors from society.

> It was the sort of idea that might easily recondition the more unsettled minds among the higher castes—make them lose their faith in happiness as the Sovereign Good and take to believing, instead, that the goal was somewhere beyond, somewhere outside the present human sphere; that the purpose of life was not the maintenance of well-being, but some intensification and refining of the consciousness, some enlargement of knowledge. (Huxley, 1932/2013, p. 150)

This passage is the key to understanding Huxley's novel and it is the key to unlocking the discussion of school and society in my classroom. Here, Huxley enters the philosophical argument of his time and of our time. He was experiencing the beginning of a society in which the psychological understanding of human beings was becoming influential in the promotion of individual purpose, comfort, and happiness. In other words, the goal is an equitable society in which every person has not only what they need to survive but also what they need to be comfortable and happy. I have found that this is the understanding of purpose that most preservice teachers have at the beginning of my class. What Huxley promotes, however, is a more classic understanding, one that looks more like Plato or Aristotle or like the teaching in many religious texts. Huxley is promoting a society where the pursuit is not happiness or comfort, but fulfillment and service. If the purpose of education is only to prepare students to be happy performing a job, then what is lost? What kind of society should we expect from a system of education built around trivia rather than critical thinking and understanding? What things in our society provide happiness, and what things might provide, as Mustapha Mond says, some intensification and refining of the consciousness, some enlargement of knowledge? Is Huxley right or is he missing something that only our modern perspective can see?

What is lost in a society built around happiness, supported by an education of conditioning for participation in that society? In Chapter 16, Mustapha Mond begins to explain what must be left behind in order to preserve the utopia. He says, "You've got to choose between happiness and what people used to call high art. We've sacrificed the high art" (p. 188). Art can be a great educational tool; it requires conceptual understanding, technique, and the ability to challenge. Good art causes discomfort because it requires the artist and the observer to think critically. Good art is not easy. The society of *Brave New World* is full of simple art requiring no thought to experience. It may be pretty or pleasurable, but it is lacking in its ability or desire to help the artist or observer seek greater truth or understanding. What offerings do we provide in education that authentically encourage a student to expand conceptual understanding? Should teachers encourage student work that goes beyond the replication of process? What are the implications of a classroom focused on meaningful connection to curriculum rather than acquisition of a set amount of knowledge?

Preservice teachers in my class are encouraged to question what lies at the heart of the system they are about to enter and where they see themselves fitting into, or fitting out of, that system. It is easy and comfortable to accept a system already in place but is that the nature of a real education? At the end of Chapter 16, Mustapha Mond gives a reminder that the common practices of a system are the results of the society in which the system exists.

> Our Ford Himself did a great deal to shift the emphasis from truth and beauty to comfort and happiness. Mass production demanded the shift. Universal happiness keeps the wheels steadily turning; truth and beauty can't. And, of course, whenever the masses seized political power, then it was happiness rather than truth and beauty that mattered. (p.194)

A society that relies on status quo, stability, and leisure does not desire to create opportunity for criticism, improvement, or novelty. What kind of society are we inhabiting? How does society expect our graduates to look or act? What can education offer students that is meaningful to their hopes, fears, or passions?

Efficiency

"Hell is empty and all the devils are here." (*The Tempest*, Act I, Scene 2)

Human beings love efficiency. It is evolutionary. It has always been a part of human survival. The love of efficiency is built into societal and economic systems. People want to get the most in exchange for the least; they look for sales, shortcuts, and fast tracks, all to get more product for less cost. Humans also go to great lengths to measure efficiency and then use those measurements to make important decisions about the ways in which the living of life should be carried out. This truth is incredibly evident in both the auto and fast-food industries, where assembly line techniques lead to construction of cars measured in minutes, and the cooking of meals measured in seconds. Efficiency is a principle of modern life and one that creates immense societal pressure on education.

The fear of inefficiency is a fear of waste. Waste, however, is a matter of perspective. I find an afternoon reading in a lawn chair to be an excellent use of time for growth or relaxation; however, it may also seem an incredible waste of time given a sink full of dirty dishes or a pile of unfolded laundry. A corporation sending out a pregenerated email saves a considerable amount of time but sacrifices personal acknowledgement of the customer. Determining waste is all a matter of intention. What is it that a person wants? What is the goal or intention? Only once these questions have been answered can a discussion of efficiency begin.

Students in my classroom often jump to discussions about efficiency right from the start. This is no surprise since their preservice teacher training has consisted of investigations about best practices for the delivery of curriculum and how to properly assess a student's mastering of that curriculum. There is also the fact that behaviorism (Skinner, 1971) still influences a great deal of pedagogy. Today, we can easily recognize behaviorism as a tool used in most schools. In fact, B.F Skinner's research is often quoted in educational texts provided for preservice teachers and administrators alike. This view is juxtaposed to the idea that intrinsic motivation is the path to a meaningful education. Much of the research around intrinsic motivation can be found in the work of Alfie Kohn (1993) who said of B.F. Skinner: "a man who conducted most of his experiments on rodents and pigeons and wrote most of his books about people" (p. 6).When looking at the long list of teacher responsibilities, it is no surprise that future teachers want to know how to get the job done as efficiently as possible in order to reserve time for all the other duties that go along with the job. There is also the personal life of the teacher, which is easily sacrificed as job-related tasks pile up.

I have found that a discussion of efficiency is best begun by referring to the previous section's discussion of purpose. After all, efficiency is meaningless without purpose. So, my students must first begin to understand what it is they are attempting to accomplish through education before they can fully understand the conversation around efficiency in education.

Education is full of systems and practices rooted in efficiency. There are grade levels, bells, lines, letter grades, and multiple-choice tests, just to name a few. These are all products of what Frank Smith (1999) calls "the official view" of learning: a perspective on education where the organization, management, and efficiency of the 19th century Prussian army are crucial to success. This view is often adopted by parents, students, and teachers, citing a fear of waste. The idea of wasted time or resources in education can seem much like a wasting of life. This is due to the fact that education is not merely a step on the road of life, but the road itself. As John Dewey (1897) puts it: "I believe that education is a process of living and not of preparation for future living." The questions must be asked: What is lost when efficiency is the focus of education? Is there room for failure in an efficient education? Is there room for originality, novelty, or individualism in the modern American education system?

Efficiency in *Brave New World*

> "You taught me language, and my profit on't is I know how to curse."
> (*The Tempest*, Act I, Scene 2)

Huxley was writing at a time when the exploration of humanity was driven by psychology, sociology, and the need for greater efficiency, manifesting itself as industrialism. These pursuits were just beginning to establish their hold on the American education system and to influence the international culture of thought when Huxley penned the first draft of *Brave New World*. His novel examines the influence of these scientific pursuits—which became cultural obsessions—and their effects on civilization. Huxley was interested in the way humans are grown, trained, developed, and used by a society. These concerns align directly with questions educators ask about their own pursuits and practices.

The focus on efficiency is incredibly prominent right from the beginning of *Brave New World*. The first chapter is a description of the industrialized reproductive process. It is a tour of a factory that makes humans. This factory has removed emotion from reproduction; there is no love or beauty, only efficiency. This efficiency helps ensure that each human turns out exactly as desired. Specifically, "[this] process is one of the major instruments of social stability. Standard men and women; in uniform batches" (p. 8).

Is this the expectation of the school? The education system currently runs on standards and standardized testing. The last five American presidents have required such testing to ensure equality in education. Every student must learn the same things in the same way. Such uniformity does not allow for creativity, ingenuity, or critical thinking. Why do legislators, regardless of political party or agenda, seem to agree on standardization of education? Is that good or bad?

In the first chapter of *Brave New World*, this quote from the director of the facility can be found: "An Epsilon must have an Epsilon environment as well as Epsilon heredity" (p. 14). In education, this is known as tracking. Students' outcomes are predetermined and they are placed in classes or environments that will guarantee those outcomes. There are any number of examples of this in education; some students are placed in slower moving math classes or required to enroll in vocational electives, while higher achieving students are given requirements that deny their ability to take those same vocational classes. *Brave New World* denies citizens future freedoms by limiting their curricular access. Finding ways to connect students to all curricular possibilities is difficult and inefficient. Instead, students are limited, organized, tracked, siloed, and specialized until they are equipped to join the workforce and become a specific functioning member of the brave new world . . . or contemporary American society. Is there a difference? It is easy to scoff at the caste system within the novel, but is it really so far from the stratification of students done in the American education system? Should students be taught curriculum that has nothing to do with their future career? Are educators wasting students' time by requiring art classes or physical education classes? Who gains and who loses when students are given the most efficient route to the workforce or to a university?

There exists still an even darker outcome of the societal economy in *Brave New World*, one that teachers should pay careful attention to when thinking about what might lie in the hidden curriculum of efficiency. In Chapter 3, Mustapha Mond, speaking to the upper caste students, is discussing the importance of providing distraction to the masses in order to keep them happy: "You can't consume much if you sit still and read books" (Huxley, 1932/2013, p. 44). This is a simple statement but it points to a perspective on the value of learning as a lifelong pursuit. The utopian society doesn't need people seeking truth and beauty. Rather, it needs people performing their proper tasks and when not doing so, it is important to keep them distracted so as to not upset the established routine. This becomes so important in the novel that the society has invented a perfect drug to provide instant contentment at a moment's notice. The drug is called Soma and is described by Mustapha Mond as having "all the advantages of Christianity and alcohol: none of their defects" (p. 47).

By encouraging educational efficiency that denies room for creativity, or novelty in search of truth, what kind of lives are we encouraging students to live? Does efficiency play a role is the desire for distraction? What distractions exist in society to quell deeper thought? Is there a difference between Soma and an opioid or alcohol? What about social media or a smartphone? Where do popular educational phrases like "21st century skills," "critical thinking," "high rigor," or "equity in education" fit with an educational system using standards, pacing guides, and uniform testing to ensure the most efficient delivery of curriculum?

What Am I to Do?

"Your tale, sir, would cure deafness." (*The Tempest*, Act I, Scene 2)

The discussion of educational purpose and practices rooted in efficiency can sometimes leave the heads of my students spinning. "Well, what are we supposed to do?" This is often the question asked as my students and I make our way through Huxley's narrative. Many of the answers I have to that question come in the form of additional reading that, having had their preconceptions unchained by Huxley, my students are now prepared to investigate. However, there are two important methods that exist in *Brave New World* that I think are worth a quick look.

Subject as Access

> "Me poor man, my library was dukedom large enough." (*The Tempest*, Act I, Scene 1)

This is perhaps one of my favorite concepts to discuss with future educators. All teachers spend a great deal of time looking for ways to make their curriculum more interesting. This includes things like gamification, creating songs, or attempting to find videos that anecdotally relate to what they are teaching. But if a person were to read the works of those thinkers mentioned already in this chapter—John Dewey, Kieran Egan, Neil Postman, and Frank Smith—they might find that all seem to agree that it is not a matter of making the curriculum interesting; the curriculum is already interesting. The job is to help students understand what it has to do with them. The job is to show students that what teachers are offering is not a list of stale facts for use at some later date, but access to understanding the universe and their place within it. Who am I? What am I doing here? How does this work? If students can see the everyday curriculum as providing pieces to a puzzle that begins to answer these questions, then the need for quaint songs and contrived games all but evaporates.

Where does this exist in the text? One of the most compelling characters, and arguably the protagonist, is the character of John. John is brought to the utopian society from a "savage reservation." As he experiences the society, he has no prior knowledge with which to understand the strange things he sees. What he does have is a book of all of William Shakespeare's plays. There are over 40 quotations from Shakespeare in Huxley's novel, and the majority of them all come in the same context. John uses Shakespeare to make sense of a world he does not understand. One of my favorites comes when John is attempting to tell Lenina, a member of the world society, how he feels. Neither character has any societal understanding of love and so as John attempts to explain a feeling he doesn't understand, he reaches into Shakespeare's *The Tempest*:

> "Anything you tell me, there be some sports are painful—you know. But their labour delight in them sets off. That's what I feel. I mean I'd sweep the floor if you wanted."
>
> "But we've got vacuum cleaners here. It isn't necessary," said Lenina in bewilderment. "It isn't necessary."

> "No, of course it isn't necessary. But some kinds of baseness are nobly undergone. I'd like to undergo something nobly. Don't you see?"
>
> "But if there are vacuum cleaners . . ."
>
> "That's not the point." (Huxley, 1932/2013, pp. 161–162)

John understands love, albeit incompletely, because he is given access through Shakespeare. John quotes twice from Shakespeare's *The Tempest* to explain how he feels. Lenina, who has experienced no mind-expanding education, has no way to understand that feeling that was never conditioned in her and cannot understand the complexity of what John is saying because her education never consisted of anything but memorization of facts. Student conceptual understanding does not come from memorized facts, as Lenina shows while attempting to understand love. Conceptual understanding comes from using knowledge in ways unlike when it was first encountered to make sense of the lived experiences in student lives. What can students discover through my curriculum? Am I providing access to life and the universe or am I ensuring an exact but limited understanding? Is my class about repeating a skill or understanding a concept?

Solitude/Individuality

> "I would not wish any companion in the world but you" (*The Tempest*, Act 3, Scene 1).

Big ideas are dangerous. There is a status quo and a comfortable truth that a society accepts. The society must accept it to avoid upheaval or chaos, otherwise referred to as discomfort. For the society of *Brave New World*, the threat of change is controlled by the removal of solitude and individuality. This is an important concept for teachers to understand as they develop lessons that are relevant to all students. I do not wish to disparage cooperation, social interaction, or community, but merely to identify the value of space for personal contemplation.

Where does this exist in the text? The book begins by following the character of Bernard Marx. He is a bit of an outcast in society. He is not shunned or ostracized, but he is the subject of rumor and belittlement. As the story progresses, the readers learn that Bernard has developed some suspicion of the world society and begins to long for something more that he can't seem to describe. He articulates this feeling at numerous points in the book by explaining his feeling of separateness from society and it is through this separation that he has the opportunity to think critically about the conclusions society takes for granted. In Chapter Four, Bernard identifies the way his peers take their privilege for granted, speaking specifically about the way in which they effortlessly act within the social norms, "so utterly at home as to be unaware either of themselves or of the beneficent and comfortable element in which they had their being" (p. 56). This behavior is juxtaposed with Bernard's good friend Helmholtz Watson, who is also beginning to question society. Helmholtz is purposely creating space between himself and the society in order to provide room for contemplation. Huxley makes a comparison between the space Helmholtz voluntarily creates and the space Bernard finds himself in due to his physical difference:

> A physical shortcoming could produce a kind of mental excess. The process, it seemed, was reversible. Mental excess could produce, for its own purposes, the voluntary blindness and deafness of deliberate solitude, the artificial impotence of asceticism. (p. 59)

Whether by finding oneself an outcast, or by conscious choice, solitude from society has provided both of these characters the distance necessary to think deeply about the environment in which they exist. Are students given opportunity for quiet reflection? Can students be taught to objectively think about the system in which they subsist? In a world of social media, how much time do students have to be alone with their thoughts? What space are students given in schools to individually connect with curriculum?

Final Thoughts

"How Beauteous mankind is!" (*The Tempest*, Act V, Scene 1)

Brave New World provides a wealth of social commentary, specifically about the development of human beings, told through a compelling science fiction narrative. The older this novel gets, the more relevant it seems to contemporary

American society. Using this text in the preservice teacher classroom activates students' imaginations while providing the space to explore complex ideas about humanity. I have found Aldous Huxley's masterpiece to be an excellent tool for framing my students' discussion around societal influences on education. The novel has the ability to shine light on a great number of cultural assumptions in the world of education and ask stimulating questions of educators. These questions draw the mind outside theories of pedagogy to the world at large and its forces on the individual human experience. What is the purpose of education? What is the purpose of life?

References

Dewey, J. (1897). My pedagogic creed. *School Journal, 54* (January), 77–80.

Dewey, J. (1900/1990). *The school and society & the child and the curriculum.* University of Chicago Press.

Diehl, D. E. (2006) A study of faculty-related variables and competence in integrating instructional technologies into pedagogical practices. Ph.D. thesis, Texas Southern University.

Egan, K. (2005). *An imaginative approach to teaching.* John Wiley & Sons.

Huxley, A. (1932/2013). *Brave new world.* Everyman's Library.

Kohn, A. (1993). *Punished by rewards: The trouble with gold stars, incentive plans, A's, praise, and other bribes.* Houghton Mifflin Co.

Plato, Bloom, A., translator. (2016). *The Republic of Plato.* Basic Books. (Originally published 375 BCE)

Postman, N., & Weingartner, C. (1971). *Teaching as a subversive activity.* Delacorte Press.

Shakespeare, W. (2007a). *The merchant of Venice* (J. Crawford, Ed.). Barnes and Noble. (Original work published 1600)

Shakespeare, W. (2007b). *The tempest* (G. McMullan, Ed.). Barnes and Noble. (Original work published 1623)

Skinner, B. F. (1971). *Beyond freedom and dignity.* Knopf.

Smith, F. (1999). *The book of learning and forgetting.* Teachers College Press.

EIGHT

 Homer, *The Odyssey*, and Resilience in Education

Lynanne Black

THE FIELD OF EDUCATION IS currently at a crucial crossroad. Teacher shortages have been an issue for many years; however, with the onset of the COVID-19 pandemic, the shortages are reaching crisis levels (Lurye & Griesbach, 2022; Walker, 2022). The National Education Association (NEA) conducted a survey in February 2022 where 55% of educators indicated they were considering exiting their professional roles. This represented an increase of 37% from a survey conducted only six months prior. There are a myriad of reasons why teachers are leaving the profession or not choosing it in the first place, not the least of which is the increase in mental health issues among students with limited resources to address them. While the prevalence of mental health issues among students and families and the need for systematic social-emotional learning (SEL) instruction in schools has resurged in recent years, the pandemic has illuminated the vastness of the problem. Also, the pandemic has made clear that mental health services frequently are not accessible to students and families for a variety of reasons. With all of this said, teachers remain the frontline workers in the classroom, as well as the first responders for students when addressing not only their educational, but also social and emotional needs. Indeed, it is often these skills that facilitate the learning process for students and help them be ready to learn once the teacher begins instructing. As such, it is imperative that teachers are taught the basics regarding social-emotional competence (SEC) in students; why SEC is important for student development and learning; how to identify deficits in SEC; and what to do when they encounter these deficits. If teacher education programs do not adjust to these societal pressures and teachers do not feel prepared to address their students' needs, the teacher shortage crisis will likely only become worse.

All teacher education majors take one or more courses in their degree programs regarding the social and emotional development of children. Indeed, most are required to take a class in educational psychology, which specifically outlines the application of psychological theories and concepts to the educational process. Teachers know that beyond what students bring to the classroom in terms of heritable ability, they need to possess other important behavioral and emotional characteristics to be successful. Students must be capable learners and display skills consistent with educational progress if they are going to achieve a high school diploma. The educational journey from birth to twelfth grade is a long one that necessitates a particular attitude, approach, and level of acceptance to achieve the ultimate goal. Additionally, the journey requires an understanding of the value of education and how education aids in creating competent members of society, who can critically think about their world and support themselves as they navigate life. This is no small order for students or teachers in their efforts to make it to their ultimate goal.

Because this an enormous task, it becomes essential that teacher education students are taught SEC concepts in a way that aids in comprehension and practical use. It is important for teachers to have tools in their toolkits to not only identify, but also address, the concerns they will face in the classroom daily. Thus, it becomes imperative that higher education faculty effectively teach their education students about these concepts and their application in the classroom environment. There are many ways that faculty can relate these ideas to their students, one of which is using literature to explain them and demonstrate their use in the educational setting. In this chapter, several educational and psychological concepts will be exemplified using the classical story of *The Odyssey* by Homer. Although at first it may seem the story of Odysseus has little to no relationship with the educational process, it will become clear how this epic tale epitomizes the importance of education in general, of special education services, and of resilience to students' growth, progress, and eventual success in their educational careers. First, Homer's background and impetus for writing his story will be presented. Second, the connections between various educational and psychological concepts and the story itself will be proposed. Finally, instructional methods for the use of Homer's story in the teaching of these concepts will be offered.

The Life of Homer

Homer was a Greek poet, born on the coast of Asia Minor or the island of Chios between the 12th and 8th centuries BCE (c. 800 BCE – c. 701 BCE). His exact birth date is not known as there was no recording system in existence during his time for this type of information. Homer is recognized as the first author to record the stories of *The Iliad* and *The Odyssey* in the form of writing. While most often stories of the time were transmitted via word of mouth in the oral tradition, Homer dictated the poems to a scribe to preserve Greek history and educate others about life in the area at that time. Very little is known about Homer and his life, and most biographical data are gleaned from reading and analyzing his writing. Homer is believed to have been blind; therefore, he often is depicted as a man with curly hair, a beard, and vacant eyes. Homer's literary style was to begin a story in the middle, while recounting what had already happened through character recollections, and *The Odyssey* is indeed written in this fashion. While much of Homer's life remains a mystery, it is clear that the impact of his work has been immense and substantial (A&E Networks Television, 2021).

Teacher Education and *The Odyssey*

Homer's *The Odyssey* exemplifies the field of education and various aspects of this field in quite insightful and contemplative ways. This epic story is a metaphor for an educational career including the highs and lows, obstacles and successes, challenges and accomplishments, fear and courage that define the educational path from birth to twelfth grade. Students often begin their formal education in preschool at age three to four years and continue until they graduate, typically at age 18 years. This amounts to a 14- to 15-year journey through the educational system, navigating frequent error and failure coupled with success and accomplishment. Students are not only learning, but also learning how to learn and become lifelong learners. Along the way, the students are guided by others they encounter in their path; some of these important adults become mentors while others become life lessons from all of which students learn and grow. Similar to Odysseus, students may realize at their culminating moment (earning a high school diploma) that even more important than the product earned is the process of arriving at this moment including all the experiences and adventures that have shaped the people they have become and will lead them into the next phases of their lives. The following sections will draw specific parallels between Odysseus' journey and students' educational journey and demonstrate how *The Odyssey* can help teacher education students understand both the immense and important nature of their work and how they can exert considerable influence over outcomes.

Educational Career

In *The Odyssey*, Odysseus finds himself on an extremely long journey home from the Trojan War where he had experienced great success. Throughout this journey, Odysseus faces challenge after challenge, yet despite his frustration he continues on toward his ultimate goal, which is being home with his wife and son. The fact is that for children and adolescents, education is an extremely long journey to a high school diploma. Additionally, like Odysseus, students face many challenges and uphill battles as they progress toward their goal. They must face fears, encounter hurdles, overcome challenges, and maintain forward momentum.

At the beginning of *The Odyssey*, readers are presented with the current state of affairs in Ithaca with Odysseus' wife, Penelope, and son, Telemachos. Penelope has many suitors who are vying for her hand in marriage, all of them assuming that Odysseus has passed since it has been so long since the end of the war without his return. Unfortunately, rather than respecting Penelope, her son, and their home, the suitors are pillaging through animals/food, wine/drink, etc., as well as giving Penelope ultimatums and urging her to admit her husband's death and choose a new husband. Penelope is not ready to acknowledge that Odysseus could be dead or move on as if he is gone from her life. Telemachos is appalled by the way these suitors are treating his homestead and disrespecting his mother, father, and himself. Telemachos is trying to determine what his next steps need to be; he is fearful of standing up to the suitors and defending his parents' honor but knows that something needs to be done.

Meanwhile, Odysseus has made his way to the house of Alcinoos, who has offered him assistance to reach home on the final leg of his journey, at which time Alcinoos asks Odysseus to recount all of the adventures he has encountered prior to arriving at this place. Odysseus obliges and recounts all of his challenges to date, including the Lotus-Eaters, the Cyclops, Circe, Scylla and Charybdis, the Sirens, and Calypso. Each one of these events presents a significant challenge to Odysseus that he needs to face and resolve to continue forward with reaching his goal. Similarly, students must meet certain standards in each grade to move forward to the next grade and continue toward reaching their goal of graduation. Various milestones need to be reached; tests need to be passed; and standards need to be met at each grade level to ensure progression to the next grade and skill development. Many of these milestones can be quite difficult and challenging for students to attain and require their persistence to keep moving forward.

One example of such a milestone is students learning to read. This is perhaps one of the most important and influential milestones that students accomplish early on in their academic career. Indeed, it is the primary focus of instruction beginning in preschool through the elementary years of education. Moreover, research has shown that the near and far outcomes for students who do not become competent readers can be quite negative and exert a significant influence over the trajectory of their entire lives (Smart et al., 2017; McNamara et al., 2011; Lyytinen & Erskine, 2006). Students who do not master the skill of reading are more at risk than their counterparts who are competent readers for failing to graduate high school and earn their diplomas; failing to pursue post-secondary education or training; failing to secure gainful employment; earning less income over the lifespan; engaging in delinquent behavior; becoming involved in criminal behavior, etc.

While having difficulty reading does not guarantee these risk factors will become a reality, it does exhibit why reading is so important and what could happen if this milestone is not reached. At first glance, it does not seem that a milestone occurring so early in an individual's life could exert such long-lasting effects on their lives. However, it elucidates for parents, teachers, etc. the importance that such a milestone holds for students. Further, it speaks to the overall significance of education in people's lives. Education has been termed the great equalizer which can close the gap caused by other risk factors, such as low socioeconomic status. Despite the import of this experience for students, individuals need to complete the journey if the benefits are to be reaped. Similar to Odysseus and his life-and-death journey, education can be viewed as a journey that determines how students' lives progress and culminate.

Special Education

Special education is a service provided within the educational environment to address the needs of students who have been classified as having an educational disability according to the Individuals with Disabilities Education Improvement Act (Yell et al., 2017). This service is provided by a certified special education teacher, in other words one who has been trained to work with students who are exceptional and helps them to make academic gains similar to those students in the regular education environment. These service providers or special education teachers equalize the playing field for these students and accommodate their differences in order to ensure their continued educational progress. These more capable adults/teachers have the skills to be able to help students work around and through their deficits using student strengths and instructional strategies and supports.

Odysseus is described in *The Odyssey* as a larger-than-life character with extraordinary strength, intelligence, and resolve. Although Odysseus is blessed with these gifts, they are not enough for him to reach home on his own. Throughout the many trials and tribulations Odysseus faces, he often needs the assistance of others in order to continue forward progress toward his overall goal. Indeed, his capture and imprisonment by Calypso is a perfect metaphor for understanding how special education works. In this scenario, Odysseus' capture and imprisonment represents the regular education setting, while Odysseus is the student with special needs requiring assistance. Calypso is the regular education teacher, who is doing all within her skill set to help Odysseus to be successful in her environment. However, it simply is not working. Finally, Athena, the embodiment of the special education teacher, appears to provide assistance, guidance, and mentorship to facilitate Odysseus' escape and arrival to Alcinoos, which eventually leads him home to his wife and son.

Another example of the special education process is the story of Telemachos. When the reader first encounters Telemachos, he is presented as weak, floundering, and lacking the problem-solving skills to determine how to help his mother face her suitors and protect their home. After four years of struggling, Athena comes to his aid and provides the instruction and mentorship he needs to not only succeed, but also discover his own physical and inner strength, aptitude, and acumen. In addition, Athena provides Telemachos with the means to increase his confidence, steadfastness, and determination to find resolution for his problems. In this scenario, Telemachos' present situation represents a student in the regular education environment with Penelope representing his regular education teacher. Athena again embodies the special education teacher who provides the instructional accommodations and supports to assist Telemachos with doing what needs to be done to accomplish his goal. Her assistance, guidance, and mentorship serve to help Telemachos recognize his own strengths and use those to develop skills in his weaker areas. Thus, he is able to step up, take action, and help to take back their home for his mother.

While Odysseus and Telemachos are very different "students," needing various instructional strategies and techniques to be successful, Athena, "the teacher," is able to meet both of their special needs and assist them toward their individual goals. Further, Athena is able to work collaboratively with others in their respective environments, i.e., Penelope and Calypso, so that both the "special education teacher" and the "regular education teacher" can work together to aid the "students" toward their goal. Indeed, Rouse (1937), in his translation of the story, describes the following situation for Odysseus that reveals this concept of special education:

> After that, he tossed about for two nights and two days on the rolling waves, always looking for death. But the third day broke with rosy streaks of dawn and when the light was full, the wind fell and there came a breathless calm. Odysseus lifted high on a great swell, took a quick look forward, and there close by he saw the land. As a father's life is welcome to his children, when he has been lying tormented by some fell disease, and in his agony long drawn out the hateful hand of death has touched him, but god has given relief from his troubles; no less welcome to Odysseus was the sight of earth and trees, and he swam on, longing to feel his feet on solid ground. (p. 70)

Another special education concept tangentially relevant to the story of *The Odyssey* is the idea of labeling. The special education system is designed so that in order for a student to receive special education services, they must be eligible for services under a specific educational classification. Examples include specific learning disability (SLD), autism, and intellectual disability (ID). Over the years, classification names have changed to be more reflective of current terminology and less stigmatizing. However, having to classify a student at all for services to be delivered necessitates labeling them as having some sort of disability. Several issues related to labeling have arisen over the years that special education has been in existence with the primary issue being that a label often results in the student being known only for the difficulties they face related to their diagnosed disability. Several strategies and practices have been recommended to counter these stigmatizing effects including the use of person-first language and inclusion of student strengths in their Individualized Education Plan (IEP), though students often are viewed through the lens of disability regardless of these efforts (Arishi et al., 2017; Lockwood & Coulter, 2017; Gold & Richards, 2012).

Difficulties related to the act of labeling exacerbates the overall perception that a person is only defined by their disability. The reality is that all humans have strengths and weaknesses they face in their lives, but these may not impact their primary activities (i.e., school and work) and do not require identification or services. Others have weaknesses that do affect their daily activities and as such necessitate identification and services in order to level the playing field for them and allow for their participation in the world similar to their nondisabled counterparts. As educators in the educational system, we need to advocate for these students and ensure that they are known for their strengths and attributes rather than only for the challenges. Each individual deserves to be seen for who they are not for whom they are perceived to be because of a label, diagnosis, or classification ascribed to them.

Another complication related to labeling is the misunderstanding that all individuals who possess the same label present in the same manner. In other words, the label is viewed similarly to a medical diagnosis whereby individuals diagnosed with the same medical conditions tend to exhibit many of the same symptoms. Special education students, on the other hand, experience their disability/classification in varying ways. If 15 students diagnosed with attention-deficit hyperactivity disorder (ADHD) described their ADHD experience, likely they would touch on behaviors related to impulsivity, distractibility, and hyperactivity. On the other hand, the likelihood that these 15 students would describe the same or similar experiences in their lives based on their diagnosis of ADHD is slim. Therefore, while ascribing a label does provide a starting point from which to examine a student's educational needs, it does not imply that all students within that group or ascribed with that label will present in the classroom in exactly the same manner. This creates a stereotyping situation, which does not help anyone, least of all the student, in the educational process.

In *The Odyssey* Odysseus is presented to the reader as a larger-than-life character, who exhibits incredible power and ability, displays excellent leadership skills, and is courageous even in the face of certain death. However, Odysseus still has significant difficulty finding his way home to Ithaca from the war. He is required to face obstacle after obstacle, and when the reader encounters him in the story, Odysseus is in his 20th year of trying to make it home to his family. Despite Odysseus' strengths, he needs assistance and guidance to level the playing field and allow him to complete his journey and accomplish his goal. He is the embodiment of the individual who is highly capable but requires some accommodations and supports to be successful. Telemachos, on the other hand, initially is presented in the story as an individual with many weaknesses who is struggling to make decisions, defend his mother and home, and determine whether his father is alive. After receiving help and guidance from Athena, Telemachos is able to recognize his own strengths and employ them to solve his problem of the suitors pillaging his father's land and valuables. Both of these characters demonstrate the notion of the special education student who needs assistance to be more successful in their current situations. Both characters have similar difficulties but display those difficulties in varying ways through varying behaviors. They show clearly that lumping individuals into labels/categories does not tell the entire story of the individual, although it can provide a jumping off point for understanding what that character may be experiencing.

Resilience

Luthar et al. (2000) define resilience as a "dynamic process encompassing positive adaptation within the context of significant adversity" (p. 543). Resiliency is an important concept in education as it can make the difference between one who overcomes hardship and one who succumbs to it. There are many facets related to resilience and factors influencing one's level of resiliency, though a discussion of these is beyond the scope of this chapter. For the purposes of this chapter, a basic understanding of resilience suffices to make the connections between the concept and *The Odyssey*. Regardless, resilience remains an important trait for educators to understand and employ in their work to shelter students and keep them moving toward their goals (Gardner & Stephens-Pisecco, 2019; Coyle, 2011).

The story of Odysseus very clearly demonstrates resiliency and personifies various aspects of this construct through many characters, problems, situations, and solutions presented in the tale. At a basic level, certainly the eventual return of Odysseus to Ithaca and reunification with his wife and son, which was his primary goal from the beginning after years of fighting in the Trojan War and traveling home, is the ultimate example of resilience. Many individuals, when faced with these types and the sheer number of tribulations Odysseus faced, would have given up seeking out this goal and striving for success. Various factors related to resilience are outlined in *The Odyssey* and will be discussed. These include mentorship, delay of gratification, goal-seeking, and persistence and perseverance.

Mentorship

In *The Odyssey* mentorship can be observed in numerous relationships throughout the story. The focus here will be on Athena as mentor to Odysseus and Telemachos, though there are other examples present in the story. At various times during this tale, Athena advocates for her students (i.e., Odysseus and Telemachos), provides them with direct instruction, works collaboratively with them, watches from afar as they demonstrate their knowledge, and celebrates their successes with them. Athena is the complete metaphor for the role of teacher, whether regular or special education, in the educational system. Teachers are required to take content information that is novel and/or difficult to understand and translate it in ways that promote students' understanding of and memory of that knowledge. Additionally, when their students find themselves faced with difficult problems to solve and need a helping hand, teachers provide the instructional supports and scaffolding necessary for them to be successful. Further, when students are faced with troublesome situations, teachers often are their most ardent advocates in the pursuit of extra assistance, support, and justice. Athena is the epitome of the teacher/mentor for Odysseus and Telemachos.

Examples of Athena's role as mentor and her commitment to her mentees are scattered throughout the story of Odysseus. Athena serves as advocate for Odysseus when she disguises herself as a King's herald to announce that the stranger (i.e., Odysseus) who had arrived at the palace in Ithaca "seems like a visitor from heaven" (p. 88). Undeniably, she cares for Odysseus when she sees him in Ithaca, pats him with her hand, and smiles over him with a loving and adoring gaze. Further, when needed, Athena would provide direct instruction to Odysseus to ensure success. Athena says to him, "Prince Laertiades, you are a man ever ready! Now is the time to speak to your son! Hide nothing from him, contrive with him death and destruction for the pretenders, and then return to the town. I will not be far from you and your son in the thick of the fight" (p. 184). Finally, one last example is when Athena describes that Odysseus will meet the singing sirens and Scylla and Charybdis on the final leg of his journey home. Prior to Odysseus' departure, Athena walks him through these situations step by step and states what Odysseus must do to survive and make it through these trials. She insists that if he follows these steps and guidelines, he will conquer these obstacles and make his way home to Ithaca. Athena cautions him that if he does not follow these steps exactly as she states them, he will not be successful with this endeavor and will certainly perish. Odysseus does follow the guidelines laid before him and conquers the singing sirens and the Scylla and Charybdis obstacle. Surely, if Odysseus would have strayed from Athena's instructions in any way, the same outcome would not have been achieved (Day, 2006; Southwick et al., 2006; Brown, 2004).

Mentorship is critical to education and student development, as relationships, both positive and negative, can have a significant impact on student progress. Ask any students if they can recall their favorite, most influential teacher and/or the teacher who impacted them the most negatively, and usually memories immediately begin flooding. Both types of relationships can influence the trajectory of students' progress during their educational careers. Mentorship refers to a positive relationship where more competent individuals take less competent individuals under their influence to facilitate their growth and development (Cardinot & Flynn, 2022; Dawson et al., 2022; McCarron et al., 2022). A mentor not only teaches, but also guides, inspires, and supports mentees toward successful completion of their goals. A dissertation advisor/mentor serves in this capacity for doctoral students attempting to complete their doctoral degree. Many times, the dissertation is termed an exercise in persistence as much as an academic exercise. There is a term for students who complete all doctoral requirements save the dissertation called "all but dissertation" (ABD), meaning that the student was able to fulfill all requirements of the doctoral degree with the exception of the dissertation project. Often, life circumstances are the cause of this inability to complete the project, and many times a mentor relationship can be the difference between the doctoral student's ability or failure to complete their degree.

The same is true of students who are pursuing their high school diplomas and traversing elementary, middle, and high school experiences. One significant, positive relationship can exert influence over the students' ability to face and overcome adversity, persist with their education despite difficulties and obstacles, and ultimately reach their goal of earning a high school diploma. These mentorship relationships can make all the difference for these students. Teachers are in the unique position to be that mentor or positive relationship that makes the difference for students at risk of adversity during their educational journey. These risk factors can include, but are not limited to, birth trauma, developmental delays, low socioeconomic status or living in poverty, limited access to educational materials and/or quality preschool experiences, and many more. Risk factors do not ordain an individual's fate; however, protective factors, of which mentorship is one, can reduce the possible negative effects of those risk factors (Wu & Farmer, 2022). In this way, teachers have the unique ability, given their proximity to and frequency of contact with the student population, to develop these relationships or link students with other individuals in a good position to form a strong mentorship relationship with them.

Delay of Gratification

To delay one's own gratification is to resist the desire to give in to needs and weaknesses realizing that other expectations and responsibilities need to be faced first (Bembenutty, 2011; Bembenutty & Karabenick, 2004). The easier path to take is the former, while the latter relates to the ability of the individual to put aside their own satisfaction for a greater benefit. Anyone who has read the labors of Odysseus can easily see that Odysseus must have possessed this virtue in abundance based on the number and intensity of obstacles he faced. Odysseus had the distinct ability to deny his own wants and needs to stay true to his overall goal of going home. This is no easy feat but speaks to the will and resolve of Odysseus and the importance of his desire to be home with his wife and son. In *The Odyssey*, Odysseus muses regarding what he has been through already and considers how he can go on from here:

But Odysseus was left in doubt. How much had he endured patiently already! And he was angry as he said to himself: "More trouble for me! I can't help thinking that some god or other is weaving another snare, when she tells me to leave the raft. At all events I won't do it yet; she said I should get ashore there, but the land was a long way off when I caught sight of it. Well, I know what I'll do; this seems the best thing. As long as these sticks hold together, I'll stick to them, and make the best of my hard luck; but if the sea smashes them up, I'll swim for it, since I cannot see anything better to do." (p. 69)

Possessing the ability to delay gratification also is a fundamental skill needed for educational success. Frequently, students need to make intentional decisions to forego their own immediate wants and needs to pursue the greater goal of earning an education. Students are faced with these challenges daily, starting with the choice to get up in the morning and come to school. Students must resist peer pressure to avoid educational work and surrender to their proximate wants and needs. When these pressures are not managed and appropriate choices are not made, significant repercussions are possible and more likely. While occasional dalliances may not exert broad negative impact, a repeated pattern of inability to delay gratification could have substantial influence over progression toward and eventual goal accomplishment.

Goal Seeking

Having a goal for which to strive often can be a motivating factor for continuing despite obstacles and challenges. It also contributes to an individual's understanding of their own progress toward that goal. This can be a motivating factor to the individual as they view their advancement and/or improvement toward that goal (Gerani et al., 2020; Sides & Cuevas, 2020). Any forward momentum, no matter how slight, can be enough to spur the individual on toward the goal. In *The Odyssey*, Odysseus' goal is to be home with his wife and son. Clearly, this goal is extremely important for him to persist through so many life-and-death struggles; keep pushing forward despite losing all of the men who served at his command; and make strides when he has been away from his family for such an extended period of time. An example presented in the story by Rouse (1937) is this quote in which Athena is speaking to Odysseus regarding his resolve. She states that:

Ah, you are always the same, no one can catch you napping; and that is why I cannot desert you in misfortune, because you are so charming and discreet and always ready for anything. Any other man after those long wanderings would have been eager to see home and wife and children; you do not choose to ask anything of any one until you make sure of your wife by your own observation—and she, let me tell you, just stays at home, while she weeps the nights and days away.

In order to reach a goal, individuals need to be motivated to attain that goal. Motivation is that force that assists the individual with starting a project, seeing the project through to fruition, and continuing to work on the project even when there are bumps in the road. Psychologists describe two primary types of motivation including intrinsic and extrinsic (Morris et al., 2022). Intrinsic motivation occurs when individuals are eager to complete a task simply for the sake of completing it. In other words, the task itself is motivating enough on its own for the individual to work toward task completion. Extrinsic motivation occurs when individuals need some reward from outside of themselves to continue working toward task completion. In other words, the intrinsic motivation to complete the task has not yet developed; thus, an external motivator is necessary. Often, educators begin by using extrinsic types of motivation to encourage students to engage in nonpreferred tasks until they achieve enough success with those tasks that the intrinsic motivation is present. The ultimate goal most often is to develop this intrinsic motivation because ultimately that type of motivation will be the catalyst for the individual to follow through with the task. While this may not always be possible, it is the primary goal for educators. Odysseus clearly is intrinsically motivated to achieve his goal and will move forward until the goal is reached without a great deal of extrinsic motivation needed.

Persistence and Perseverance

Without the virtues of persistence and perseverance, Odysseus would never have seen his journey come to fruition when he takes back his home, wife, and son and reclaims his place in Ithaca. Odysseus encounters so many hindrances along the way home that it would have been easy for him to give up at any point. Instead, Odysseus braves the challenges and forges on his path toward his goal. Persistence and perseverance are necessary skills to possess if

Odysseus is to see his goal come to fruition; he must have the fortitude within him to keep moving forward regardless of the dangers or impediments in his path. The same is true of students pursuing their education and moving toward their high school diploma. No student leaves the educational system completely unscathed without encountering some sort of challenge that must be overcome to achieve the goal. The question becomes ... what will the student do when the challenge is encountered? Will the student choose to avoid the challenge, face the challenge head on, or wilt in the midst of the challenge? The answer to this question will impact the trajectory of the student's movement toward the eventual goal. Each choice has the potential to send the student on a different path, which will either allow, delay, or prohibit the student from reaching that goal. Persistence at one challenge could reduce challenges later on the journey, while avoiding or succumbing to a challenge could exacerbate future challenges and necessitate increased persistence or perseverance farther along the journey.

Odysseus demonstrates his willingness to pursue all challenges before him no matter the intensity on several occasions throughout the story. At one point when speaking with Calypso about his reaching his homeland, they have the following conversation:

> "Prince Odysseus Laertiades, now is the time to show your famous cleverness! So you want to go home at once? Well, I wish you luck all the same. If you knew what troubles you will have before you get to Ithaca, you would stay where you are and keep this house with me, and be immortal, however much you might want to see your wife whom you long for day in and day out. Is she prettier than me? I think not. I don't think it is likely that a mortal woman would set herself up as a model of beauty against a goddess!"
>
> Odysseus knew what to say to that, and he answered at once: "Gracious goddess, don't be cross with me! I know all that as well as you do. My wife is nothing compared to you for beauty. I can see that for myself. She is mortal, you are immortal and never grow old. But even so, I long for the day of my homecoming. And if some god wrecks me again on the deep, I will endure it, for I have a patient mind. I have suffered already many troubles and hardships in battle and tempest; this will be only one more." (Rouse, 1937, p. 66)

This passage within the tale indicates the determination of Odysseus, as well as his overall commitment to achieving his goal no matter how long it takes or how many obstacles are placed before him. Students need to exhibit this level of persistence and perseverance as they are progressing through the grades toward earning a high school diploma. Academic milestones—including learning to read; making the transition to reading to learn; navigating elementary, middle, and high school; passing state tests; deciding on a post-secondary transition plan, etc.; as well as social and emotional milestones—can be difficult to manage depending on the student's individual experience. Possessing the quality of perseverance helps students to continue moving forward in the face of adversity they may encounter (Tovar-Garcia, 2017; Simon et al., 2015).

Learning via *The Odyssey*

Given the connections that have been presented between the story of *The Odyssey* and the educational process, it is clear that this epic tale could be used in the higher education classroom to educate future teachers about various concepts related to the educational process. Concepts are abstract by nature and difficult to understand without the ability to make connections between these concepts and more concrete understandings. Using literature, the story can be used to show how these concepts can be applied to characters and scenes within a literary story. Rather than simply presenting concept definitions, including examples and nonexamples of those concepts or real-world examples or applications of these concepts, faculty can aid students in drawing connections between characters and/or a story and abstract concepts. These linkages serve to help students comprehend these concepts in action and applied to human stories and scenarios. Employing literature in this way has the ability to bring abstract concepts to life and reinforce students' ability not only to understand what is being taught, but also to analyze the information as it relates to the field of education and the education process. Three possible ways to accomplish this would be through the use of analogy, character analysis, and literary analysis.

Analogy

First, the use of comparison through the technique of analogy provides a plausible strategy for helping students to understand educational concepts. An analogy is a similarity between like features of two objects, individuals, concepts, etc., on which a comparison can be based (dictionary.com). Analogy allows teacher education students to make comparisons between characters, plots, problems, etc. in the story to students, teachers, instructional techniques, etc. they may have encountered in their own lives, via video representations, or through observations/student teaching experiences. Teacher education faculty can use activities employing analogy to assist teacher education students in understanding broad, abstract educational concepts. Teacher education students should read *The Odyssey* and discuss the story in depth before any other tasks are required. An educational case study, along with an excerpt from *The Odyssey*, can then be provided to students. Teacher education students can read both passages, critically analyze the information, and draw connections between the story of *The Odyssey* and various educational concepts present in the educational case study. This type of activity should be done after the abstract concept has been defined and students have been provided examples and nonexamples of the concept. The analogy activity can aid teacher education students in their comprehension and analytical thinking regarding abstract educational concepts.

Character Analysis

Second, character analysis can be utilized to help teacher education students analyze literary characters in the story in order to describe and understand their personalities. According to study.com (*Character Analysis*, 2015), there are five methods of character analysis including physical description, action, inner thoughts, reactions, and speech. Subsequent to reading and discussing *The Odyssey*, teacher education students can be assigned various characters within the story to analyze. They can accomplish this by gathering information from the story related to the five methods presented above. This information can be organized through the use of a graphic organizer. Figure 1 shows a template that might be used to show the students what is required of them, while Figure 2 demonstrates a completed analysis for illustration purposes. Once this information has been collected, the teacher education student can write a summary of the data collected regarding the personality and characteristics of the character in the story. The next step would be to draw comparisons between the character in the story and various educational concepts they are learning within their course. Talking about these analyses in small groups and sharing information with others who had the same characters first could help the students to understand their own character and analyses better. Shifting then to small groups and sharing information with others who had different characters second could aid in the transfer of information and learning of additional educational concepts beyond the character analysis that a student was assigned.

Literary Analysis

Third, literary analysis can be utilized to help teacher education students analyze the literary work itself and make interpretations about the work that they can relate to what they are learning in education. According to germanna.edu, a literary analysis is an argument about the literary work that expresses a writer's personal perspective, interpretation, judgment, or critical evaluation of the work and includes four elements: plot, conflict, characters, and setting. Subsequent to reading and discussing *The Odyssey*, teacher education students can be assigned one of the elements within the story to analyze. They can accomplish this by gathering information from the story related to the element they are assigned. This information can be organized through the use of a graphic organizer. Figure 3 shows a template that might be used to show the students what is required of them, while Figure 4 indicates a template with assigned element and educational/psychological concepts. Figure 5, then, demonstrates a completed analysis for illustration purposes. Once this information has been collected, the teacher education student can write a summary of the data collected regarding the element, i.e., plot, conflict, characters, and setting. The next step would be to draw comparisons between the element in the story and various educational concepts they are learning within their course. Talking about these analyses in small groups and sharing information with others who had the same element first could help the students to understand their own element analyses better. Shifting then to small groups and sharing information with others who had different elements second could aid in the transfer of information and learning of additional educational concepts beyond what element a student was assigned.

Homer, The Odyssey, and Resilience in Education 137

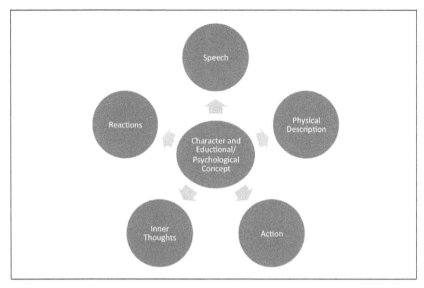

Figure 8.1. Character Analysis Template.
Note: By the author.

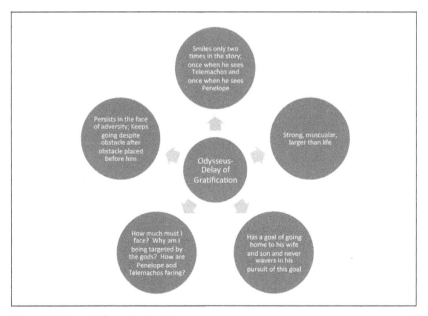

Figure 8.2. Sample Character Analysis.
Note: By the author.

138 LITERARY IMAGINATION AND PROFESSIONAL KNOWLEDGE

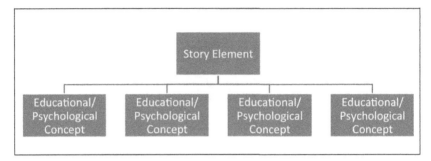

Figure 8.3. Literary Analysis Template.
Note: By the author.

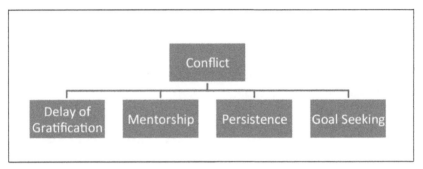

Figure 8.4. Literary Analysis Template with Element and Concepts.
Note: By the author.

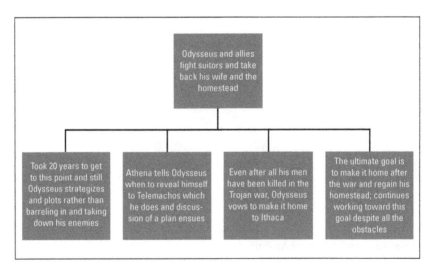

Figure 8.5. Literary Analysis Example.
Note: By the author.

Conclusion

Undoubtedly, literature benefits the reader on its own based on the story presented and the writing itself. There are lessons to be learned, characters to be explored, language to be interpreted, and stories to comprehend. This chapter has endeavored to further demonstrate that a literary work can be used to teach abstract concepts related to a seemingly unconnected field—in this case education. Having the ability to understand the story being read and make meaningful connections to the concepts being taught serves to increase conceptual understanding as well as practical application and use. Making the comparisons solidifies important concepts in teacher education students' minds and facilitates internalization and employment of these concepts and related strategies in the classroom. Having effective tools in their toolboxes ready for use when working with students can reduce stress for the teachers helping them to be more effective, which will hopefully keep these talented and exceptional individuals in their positions, educating students and informing the next generation.

References

A&E Networks Television. (2021, March 31). *Homer*. Biography.com. Retrieved October 25, 2022, from https://www.biography.com/writer/homer

Arishi, L., Boyle, C., & Lauchlan, F. (2017). Inclusive education and the politics of difference: Considering the effectiveness of labelling in special education. *Educational & Child Psychology, 34*(4), 9–19.

Bembenutty, H. (2011). Academic delay of gratification and academic achievement. *New Directions for Teaching and Learning, 126*, 55–65.

Bembenutty, H., & Karabenick, S. A. (2004). Inherent association between academic delay of gratification, future time perspective, and self-regulated learning. *Educational Psychology Review, 16*(1), 35–57.

Brown, W. K. (2004). Resiliency and the mentoring factor. *Reclaiming Children and Youth, 13*(2), 75–79.

Cardinot, A., & Flynn, P. (2022). Rapid evidence assessment: Mentoring interventions for/by students with disabilities at third-level education. *Education Sciences, 12*(6), 384. https://doi.org/10.3390/educsci12060384

Character Analysis (2015, August 21). Examples; What is a character study? Retrieved from https://study.com/learn/lesson/character-analysis-examples-study.html.

Coyle, J. P. (2011). Resilient families help make resilient children. *Journal of Family Strengths, 11*(1), 5.

Dawson, S., McCormick, B., Knapp, D., & Piatt, J. (2022). Analysis of a year-round mentoring program for youth with physical disabilities attending a medical specialty camp. *Journal of Outdoor Recreation, Education, and Leadership, 14*(3), 74–92. https://doi.org/10.18666/jorel-2022-10906

Day, A. (2006). The power of social support: Mentoring and resilience. *Reclaiming Children and Youth: The Journal of Strength-Based Interventions, 14*(4), 196–198.

Dictionary.com. (n.d.). *Analogy definition & meaning*. Dictionary.com. Retrieved October 25, 2022, from https://www.dictionary.com/browse/analogy

Gardner, R. L., & Stephens-Pisecco, T. L. (2019). Fostering childhood resilience: A call to educators. *Preventing School Failure: Alternative Education for Children and Youth, 63*(3), 195–202. https://doi.org/10.1080/1045988x.2018.1561408

Gerani, C., Theodosiou, A., Barkoukis, V., Papacharisis, V., Tsorbatzoudis, H., & Gioupsani, A. (2020). The effect of a goal-setting program in physical education on cognitive and affective outcomes of the lesson. *Physical Educator, 77*(2), 332–356.

Gold, M. E., & Richards, H. (2012). To label or not to label: The special education question for African Americans. *Educational Foundations, 26*(1–2), 143–156.

Lockwood, A., & Coulter, A. (2017). Rights without labels: Thirty years later. *Communique, 45*(6), 1–29.

Lurye, S., & Griesbach, R. (2022, September 12). *Teacher shortages are real, but not for the reason you heard*. AP NEWS. Retrieved October 25, 2022, from https://apnews.com/0785042a3da15bcbcc58922c747fd961

Luthar, S. S., Cicchetti, D., & Becker, B. (2000). The construct of resilience: A critical evaluation and guidelines for future work. *Child Development, 71*(3), 543–562. https://doi.org/10.1111/1467-8624.00164

Lyytinen, H., & Erskine, J. (2006). Early identification and prevention of reading problems. *Learning Disabilities*, 1–5.

McCarron, E., Curran, E., & McConkey, R. (2022). Promoting the wellbeing of youth with disabilities through music mentoring. *Youth, 2*(3), 258–270. https://doi.org/10.3390/youth2030018

McNamara, J. K., Scissons, M., & Gutknecht, N. (2011). A longitudinal study of kindergarten children at risk for reading disabilities. *Journal of Learning Disabilities, 44*(5), 421–430. https://doi.org/10.1177/0022219411410040

Morris, L. S., Grehl, M. M., Rutter, S. B., Mehta, M., & Westwater, M. L. (2022). On what motivates us: A detailed review of intrinsic v. extrinsic motivation. *Psychological Medicine, 52*(10), 1801–1816. https://doi.org/10.1017/s0033291722001611

Rouse, D. W. H. (1937). *Homer: The odyssey*. Mentor. (originally published in 1488)

Sides, J. D., & Cuevas, J. A. (2020). Effect of goal setting for motivation, self-efficacy, and performance in elementary mathematics. *International Journal of Instruction, 13*(4), 1–16.

Simon, R. A., Aulls, M. W., Dedic, H., Hubbard, K., & Hall, N. C. (2015). Exploring student persistence in STEM programs: A motivational model. *Canadian Journal of Education, 38*(1), 1–27.

Smart, D., Youssef, G. J., Sanson, A., Prior, M., Toumbourou, J. W., & Olsson, C. A. (2017). Consequences of childhood reading difficulties and behaviour problems for educational achievement and employment in early adulthood. *British Journal of Educational Psychology, 87*(2), 288–08. https://doi.org/10.1111/bjep.12150

Southwick, S. M., Morgan, C. A., Vythilingam, M., & Charney, D. (2006). Mentors enhance resilient in at-risk children and adolescents. *Psychoanalytic Inquiry, 26*(4), 577–584.

Tovar-Garcia, E. D. (2017). The impact of perseverance and passion for long term goals (GRIT) on educational achievements of migrant children: Evidence from Tatarstan, Russia. *Psicologia Educativa, 23*(1), 19–27. https://doi-org.proxy-iup.kinpa.org/10.1016/j.pse.2017.02.003

Walker, T. (2022, October 4). *Real solutions, not band-aids, will fix educator shortage*. NEA. Retrieved October 25, 2022, from https://www.nea.org/advocating-for-change/new-from-nea/nea-real-solutions-not-band-aids-will-fix-educator-shortage

Wu, S., & Farmer, A. Y. (2021). Risk and protective factors of youth prescription drug misuse: Variations across racial/ethnic groups. *Child and Adolescent Social Work Journal, 39*(4), 499–514. https://doi.org/10.1007/s10560-021-00752-1

Yell, M. L., Shriner, J. G., & Katsiyannis, A. (2017). Individuals with disabilities education improvement act of 2004 and IDEA regulations of 2006: Implications for educators, administrators, and teacher trainers. *Focus on Exceptional Children, 39*(1). https://doi.org/10.17161/fec.v39i1.6824

NINE

 Developing Preservice Teachers' Beliefs About Cultural Diversity Through Multicultural Children's Literature

Brian Hibbs

According to Alred et al. (2002), being intercultural involves "the awareness of experiencing otherness and the ability to analyze the experience and act upon the insights into self and other which the analysis brings" (p. 4). This definition identifies several important steps in the process of becoming intercultural. First, students need to be immersed in a situation in which they come into contact with some cultural variable that is not part of their own cultural/linguistic background. Second, students need to be provided with opportunities to try and make sense of the situation and consider what the situation has taught them about others' cultural identities as well as their own. The reflective portion of this process is essential to deepen students' evolving understanding of other cultures; mere exposure to other cultures is not sufficient. This chapter explores a research study that exposed pre-education students to numerous sociocultural variables through the reading and analysis of multicultural children's literature and provided opportunities for students to reflect on how these books contributed to their developing awareness of the role these sociocultural factors play in education.

Numerous scholars have identified a variety of ways to promote education students' intercultural competence. For example, Burton (2011) describes a collaboration on a year-long music education course between students and instructors from the United States and Sweden. The fall semester of the course included several synchronous virtual conferences between both groups, and the spring semester included two 10-day immersion experiences, one for the students from the United States to travel to Sweden, and the second for the students from Sweden to travel to the United States. Students' journal entries revealed that they noticed important similarities and significant differences between both cultures and thus were able to adopt multicultural perspectives regarding these phenomena.

Reidel and Draper (2013) outlined the incorporation of an interdisciplinary unit in a social studies methods course for preservice teachers designed to enlarge their understanding and appreciation of Indian and South Asian cultures. To this end, students reflected on their background knowledge and experiences concerning India, read and responded to a children's book on India, engaged in a museum exhibit consisting of various cultural artifacts from India, and reflected on how their perspective on Indian culture had changed through their participation in these activities. To move beyond the superficial level of cultural analysis, students then viewed the film *Going to School in India* and discussed the similarities and differences between the education systems in the United States and India.

Finally, Siwatu (2011) described a research study intended to identify preservice teachers' perceptions concerning the contribution of a university teacher education program to their views on culturally responsive teaching. The study measured 192 preservice teachers' beliefs concerning culturally responsive teaching via the Culturally Responsive Teaching Self-Efficacy (CRTSE) scale (Siwatu, 2011) followed by semistructured face-to-face interviews with eight of these teachers in order to collect information regarding the influences of the teacher education program they were enrolled in on their perspectives regarding culturally responsive teaching. Participants indicated that they were exposed to culturally responsive teaching in some of their coursework and believed that these experiences were valuable to their ongoing development as future teachers. However, many of the participants noted that these experiences were often disparate in nature and, if they were included, consisted mainly of class discussions and demonstrations with few opportunities for them to incorporate such practices in their own teaching contexts.

Other researchers have explored the contribution that literary texts can make in the development of students' intercultural competence. For example, Short (2011) argues that, despite the globalization of our modern world, many students "are ignorant of world cultures, international issues, and foreign languages" (p. 130) and that the knowledge of those students who are cognizant of other cultures is often superficial and grounded in stereotypical views of these cultures. Short proposes that literature is one way to overcome these deficiencies in cultural learning in several ways. Firstly, literature allows students to move beyond a superficial view of other cultures towards understanding other cultures at a deeper level. Secondly, by immersing themselves in the story worlds found in literature, readers are able to learn about how people of other cultures live, think, and feel; as a result, students develop more empathy and understanding towards these cultures. Thirdly, literature gives students opportunities to see similarities they share with other cultures while also valuing the unique differences of each culture. Fourthly, literature helps students not only learn about other cultures but also learn about their own culture as well. In sum, literature "provides a means of building bridges of understanding across countries and cultures" (p. 131). Short (2012) indicates that literature promotes intercultural understanding because readers enter the story worlds of the books they read and experience first-hand the characters' life experiences. Thus, students are immersed in "cultural input" in the same way that children are exposed to linguistic input; consequently, by reading literary texts, students can acquire both cultural and linguistic input. Students' comments suggest that the children's books provided them with cultural input by immersing them in the story worlds of the books and that, as a result, students learned about Latino culture in a deep and profound way.

Matos (2005) suggests that reading literature can facilitate the development of one's intercultural competence since literature "has the value of mobilizing a critical awareness of self and other" (p. 68). Literature allows readers to inhabit other worlds and move constantly between their individual perspectives and social perspectives of cultural phenomena so that they are able to see the world from different perspectives. Building off Kramsch's (2009/2011) notion of third space, Matos argues that texts contain "touchpoints" or unclear and ambiguous moments that "offer a pretext for reflection on the intercultural (dis)encounters portrayed [in texts] and the [dialectical] struggle that they prefigure" (p. 63). In other words, these textual touchpoints allow readers to see how characters negotiate different cultural worlds that then serve as models for readers' own cultural negotiations. Lütge (2013) concurs, noting that such texts encourage readers to put themselves in the position of others and see the world from their eyes and that children's literature "offers a fascinating platform for exploring questions of identity, values and worldviews, the basic ingredients for intercultural learning" (p. 104). Lütge (2013) also contends that an important step in reading multicultural texts is the analysis of one's personal response to the text, which can lead to a reflective examination of their own cultural identity: "aesthetic reading has a strong bearing on the development of identity formation processes that relate the student's 'self' with potential 'others' through literary encounters" (p. 98).

The current study brings these two perspectives together in that multicultural children's literature is used as a vehicle to expose pre-education students to a variety of sociocultural variables they may (not) be familiar with and provide opportunities for them to consider the extent to which these books contributed (or not) to their developing understanding and appreciation of others whose cultural identities may be different from their own.

Theoretical Framework

One valuable way to promote students' evolving awareness of the multicultural nature of the world around them is the framework adopted by Mansilla and Jackson (2011) (see Figure 9.1). The framework outlines four steps to help students better understand issues and problems in their community and/or the world. In the first step, "Investigate the World," students pinpoint and gather information about a given question or dilemma of significance to them and/or their community. In the second step, "Recognize Perspectives," students become aware of the fact that there are multiple ways to make sense of a given situation and that one perspective is not inherently superior or inferior to another. In the third step, "Communicate Ideas," students share the information they've gathered and what they have learned about the question or dilemma with others. In the final step, "Take Action," students apply their learning in an attempt to implement an authentic and real-world solution to the question or dilemma they investigated. This study focused on the first two steps of the framework in that the children's books contributed to their awareness of the role various sociocultural factors play in education while also learning to understand a variety of viewpoints others may have regarding these sociocultural factors.

Research Question

The research question that guided this study is: In what ways can multicultural children's literature contribute to pre-education students' personal and professional beliefs about sociocultural diversity in education?

Developing Preservice Teachers' Beliefs About Cultural Diversity   147

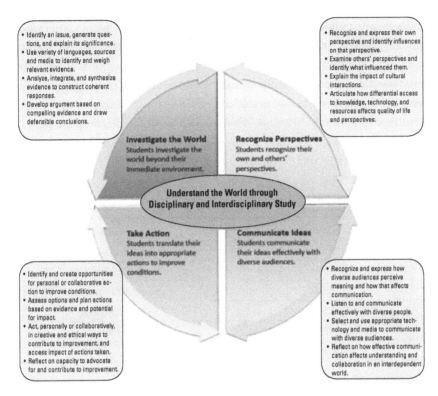

Figure 9.1. Understanding the World through Disciplinary and Interdisciplinary Study.
Note: From Mansilla, V. B., & Jackson, A. W. (2011). *Educating for global competence: Preparing our youth to engage the world.* Asian Society Council of Chief State School Officers (CCSSO). Retrieved from https://asiasociety.org/files/book-globalcompetence.pdf

Research Context

This study was conducted during the spring semester of 2019 in a small four-year institution of higher education in southeastern United States. The study was conducted as part of a 2000-level course on multicultural education for pre-education majors; 27 students in the course (17 females and 10 males) ultimately consented to participate in the study.

The textbook that was used in the course was Gollnick and Chen (2016). The textbook is organized into 11 chapters with 9 of these chapters focusing on a specific sociocultural variable (race and ethnicity, class and socioeconomic status, gender, sexual orientation, exceptionality, language, religion, geography, the youth culture) with the introductory and concluding chapters centering on multicultural education in general. The class met twice per week for 75 minutes per session. Both sessions in a given week were dedicated to a specific chapter from the Gollnick and Chen (2016) textbook. During the first session of the week, students discussed the chapter from the textbook, and during the second session, students read and discussed one or more multicultural children's books aligned with the theme of the chapter the class was exploring that week. See Table 9.1 for a list of sample books that were used for each chapter/sociocultural variable.

Table 9.1. A List of Sample Books for Each Sociocultural Variable

Sociocultural Variable	Sample Book
Race & Ethnicity	Alko & Qualls (2015)
Class & Socioeconomic Status	Boelts & Jones (2009)
Gender	Schwartz & Santat (2014)
Sexual Orientation	Ewert & Ray (2008)
Exceptionality	Peete (2010)
Language	Tonatiuh (2010)
Religion	Buller (2005)
Geography	Castillo (2014)
The Youth Culture	Langston-George & Bock (2014)

In order to prepare students to read the multicultural children's texts later in the semester, we began by reading *My Name is Maria Isabel* (Ada & Thompson, 1995). The book describes the life experiences of María Isabel Salazar López, a 9-year-old girl from Puerto Rico who emigrates to the United States with her family. On her first day in her new school, she introduces herself to her new teacher, who proceeds to tell her that, since there are already several girls named Maria in the class, her name will be changed to Mary. This begins the trajectory of María Isabel simultaneously discovering her Puerto Rican ancestry through her names while also negotiating her cultural identity in a new country. This book was chosen as it highlights the importance of fighting against those in authority who advocate for assimilation to mainstream American culture while also helping students better understand the importance of appreciating and valuing their future students' cultural and linguistic backgrounds.

Students participated in a variety of reader response activities while reading the book. In some cases, as I read the book aloud, students completed a Graffiti Board (Short et al., 1996, pp. 379–386) which allowed them to document their initial feelings, impressions, connections, etc. about the text by representing their thoughts through single words, complete sentences, pictures, and/or any form(s) they felt best showed their thinking processes. After they finished their Graffiti Boards, they turned and shared their Graffiti Boards with a partner, explaining what the drawings, words, etc. on their board represented. See Figure 9.2 for an example of a student's Graffiti Board as the student listened to a chapter of *My Name is Maria Isabel* (Ada & Thompson, 1995).

Figure 9.2. Student's Graffiti Board in Response to Chapter One of *My Name is Maria Isabel*.

In other cases, students were randomly separated into groups and read a different children's book on the sociocultural variable we were examining that week. Students read their group's book and completed a book response on which they provided a summary of the book, their group's response to the book, what they learned about the sociocultural variable by reading the book, and whether they would (not) use the book with their future students and why. See Figure 9.3 for the response sheet that groups completed as they read their group's book.

Title:	Author:
Write a **SYNOPSIS** of the book.	
Record your **PERSONAL RESPONSE** to the book.	
Describe **WHAT YOU LEARNED ABOUT SOCIOCULTURAL DIVERSITY** through the book.	
Indicate **WHETHER YOU WOULD (NOT) USE THIS BOOK WITH STUDENTS** and why (not).	

Figure 9.3. Sample Book Response Sheet.

Data Collection

Data for the study were collected via two questionnaires, a pre-questionnaire at the beginning of the semester before students began reading the children's books and a post-questionnaire at the end of the semester after students had read the children's books (see Appendix). Both questionnaires collected quantitative and qualitative data on students' perceptions of the contribution of the children's books to their emerging/developing personal and professional beliefs concerning cultural diversity. The quantitative section of both questionnaires contained statements taken directly from the Personal Beliefs About Diversity Scale and the Professional Beliefs About Diversity Scale (Pohan & Aguilar, 2001). The Personal Beliefs About Diversity Scale consists of 15 statements intended to measure participants' individual attitudes towards cultural diversity, and the Professional Beliefs About Diversity Scale consists of 25 statements intended to measure participants' views towards cultural diversity in educational settings. For this study, all of the statements from both scales were included on both questionnaires, but the scales were tweaked slightly to allow students to respond to each statement via Likert scales. On the questionnaires, students read each statement and indicated the extent to which they agreed with the statement, from "1" ("strongly disagree") to "5" ("strongly agree"). The qualitative section of both questionnaires asked students to indicate their perceptions of multicultural children's books. On the first questionnaire, students were asked to identify any books they previously read that contained multicultural characters that were similar to and/or different from their own and the relevancy of these books to their understanding of cultural diversity. On the second questionnaire, students were asked to identify any positive and/or negative experiences they had reading the children's books and the extent to which these books did (not) contribute to their beliefs concerning sociocultural diversity in education.

Although both quantitative and qualitative data were collected for the study, this chapter will focus on an exploration of the quantitative data obtained from the questionnaires.

Data Analysis

The quantitative data for the study were analyzed using descriptive statistics. Students' responses to each statement on each questionnaire were identified with the number of times students responded to a given number in the Likert scale being subsequently tabulated and averaged against the total number of participants, thus arriving at a percentage. These percentages were then compared across both questionnaires to determine whether students' personal and professional beliefs concerning cultural diversity had shifted during the course of the semester.

Findings

Tables 2 and 3 summarize the average students' responses to each statement on the Personal Beliefs About Diversity Scale and the Professional Beliefs About Diversity Scale across both questionnaires, from "1" ("strongly disagree") to "5" ('strongly agree"). See the Appendix for the actual items (statements) from the Questionnaires.

Comparing students' responses on both scales across both questionnaires yields some interesting findings. When investigating students' pre-questionnaire (Questionnaire #1) and post-questionnaire (Questionnaire #2) responses, in most cases, results show that students overall tended to have a more positive outlook regarding issues of sociocultural diversity from the beginning to the end of the course. In some cases, students tended to agree less and disagree more with statements that did not view cultural diversity in a positive light. For example, on the Personal Beliefs About Diversity Scale, it can be noted that, regarding Statement #2 ("America's immigrant and refugee policy has led to the deterioration of America"), the average rating was

Table 9.2. Students' Responses on the Personal Beliefs About Diversity Scale

Statement #	Questionnaire #1	Questionnaire #2
1	4.56	4.93
2	2.96	2.41
3	1.26	1.11
4	4.11	3.96
5	2.74	2.00
6	2.56	2.56
7	4.44	4.82
8	1.62	1.52
9	1.93	2.04
10	2.81	2.93
11	1.44	1.37
12	3.56	4.04
13	2.70	2.04
14	3.30	2.89
15	1.48	1.56

Developing Preservice Teachers' Beliefs About Cultural Diversity   153

Table 9.3. Students' Responses on the Professional Beliefs About Diversity Scale

Statement #	Questionnaire #1	Questionnaire #2
1	1.26	1.22
2	3.26	3.22
3	1.67	1.59
4	4.59	4.63
5	1.63	1.56
6	4.15	4.52
7	1.59	1.44
8	2.82	2.41
9	3.67	3.26
10	3.04	3.11
11	3.85	4.07
12	3.19	3.22
13	2.67	2.70
14	3.52	4.00
15	3.59	3.56
16	3.78	3.89
17	3.59	3.52
18	2.48	2.00
19	3.44	3.78
20	2.56	3.30
21	4.44	4.63
22	3.67	4.00
23	1.96	1.78
24	4.22	4.26
25	2.15	2.30

2.96 on Questionnaire #1 but was 2.41 on Questionnaire #2, indicating that fewer students agreed with this statement at the end of the semester. In regards to Statement #5 ("It is not a good idea for same-sex couples to raise children"), the average rating was 2.74 on Questionnaire #1 but was 2.00 on Questionnaire #2, signaling that students were much less in agreement with this statement at the end of the semester than at the beginning of the semester.

On the Professional Beliefs About Diversity Scale, with respect to Statement #8 ("The attention girls receive in school is comparable to the attention boys receive"), the average rating was 2.82 on Questionnaire #1 but was 2.41 on Questionnaire #2, signaling that students were much less in agreement with this statement at the end of the semester than at the beginning of the semester.

In other cases, students tended to agree more and disagree less with statements that did view cultural diversity in a positive light. For example, on the Personal Beliefs About Diversity Scale, it can be noted that, regarding Statement #12 ("It is a good idea for people to develop meaningful relationships with others having a different sexual orientation"), the average rating was 3.56 on Questionnaire #1 but was 4.04 on Questionnaire #2, indicating that students agreed substantially more with this statement at the end of the semester than at the beginning of the semester. On the Professional Beliefs About Diversity Scale, in regards to to Statement #6 ("All students should be encouraged to become fluent in a second language"), the average rating was 4.15 on Questionnaire #1 but was 4.52 on Questionnaire #2, signaling that students were much more in agreement with this statement at the end of the semester than at the beginning of the semester. With respect to Statement #14 ("Students living in racially isolated neighborhoods can benefit socially from participating in racially integrated neighborhoods"), the average rating was 3.52 on Questionnaire #1 but was 4.00 on Questionnaire #2, signaling that students were more in agreement with this statement at the end of the semester than at the beginning of the semester.

Results also demonstrate that, in yet other cases, students' perceptions on sociocultural diversity varied little if at all over the course of the semester. For example, on the Personal Beliefs About Diversity Scale, it can be noted that, regarding Statement #6 ("The reason people live in poverty is that they lack motivation to get themselves out of poverty"), the average rating was exactly the same on both questionnaires (2.56), indicating that students' perspectives on this statement did not vary at all during the course of the semester. With respect to Statement #15 ("Historically, education has been monocultural, reflecting only one reality and has been biased towards the dominant (European) group"), the average rating was 3.59 on Questionnaire #1 but was 3.56 on Questionnaire #2, signaling that students' attitudes changed changed very little on this statement during the course of the semester.

Analysis of the results of both questionnaires show that, in general, students' personal and professional beliefs concerning sociocultural diversity tended to improve over the course of the semester, particularly regarding race and ethnicity, class and socioeconomic status, gender, sexual orientation, and language, in addition to other areas related to education, such as immigration and standardized testing. In other areas, students' views tended to change little if at all over the course of the semester, such as exceptionality and religion, and also in the educational areas of differentiation and the western orientational bias of the American education system. Interestingly, in regard to class and socioeconomic status and gender, in some instances, students' viewpoints changed substantially over the course of the semester and yet, at other times, students' opinions changed little if at all. This may have been due to the wording of the statements; students may have felt that, in specific cases, certain statements may have been seen as more "radical" or inflammatory in nature than others.

Since the institution where the study took place is located in southeastern United States, and since the institution is relatively small in nature (less than 5,000 students), students regularly come from a lower-middle class and monolingual background, are often politically conservative, commonly subscribe to Christianity, and tend to have had little previous contact with others whose upbringing differ from their own. Consequently, one possible explanation for these results may be due to the fact that, overall, students seemed to be willing to change their views regarding statements that more closely aligned with their own cultural/linguistic backgrounds and tended to be less willing to alter their perspectives in relation to statements that did not match their own cultural/linguistic backgrounds.

Several cautionary notes should be taken into consideration when interpreting the results of this study. Firstly, since this study took place with a small number of participants in one institution of higher education in a specific geographical area, readers should remember this when extrapolating the results of this study to their own contexts. Secondly, the Personal Beliefs About Diversity Scale and the Professional Beliefs About Diversity Scale (Pohan & Aguilar, 2001) were used to collect data for the study, and the quantitative data were analyzed using descriptive statistics; it is conceivable that the findings of the study may have been different if another cultural diversity and/or other statistical procedures were used to analyze the data. Thirdly, since students read the course textbook (Gollnick & Chen, 2016) and participated in other activities during the course of the semester, it is conceivable that students' evolving views regarding sociocultural diversity were due to influences beyond the multicultural children's books.

Conclusion

The purpose of this study was to determine the extent to which multicultural children's books would contribute positively to pre-education majors' views regarding sociocultural diversity in an effort to prepare them for the multicultural and multilingual instructional environments in which they will find themselves as future teachers. Analysis of the quantitative results obtained during the study tended to demonstrate that the books did contribute to their developing understanding and appreciation of sociocultural diversity in educational settings. Pohan & Aguilar (2001) contend that "teacher educators nationwide have long been asking the question: How do we best help future and current teachers acquire the knowledge, skills, and attitudes that would result in culturally responsive teaching?" (p.160). This study represents one possible avenue educator preparation programs might consider in helping preservice teachers accomplish this lofty but worthwhile goal.

References

Ada, A.F., & Thompson, K. D. (1995). *My name is Maria Isabel*. Atheneum Books for Young Readers.

Alko, S., & Qualls, S. (2015). *The case for loving: The fight for interracial marriage*. Arthur A. Levine Books.

Alred, G., Byram, M., & Fleming, M. (2002). *Intercultural experience and education*. Multilingual Matters.

Boelts, M., & Jones, N. Z. (2009). *Those shoes*. Candlewick Press.

Buller, L. (2005). *A faith like mine: A celebration of the world's religions through the eyes of children*. New York, NY: DK Publishers.

Burton, S. L. (2011). Perspective consciousness and cultural relevancy: Partnership considerations for the re-conceptualization of music teacher preparation. *Arts Education Policy Review, 112*(3) 122–129. https://doi.org/10.1080/10632913.2011.566082

Castillo, L. (2014). *Nana in the city*. Clarion Books.

Ewert, M., & Ray, R. (2008). *10,000 dresses*. Triangle Square.

Gollnick, D. M., & Chen, P. C. (2016). *Multicultural education in a pluralistic society* (10th ed.). Pearson.

Kramsch, C. (2009). Third culture and language education. In V. Cook and L. Wei (Eds.), *Contemporary applied linguistics, Volume 1: Language teaching and learning*. Continuum, 233–254.

Kramsch, C. (2011). The symbolic dimensions of the intercultural. *Language Teaching, 44*(3), 354–367.

Langston-George, M. A., & Bock, J. R. (2014). *For the right to learn: Malala Yousafzai's story*. Capstone Press.

Lütge, C. (2013). Otherness in children's literature: Perspectives from the EFL classroom. In J. Bland and C. Lütge (Eds.), *Children's literature in second language education* (97–105). Bloomsbury.

Mansilla, V. B., & Jackson, A. W. (2011). *Educating for global competence: Preparing our youth to engage the world*. Asian Society Council of Chief State School Officers (CCSSO). Retrieved from https://asiasociety.org/files/book-globalcompetence.pdf

Matos, A. (2005). Literary texts: A passage to intercultural reading in foreign language education. *Language and Intercultural Communication, 5*(1), 57–71.

Peete, H. R. (2010). *My brother Charlie*. Scholastic Press.

Pohan, C. A., & Aguilar, T. E. (2001). Measuring educators' beliefs about diversity in personal and professional contexts. *American Education Research Journal, 38*(1), 159–182.

Reidel, M., & Draper, C. (2013). Preparing middle grades educators to teach about world cultures: An interdisciplinary approach. *Social Studies, 104*(3), 115–122. https://doi.org/10.1080/00377996.2012.698325

Schwartz, C. R., & Santat, D. (2014). *Ninja red riding hood*. G. P. Putnam's Sons Books for Young Readers.

Short, K. (2009). Critically reading the word and the world: Building intercultural understanding through literature. *Bookbird, 47* (2), 1–10.

Short, K. (2012). Story as world making. *Language Arts, 90* (1), 9–17.

Short, K., Harste, J., & Burke, C. (1996). *Creating classrooms for authors and inquirers*. Heinemann.

Siwatu, K. O. (2011). Preservice teachers' culturally responsive teaching self-efficacy-forming experiences: A mixed methods study. *Journal of Educational Research, 104*(5), 360–369.

Tonatiuh, D. (2010). *Dear primo: A letter to my cousin*. Abrams Books for Young Readers.

Appendix

Questionnaires #1 (Pre) and #2 (Post)

Note. Items for Parts A and B are the same for both questionnaires, while Part C differs for the two questionnaires.

Your Birth Date: _____

The Last Four Digits Of Your SSN: _____

Part A (Personal Beliefs About Diversity Scale). Please indicate the level of your agreement with each statement below by checking the box that matches your level of agreement with the statement.

1 - Strongly Disagree
2 - Somewhat Disagree
3 - Neutral
4 - Somewhat Agree
5 - Strongly Agree

Statement	1	2	3	4	5
1. There is nothing wrong with people from different racial backgrounds having/raising children.					
2. America's immigrant and refugee policy has led to the deterioration of America.					
3. Making all public facilities accessible to the disabled is simply too costly.					
4. Accepting many different ways of life in America will strengthen us as a nation.					
5. It is not a good idea for same-sex couples to raise children.					
6. The reason people live in poverty is that they lack motivation to get themselves out of poverty.					
7. People should develop meaningful relationships with others from different racial/ethnic groups.					
8. People with physical limitations are less effective as leaders than people without physical limitation.					
9. In general, White people place a higher value on education than do people of color.					
10. Many women in our society continue to live in poverty because males still dominate most of the major social systems in America.					
11. Since men are frequently the heads of households, they deserve higher wages than females.					
12. It is a good idea for people to develop meaningful relationships with others having a different sexual orientation.					
13. Society should not become more accepting of gay/lesbian lifestyles.					
14. It is more important for immigrants to learn English than to maintain their first language.					
15. In general, men make better leaders than women.					

Developing Preservice Teachers' Beliefs About Cultural Diversity   159

Part B (Professional Beliefs About Diversity Scale). Please indicate the level of your agreement with each statement below by checking the box that matches your level of agreement with the statement.

1 - Strongly Disagree
2 - Somewhat Disagree
3 - Neutral
4 - Somewhat Agree
5 - Strongly Agree

Statement	1	2	3	4	5
1. Teachers should not be expected to adjust their preferred mode of instruction to accommodate the needs of all students.					
2. The traditional classroom has been set up to support the middle-class lifestyle.					
3. Gays and lesbians should not be allowed to teach in public schools.					
4. Students and teachers would benefit from having a basic understanding of different (diverse) religions.					
5. Money spent to educate the severely disabled would be better spent on programs for gifted students.					
6. All students should be encouraged to become fluent in a second language.					
7. Only schools serving students of color need a racially, ethnically, and culturally diverse staff and faculty.					
8. The attention girls receive in school is comparable to the attention boys receive.					
9. Tests, particularly standardized tests, have frequently been used as a basis for segregating students.					
10. People of color are adequately represented in most textbooks today.					
11. Students with physical limitations should be placed in the regular classroom whenever possible.					
12. Males are given more opportunities in math and science than females.					
13. Generally, teachers should group students by ability levels.					
14. Students living in racially isolated neighborhoods can benefit socially from participating in racially integrated neighborhoods.					
15. Historically, education has been monocultural, reflecting only one reality and has been biased towards the dominant (European) group.					

Statement	1	2	3	4	5
16. Whenever possible, second language learners should receive instruction in their first language until they are proficient enough to learn via English instruction.					
17. Teachers often expect less from students from the lower socio-economic class.					
18. Multicultural education is most beneficial for students of color.					
19. More women are needed in administrative positions in schools.					
20. Large numbers of students of color are improperly placed in special education classes by school personnel.					
21. In order to be effective with all students, teachers should have experience working with students from diverse racial and ethnic backgrounds.					
22. Students from lower socioeconomic backgrounds typically have fewer educational opportunities than their middle-class peers.					
23. Students should not be allowed to speak a language other than English while in school.					
24. It is important to consider religious diversity in setting public school policy.					
25. Multicultural education is less important than reading, writing, arithmetic, and computer literacy.					

Part C (Free Responses, Questionnaire #1 only). Please respond to each question below.

1. Which children's/adolescent books have you read which included characters from cultural backgrounds that were similar to your own? What were the names of these books? What was the cultural background of the characters? How did these books contribute to your understanding of your own culture?
2. Which children's/adolescent books have you read which included characters from cultural backgrounds that were different from your own? What were the names of these books? What was the cultural background of the characters? How did these books contribute to your understanding of other cultures?

Part C (Free Responses, Questionnaire #2 only). Please respond to each question below.

1. What were your positive experiences reading the children's books in this course? In what ways did these books contribute to your beliefs about sociocultural diversity in education?
2. What were your negative experiences reading the children's books in this course? In what ways did these books not contribute to your beliefs about sociocultural diversity in education?

TEN

 Circles of Learning:
Teaching with Dante's *Inferno*

Lochran C. Fallon

THIS CHAPTER WILL EXPLORE A few ways that Dante Alighieri's *Divina Commedia* (hereafter referred to as "*Comedy*") and more specifically *Inferno*, may serve in a university-level teacher education classroom as an example or model text for effective, critical self-reflection, identity development, and narrative research for teachers at the university level, as well as in teacher education courses. The primary audience for this chapter is college-level teachers engaged in teacher education for preservice teachers, but the concepts may also be applied effectively by teachers at the secondary and primary levels.

The *Divine Comedy* and the Practice of Storying and Reflection

The *Comedy* is an allegorical poem, representing the soul of the protagonist on a journey towards the Christian God that begins in Hell with the recognition and rejection of sin. After, Dante must scale the mountain of Purgatory, where sinners repent for their transgressions, and finally, he enters the celestial spheres to learn of the virtues of Paradise. Beatrice, from her place in Paradise, enlists the aid of Virgil, the Roman poet most famous for his epic poem the *Aeneid*, to accompany and guide Dante on his journey through Hell and Purgatory. It is no accident that Virgil is appointed this task, as he is not only counted among the virtuous pagans of the first Circle of Hell, but the historical Virgil's own description of the classical Roman underworld in his *Aeneid* provides inspirational material for Dante's vision of Hell, populated as it is with many figures, historical and mythological, from antiquity that Virgil would doubtless recognize.

Given the journey the eponymous protagonist takes through these spiritual realms, the *Comedy* may be considered the culminating reflective narrative of Dante Alighieri's life. Storying and reflection are both educational practices well supported by research, taught in teacher-education classes, and practiced by teachers of all levels. Dante began composing the narrative journey of the *Comedy* in his forties and put the finishing touches on it very nearly at the end of his life. However, his protagonist's journey begins on the night before Good Friday in 1300, "Midway in the journey of our life," (*Inferno* I, line 1), at the age of 35, 6 years prior to the time when he began composing his great work. It is a story that frames not only his own perspective and challenges in the telling, but tells the stories of all those souls he encounters in a culminating educational journey that begins with a teacher and author meant to help him find God and the "straight way" to joy and salvation.

As a note of reference to the reader, all lines from *Inferno* that appear in this text are from the Hollanders' (2000) English translation found on the References page.

Constructing the Narrative of Our Teaching Lives

> Therefore, for your sake, I think it wise
> you follow me: I will be your guide,
> leading you, from here, through an eternal place
> 'where you shall hear despairing cries
> and see those ancient souls in pain
> as they bewail their second death.
> 'Then you shall see the ones who are content
> to burn because they hope to come,
> whenever it may be, among the blessed. (*Inferno* I, 112–120)

Whatever story we set before ourselves, as teachers or learners, and whatever analysis we may do upon it, each story is a threading, a weave of different narratives together: the tales of the characters, of course, but also those of the author and readers. If we consider our own lives to be narratives—(re)constructed, threaded, interactive, composed, read, analyzed—we find that the situation between ourselves and text becomes a conversation and congregation of narratives. This perspective is held by many scholars, who "suggest that our lives are storied. Not only is there a story of the self, but the self, itself, is narratively constructed" (Zembylas, 2003, p. 215). Dante's *Comedy* is a particularly appropriate text for understanding our lives as constructed narratives, not only for its allegorical, poetic form, but for its eponymous protagonist and autobiographic content; it is a master work that centers its main character on a journey that is as much about himself as any other character featured. We might suppose that many stories and the characters contained therein might be reflections of certain inspirational experiences and people that the author has encountered in their own life, but Dante removes some of the guesswork—he chose the same name for the protagonist as himself; he encounters various people from his life, and others from his education and culture. Rather than a tale about multiple characters from different perspectives, the *Comedy* follows one, and everything we are meant to know is filtered through his dialogic and diegetic interactions with the other entities and persons he encounters.

Taken further, we can apply this constructive narrative framing to our teaching experiences and identities as well: "The study of teachers' narratives—that is, stories of teachers' own experiences—is increasingly being seen as crucial to the study of teachers' thinking, culture, and behavior" (Zembylas, 2003, p. 214). Understanding our lives and identities as teachers through narrative research can open up pathways "for understanding teachers' culture; that is, teachers as knowers of themselves, of their situations, of children, of subject matter, of teaching, and of learning" (Zembylas, 2003, pp. 214–215). Dante revisits the people of his life, and those of his learning, and uses them as guides, mirrors, and reflections of various aspects of human sin and virtue—for his protagonist's own reflection and developing awareness. Teachers are encouraged to walk a similar path towards new awareness and identity by (re)constructing the narrative of their lives and threading them in interaction with others, through such practices as journals, diaries, autobiographies, and other self-reflective forms of storying.

Storying Our Lives as Educational Practice

'not tenderness for a son, nor filial duty
toward my agèd father, nor the love I owed
Penelope that would have made her glad,
'could overcome the fervor that was mine
to gain experience of the world
and learn about man's vices, and his worth.
'And so I set forth upon the open deep
with but a single ship and that small band
of shipmates who had not deserted me. (*Inferno* XXVI, 94–102)

Leshem and Trafford (2006) wrote about two education experiences that involved "learner-directed engagement in reflective, and personal, accounts" (p. 9). One was focused on a supervisor's experiences with preservice teachers on their journey to teaching English as foreign language in Israeli classrooms; the other on a supervisor's experiences with doctoral candidates engaging in practice-based inquiry in the United Kingdom. Both cases featured reflective assignments that helped the supervisors to story their own lives and share those stories with their students, making critical realizations along the way that they—the supervisors and students—were not aware of through this process (p. 21). For example, Leshem tells how, as a supervisor, "My assumption was that modelling and presenting my own story would change my students' attitude to the assignment. I was proved wrong! They were intimidated by my story, claiming that they had nothing to write about" (Lesham & Trafford, 2006, p. 12). Trafford speaks to how their research diaries "opened deeper understandings of their research and themselves" and how they discovered "multiple selves" of "'I,' 'me,' and 'we' levels of audience in writing about themselves" (Lesham & Trafford, 2006, p. 20). Because it can be applied across the experiences of teachers and students, storying allows the opportunity to thread, construct, and reconstruct experiences where all have an opportunity to share and reveal emotional dimensions through acts of speaking and listening. By doing so, Leshem was able to recognize and appreciate the emotions of their students after sharing their story: "I was definitely meeting some second-language acquisition road posts—I was the 'tongue-tied learner' and 'the risk taker' a little later" (p. 12).

Dante's journey through the *Comedy* is characterized by the accounts and stories of the souls he encounters. His understanding of these realms and himself is changed and developed by way of interacting with them, asking them who they are, and hearing their perspectives. Dante reveals these integral acts of speaking and listening to each soul he encounters as critical to his learning and understanding of his own life and story. Leshem and Trafford (2006) drive home the point that, "from these functional perspectives, storying is an integral component of educational life for learners as well as teachers" (p. 22). Moreover, when looking at Dante's journey as an act of storying and reflection, we, as storytellers, are compelled to confront questions about his and our own storying such as:

> How to set and respect boundaries, What to include, What to exclude, What levels of personal disclosure are acceptable, Who is the audience, What does the audience expect of the story, How to handle accuracy and truth. . . .
> Readers and listeners of stories face complementary choices to those of tellers/writers as audiences: How to listen to/read the story, How to interpret the story, How to construe incomplete stories or deliberately non-linear stories, How to reconcile contradictory stories. . . . and What 'to do' with the story as a social artefact. The situation is compounded for researchers who study this interchange. Not only do they experience all the choices of 'audiences' but additionally they have to cope with methodological considerations of comparability, consistency, replicatability, motive, honesty and trustworthiness of both tellers and writers.
> . . . Thus, the stories that we heard or read became both a means and an end of learning in their respective settings. (Lesham & Trafford, 2006, p. 22)

Our teaching journey through narrative (re)construction and practices is a transformative one, not only through interaction with the text of our lives, but in those contexts wherein we are not just the lecturer, teacher, and author, but also critical listener, to ourselves and others. In this reflective listening, we may arrive at a place where we are open to transformation liberated from previous constructs of our identities, ourselves, and our teaching practices:

> Critique, I believe, is most powerful when it leaves open the possibility that we might also be remade in the process of engaging another's worldview, that we might come to learn things that we did not already know before we undertook the engagement. This requires that we occasionally turn the critical gaze upon ourselves, to leave open the possibility that we may be remade through an encounter with the other. (Mahmood, 2005, pp. 36–37)

Dante emerges in the first Canto as a character who is lost, harried, and pursued by three wild beasts that represent the major categories of sin in his version of Hell. Critically, the author begins this reflective, constructed narrative in a place where he is implicitly viewing his situation as a problem in need of addressing, and the practice by which he finds his way is by being ready to listen. This is essential to effective reflective practice: "If a teacher educator simply states the problem for others (student teachers), it will not necessarily then make it visible to them, as the differences in experience influence not only what the problem is but also how it might be seen. There needs to be a reason to be able to see the problem in different ways" (Loughran, 2002, p. 35).

Reflecting: Limits and Limitations

> And he to me: 'This miserable state is borne
> by the wretched souls of those who lived
> without disgrace yet without praise.
> 'They intermingle with that wicked band
> of angels, not rebellious and not faithful
> to God, who held themselves apart.
> 'Loath to impair its beauty, Heaven casts them out,
> and depth of Hell does not receive them
> lest on their account the evil angels gloat.' (*Inferno* III, 34–42)

Upon passing through the ominous doorway to hell, on which the infamous line "Abandon all hope ye who enter here" (*Inferno* III, 9) is written, Dante and Virgil encounter a group of souls beset "by stinging flies and wasps" (*Inferno* III, 66), with "loathsome worms" (*Inferno* III, 69) at their feet. This is typically referred to in maps of Hell as the "vestibule" area, where these souls are condemned to forever chase a "whirling banner" (*Inferno* III, 52). These souls are here because they never really committed to a side; they "held themselves apart" (*Inferno* III, 39). It is easy to imagine these people as simply doing what they did without any kind of authenticity to their actions; their actions are as devoid of personal meaning as the blank banner they chase after, in whatever direction it flies. Their lives are a pantomime of life; their acts pro forma in their entirety. My own mentor teacher told me during my semester of student teaching that I should never teach in a way that I don't believe in; that I should always be authentic and true to myself in my teaching. He cautioned me that should I do otherwise, it would quickly become apparent to my students that I did not truly believe in what I was teaching.

For any teacher who values their employment—particularly those without measures of job security—to simply do as they're told without question is an understandable course of action. This is especially true if their own professors, supervisors, or administrators are adamant that they do so and have no inclination to allow those beneath them to do otherwise. A tyrannical environment, whether in the classroom or workplace, that places blind obedience above all else fosters the kind of pro forma, empty subservience to whatever direction the banner whirls. Such an environment doesn't allow freedom enough for authentic questioning of direction, nor sharing of thoughts that may lead to a more truthful, insightful reflection.

Circles of Learning 169

In the same way that reflection as practice can be essential to effective teaching, it can also lock the teacher into phallological expectations for how their reflections should be done and what content they should contain. Inside this phallological framework of expectations, the teacher's reflections become required products that determine their readiness:

> Reflection becomes an essential aspect of teaching that has to be mastered, reflecting the dominating representation of the mastery of the teacher at the same time. Reflective practice in a system set by standards in this manner would function in a way that a phallocratic symbol does, its ends becoming transcendental, determining the law by which one could define one's being in relation to a predominant masculine imaginary. (Galea, 2012, p. 249)

Drawing on the work of Luce Irigaray, particularly from *Speculum of the Other Woman* (1985a) and *This Sex Which is Not One* (1985b), Galea cautions against the dangers of mandating or performing reflective practice that minimizes risk taking, enacted for the sake of itself, to measure up to an expectation of mastery that turns the entire process into a "fabricated representation of knowing enacted and the rituals of coming to know" (p. 248). Such a system of mandated reflective practice ends up (re)producing imitations of reflection, reducing each to a known product that the system evaluates and recognizes according to its own terms repeatedly (pp. 251–252).

In opposition to this, Galea presents Irigarayan forms of feminist educational practice that offer a means for resisting "hegemonic masculinity," "encourage multiple forms of teaching," and "subvert the systems they support" (p. 254). Drawing on the writings of one newly appointed teacher named Anna, who as a student teacher "never envisaged anything but reflection," it became clear that during one of her last meetings in her undergraduate training, "Her doubts were not only concerned with the limitations of imposed forms of reflection but also to the possibilities of articulating the limitations" (p. 256). Anna went into detail about these doubts in her written reflection below:

> A requirement for our teaching practice experiences was that of producing a set of weekly reflections about our effectiveness as educators, our pedagogy and methodology. While prospective teachers are, and should, be introduced to the importance of written reflection as a necessary meta-cognitive process, students should also be aware that reflection should not be limited and that it can take

multiple forms. The above-mentioned requirement has the disadvantage of causing the reflective process to be viewed in a somewhat systematic light. Reflection can start being regarded as a mechanical process, associated with writing of a routine nature rather than a meta-cognitive, continuous and internal process. This being said, however, I do understand that in order for effective assessment and monitoring during teaching practice, the reflective process needs to be written regularly as proof of one's own professional development. However, this also has its disadvantages. One might feel inhibited when documenting teaching experiences due to the fact that these accounts will be read by examiners. While reflective writing is produced, this might not be done as a process which is conducive to one's professional growth, but as a guarded and superficial account. Moreover, one might not feel comfortable with the prescribed reflective style. (Anna's written reflection on reflective practice, 7/7/2009) (Galea, 2012, p. 256)

We must grant ourselves and our students permission to reflect authentically, critically, and meaningfully. Dante embarked on his journey to change himself. He does this through inquiry and conversation with Virgil, Beatrice, and those souls he encounters along the way. However, Dante's journey is distinctly personal—it is a narrative filled with entities and people that he has either read about, heard about, or encountered in his life. His journey is a critically insightful reflection on his own life: he begins by recognizing that he is lost; he is no longer on the path he feels he should be on. Each of us is likewise on a journey as teachers and human beings, and we must allow ourselves and our students the freedom to reflect in a way that is meaningful for each of us and permits critical questioning of personal and external expectations.

The Formation of Teacher Identity

'But why should I go there? who allows it?
I am not Aeneas, nor am I Paul.
Neither I nor any think me fit for this.
'And so, if I commit myself to come,
I fear it may be madness. You are wise,
you understand what I cannot express.' (*Inferno* II, 31–36)

This kind of authentic reflective practice can be essential to the development of teacher identity, "where identity references individuals' knowledge and naming of themselves, as well as others' recognition of them as a particular sort of person" (Clarke, 2009, p. 186). However, like Dante's journey, the formation of teacher identity is path upon which one inevitably encounters many other voices and perspectives:

> ... identities are the result of the inescapable and ongoing process of discussion, explanation, negotiation, argumentation, and justification that partly comprises teachers' lives and practices (MacLure, 1993; Coldron & Smith, 1999). Our identities are thus partly given yet they are also something that has to be achieved, offering a potential site of agency within the inevitably social process of becoming. (Clarke, 2009, p. 187)

Countless teacher education books have been written with reflections about specific students and situations their teacher-authors have encountered during their experience as educators; a couple that immediately spring to mind for me are Fecho's "*Is This English*" (2003) and Johannessen and McCann's *In Case You Teach English* (2001), both of which are teacher-educator texts that feature reflective accounts of actual teachers, students, and situations the authors encountered during their practice and research. In Dante's case, there are many figures in the *Inferno* alone that lived around the same time as the historical Dante, and with whom he either had personal experience, or would be informed about, including Fillipo Argenti (*Inferno* VIII, 31–66), Branca D'Oria (*Inferno* XXII, 88–90), Francesca da Rimini and Paolo Malatesta (*Inferno* V, 73–138), Pope Nicolas III (*Inferno* XIX, 76–77), Brunetto Latini (*Inferno* XV, 110), Farinata Degli Uberti (*Inferno* X 52–72), and of course Beatrice Portinari, who is mentioned in the *Inferno* (*Inferno* I, 121–123; *Inferno* II, 53–74, 103–114; *Inferno* X, 130–132; *Inferno* XII, 88; *Inferno* XV, 90), and encountered at the end of *Purgatorio* to guide him through *Paradiso*. Each of these figures play a part in Dante's reflective practice and transformation from a man who is lost at the midpoint of his life, unable to take the straight path to the "peak that gives delight, origin and cause of every joy," (*Inferno* I, 77–78), to one that may enjoy salvation under the stars by the end of the poem. This journey requires Dante to let go of his former self to embrace a new identity, and it's no surprise that the first leg of this three-realm sojourn is down into the darkest depths of Hell, because letting go of the "safe anchor of an unchanging, stable self," can be "daunting," especially at first (Clarke, 2009, p. 194), for teachers as much as our eponymous protagonist in the *Comedy*.

The Importance of Emotion to Identity and Reflection

> 'I am of your city. How many times
> I've heard your deeds, your honored names resound!
> And I, too, spoke your names with affection. (*Inferno* XVI, 58–60).

Throughout his journey, Dante interacts with and asks questions of those souls he encounters (along with his guides). By gathering each of their stories and perspectives, he transforms his heart and feelings about divine justice, offering a model of critical self-reflective identity transformation for each of us to explore and apply to our own lives. Zembylas (2003) points out that "One such resource for crafting teacher identity is emotion. As Hochschild (1983) reminds us: 'It is from feelings that we learn the self-relevance of what we see, remember, or imagine' (p. 196)" (p. 215). There are, of course, a few special places in the *Comedy* where Dante displays emotions in his interactions with souls; one among them stands out for Hollander (1996):

> Dante's response to Iacopo's speech is extraordinary. We have not seen (again with the exception of Limbo) and will not see anything like it, not even in his ardor to meet Ulysses: he would have jumped down among them, but for the fire that would have burned him, and he now believes that his guide would have allowed him to (as Virgil's opening words would indeed vouchsafe); Dante refers to his strong feelings for them as "la mia buona voglia / che di loro abbracciar mi facea ghiotto." Nowhere else in Hell, after Limbo, do we hear such affection expressed for damned souls. And, given the fact that these are sodomites, Dante's desire to embrace them has a strange reverberation. (para. 7)

Given the way that Dante, the poet, treats this encounter with the Florentines of Circle 7, "with greater respect than any other infernal figures except those in Limbo" (Hollander, 1996, para. 2), combined with the strong affection his protagonist expresses toward the Florentines, we would be remiss to pass over this part of his narrative without a second, critically insightful glance, if "emotions are the beacons of our true selves" (Zembylas, 2003, p. 215). Taken together, we arrive at a place where reflective practice, teacher identity, and emotions are developed and better understood through the lens of narrative research. Our lives and experiences as teachers are stories unfolding and co-written in collaboration with each other, within "social, cultural, and institutional discourses [that] set the 'conditions of possibility' for who and what a teacher might be" (Zembylas, 2003, p. 215). There are several ways teachers and students could explore and reflect on important experiences in their own developmental journeys through a literary work like the *Comedy*. A couple of these—transactional learning, project-based learning—are focused on in the following sections.

Exploring with Dante: Transactional Learning and Close Reading

The first of these is a concept that I found in Smagorinsky's *Teaching English by Design*, which he credits Louise Rosenblatt for, known as "transactional learning" (2008, pp. 125–128). Smagorinsky sums up Rosenblatt's argument and theory as advocating for "a democratic view of reading that gave the ordinary reader as much authority in determining a literary work's meaning as that accorded to a professional literary critic" (p. 125). This concept aligns with and supports not only a project-based learning approach, but also a close-reading approach wherein readers "attend carefully to the words a writer uses" (p. 125); however, the goal of this close reading is not meant to discover the author's intended meaning of the words, but rather to empower the readers to construct their own, based on and supported by what they've read. As Smagorinsky indicates, this construction would include the following content:

- a reader's personal experiences
- the cultural factors that shape both readers and texts
- the social environment of a classroom and its effects on a reader's response
- the psychological makeup of individual readers that provides a particular frame of mind for interpreting events in particular ways. (2008, p. 126)

Dante's *Inferno* features a wide assortment of human issues on display that we contend with to this day ranging from war and violence against others and oneself in many forms (many of these represented in Circle 7, but also in a number of other places like Circles 5, 8, and 9), to excess that leads to socioeconomic inequality (Circle 4), to social and political divisions and polarization caused by the media (Circle 8), to personal daily struggles that may take a variety of forms from betrayal and infidelity to sullenness and anger

(Circle 5). Their continuing relevance offers teachers and students an array of possible connections to their own lives and experiences where these issues have manifested. In this way, the *Comedy* can serve as a jumping-off point into a deeper, reflective exploration that is personally relevant and meaningful to the individual teacher or student and provide them another step on their journey of identity transformation and teaching development.

Being mindful of Galea's warning against prescriptive reflective exercises, teachers and students are encouraged to respond to the *Comedy* (or other central text) in a way that feels most authentic to their own voice and experience. Anyone engaged in a truly meaningful reflection and dialogue with the *Comedy* should feel empowered with the critical authority to challenge the representation and suffering of those individuals in *Inferno* and *Purgatorio*, in particular, or the representations of virtue in *Paradiso*. Teachers and students should consider the ways our modern social, cultural, and institutional perspectives might inform different outcomes and representations than those offered by Dante. Even raising questions meaningful to our own lives while reading the *Comedy* can be the first inquiry-based step on a journey towards self-reflective identity formation.

Project-Based Learning (PBL)

Larmer (2018, p. 2) outlines five steps to successfully teaching project-based learning in the classroom, the first of which involves developing an idea and connecting it to standards and other learning goals: "Ideas for projects can come from issues in students' lives and communities, current events, real-world problems, and content standards. Frame the students' task with a driving question to focus their work. Students can have input by identifying problems they want to address, and helping decide what content and skills they can demonstrate in the project" (Larmer, 2018, p. 2). Each of these ideas is meant to be explored through a driving question. There are many other possible driving questions and topics students might explore that tie in directly with Dante's *Inferno*, based in the social, cultural, and ethical issues that provide a foundation for the structure and population of his version of Hell.

The second step asks teachers to decide "what major products or performances students will create" with a requirement for presenting them to an audience. The third and fourth steps dive into planning lessons and activities and mapping out steps in the project and assisting students in creating a timeline and organizing their time and tasks, as well as monitoring their progress, while the fifth and final step includes an "entry event" that "grabs students' interest and provokes curiosity" starting them on the path of project creation (Larmer, 2018, p. 2).

Educators are encouraged to engage in their own project-based learning journey that may likewise pursue issues and challenges they confront within the classroom or in their own identity development as teachers. Teachers addressing topics like the treatment of sexuality, the application of retributive justice as a punitive measure, or the culturally reflective characteristics of each of the three spiritual realms can find themselves engaged in self-reflective practice that explores these or other issues and challenges that they find personally meaningful in their own lives. Such a journey is supported by the research included in this chapter as essential and valuable to authentic teacher-identity development. Below are a few possible examples of PBL units centered around Dante's *Inferno*:

Exploring Human Sexuality (secondary level or college-level course)

Driving question: How might we re-envision representations of human sexuality in modern media as well as creative work to make them more positive?

Students or teachers may explore sexual positivity and collect representations in media and other creative work, consider and explore the way sexuality is treated in Dante's Inferno, and which elements may be reimagined in a positive way. Teachers may explore the treatment and exploration of body positivity and culturally informed perspectives of gender and sexuality, and how those may be reflected in their institutions and classrooms.

Depictions of the Afterlife (secondary-level or college-level course)

Driving question: What would an afterlife that reflects our cultural beliefs and value systems look like?

Students and teachers may explore different depictions of afterlifes, including Dante's Inferno, and examine the ways in which these spiritual worlds reflect the beliefs and value systems of their respective cultures. Teachers may consider ways in which these spiritual worlds reflect and inform their own values and pedagogy in the classroom, and how certain issues and culturally sensitive topics may be explored in their lessons.

Retributive Justice (secondary-level or college-level course)

Driving question: Is retributive justice right or effective?

Students and teachers may explore various examples of retributive justice and contrapasso punishments (Stuber, 2018, para. 5), including those in Dante's Inferno, and question their rightness and effectiveness with the opportunity to propose alternative approaches and solutions. Teachers may consider implications for discipline, punishment, classroom management, parenting, and effective classroom policies with research into different ways of responding to behavior in their classrooms.

Conclusion

Along with these two methods, which align with and support narrative research, self-reflective practice, and identity formation in teachers as well as students, educators are encouraged to consider incorporating multimedia dimensions and analysis into their coursework and units focused on the *Comedy*. Dante's *Divine Comedy*, and more specifically *Inferno*, have been depicted and referenced in numerous pieces of popular culture from the medieval period down through the 21st century in various media, including but not limited to sculptures like Auguste Rodin's *The Gates of Hell* (1890) (from which many sculptures were enlarged and became works of their own, such as *Ugolino and His Children* (1881)), Gustave Doré's illustrations of various scenes from *Inferno* (1857/1976), Franz Liszt's *Dante Symphony* (1856), films like *Hannibal* (Scott, 2001) and *Se7en* (Fincher, 1995), and video games like *Devil May Cry* (2001) and *Resident Evil: Revelations* (2012).

It is my hope that this chapter has offered educators at the tertiary and secondary levels insight into the way that Dante's *Comedy* may be used as a central or mentor text as they think about and explore narrative research, self-reflective practice, and the development and formation of their own teacher identities, as well as offering the possibility of making this journey with their own learners. By recounting and documenting their own journeys as teachers and framing these experiences as a narrative, they provide themselves with a story of their lives that includes those souls that accompany them on this journey—colleagues, administrators, students, personal friends, and relations, to name a few—which they may then reflect upon critically in their own way to discover what hidden truths and meanings come to light of which they may not have been aware. With these revelations comes the possibility for identity transformation and change in their being and becoming as a teacher and human being that may open new paths for teaching, understanding, and living, for themselves and their learners.

References

Alighieri, D. (2000). *Inferno* (R. Hollander & J. Hollander, Trans.). Knopf Doubleday Publishing Group. (Original work published ca. 1320–1471)
Clarke, M. (2009). The ethico-politics of teacher identity. *Educational Philosophy and Theory, 41*(2), 185–200. https://doi.org/10.1111/j.1469-5812.2008.00420.x
Doré, G. (1976) *The Doré illustrations for Dante's Divine Comedy: 136 plates by Gustave Doré.* Dover Publications. (Original work 1857)
Fecho, B. (2003). *"Is this English?"* Teachers College Press.
Fincher, D. (Director). (1995). *Se7en* [Film]. New Line Cinema.
Galea, S. (2012). Reflecting reflective practice. *Educational Philosophy and Theory, 44*(3), 245–258. https://doi.org/10.1111/j.1469-5812.2010.00652.x
Hochschild, A. R. (1983). *The managed heart: Commercialization of human feeling.* University of California Press.
Hollander, R. (1996). Dante's harmonious homosexuals (Inferno 16.7-90). https://www.princeton.edu/~dante/ebdsa/rh.html
Irigaray, L. (1985a). *Speculum of the other woman* (G. Gill, Trans.). Cornell University Press.
Irigaray, L. (1985b). *This sex which is not one* (C. Porter with C. Burke, trans.). Cornell University Press.
Johannessen, L. R., & McCann, T. M. (2001). *In case you teach English: An interactive casebook for prospective and practicing teachers.* Pearson.
Kamiya, H. (2001). *Devil may cry.* Capcom. https://www.devilmaycry.com/
Larmer, J. (2018). Getting started with project-based learning. ASCD.
Leshem, S., & Trafford V. N. (2006) Stories as mirrors: Reflective practice in teaching and learning. *Reflective Practice, 7*(1), 9–27. https://doi.org/10.1080/14623940500489567
Liszt, F. (1856). *Dante symphony* [Symphony].
Loughran, J. J. (2002). Effective reflective practice: In search of meaning in learning about teaching. *Journal of Teacher Education 53*(1), 33–43. https://doi.org/10.1177/0022487102053001004

Mahmood, S. (2005). *Politics of piety: The Islamic revival and the feminist subject.* Princeton University Press.

Nakanishi, K. (2012). *Resident evil: Revelations.* Capcom. https://game.capcom.com/residentevil/en/

Rodin, A. (1890). *The gates of Hell* [Sculpture]. Musée Rodin, Meudon, France. https://www.musee-rodin.fr/en/musee/collections/oeuvres/gates-hell

Rodin, A. (1881). *Ugolino and his children* [Sculpture]. Musée Rodin, Meudon, France. https://www.musee-rodin.fr/en/musee/collections/oeuvres/ugolino-and-his-children

Scott, R. (Director). (2001). *Hannibal* [Film]. Universal Pictures.

Smagorinsky, P. (2008). *Teaching English by design: How to create and carry out instructional units.* Heinemann.

Stuber, S. (2018, March 9). The Inferno today. *The Stanford Daily.* https://stanforddaily.com/2018/03/09/the-inferno-today/

Zembylas, M. (2003) Emotions and teacher identity: A poststructural perspective. *Teachers and Teaching, 9*(3), 213–238, DOI: 10.1080/13540600309378

ELEVEN

 Isabel Allende's *The Sum of Our Days*: Discovering the Extraordinary Through the Ordinary

Margarita García-Notario

Isabel Allende's literary impact, fame, and legacy are widely known, in both English language and Spanish language literature. She writes beautifully, her fiction is always sustained by in-depth investigations into the historical and social contexts she describes, and she is hysterically funny. Some of her better suited books for university students can be effective tools for future teachers to reinforce how cultural and linguistic differences, family values, sexual "rules," and religious beliefs affect and determine life choices and happiness.

Isabel Allende was born and raised in Chile. Because of her family's ties with the leftist president Salvador Allende, who was assassinated in 1973, Isabel and her family went in exile to Venezuela and later to California.

Teacher educators can use Allende's books to increase students' knowledge of Latin American geography, history, traditions, and family customs. In addition, these writings can expose American students to a deep consideration of what their own culture looks like to others, how *normality* gets redefined, how much everyone gains by adapting to new ways, and the challenges of maintaining one's values and traditions when mixed in with those of others in the new home.

In this chapter, I will focus on Allende's book *The Sum of Our Days* (2008). This book reveals Isabel Allende's family life in California, describes the sad and transforming experiences of losing a child and a stepchild, and reviews—from a foreigner's perspective—the strengths and weaknesses of American culture. *The Sum of Our Days* is also a love story between a man and a woman who go through different crises and many moments of reconciliation, as their relationship is profoundly affected by the events in the lives of their loved ones. The aesthetics of the book are remarkable as well; serious problems and tragic events are depicted with stunning hilarity, resulting in both laughter and tears.

Future teachers can use *The Sum of Our Days* in multiple ways and with different thematic and didactic goals for university students, for example, in the areas of social and moral development and of cultural literacy. In general, the book is also an obvious choice for future teachers of Spanish who, in addition to the rich linguistic exposure, will encounter a unique multicultural perspective. In this chapter I will use protagonists from Allende's writing to suggest ways to help future teachers reflect on family and group relationships, human development, and cultural, religious, and gender differences.

Isabel and Paula: Dealing With Loss

The Sum of Our Days is written in the form of a letter from a mother to her deceased daughter. We see Isabel mourning, struggling to accept this terrible loss, and trying to live as if Paula were still alive. Paula was only 29 years old when she passed and Isabel writes to her to describe what is going on in the lives of their loved ones. Future teachers may need to help students deal with the despair that dominate in similar circumstances. The lesson of *The Sum of Our Days* is that despite these losses, life persists along with the ordinary tasks and responsibilities of daily living. Writing to Paula becomes Isabel's main coping mechanism with her grief and helps her to reflect on *how* she is keeping up with her roles as mother, wife, friend, and grandmother. Future teachers may suggest journaling to mourning students as a proven healing tool.

The book starts with Paula's burial. The family takes Paula's ashes to a special place after going to Mass. In the United States there is an impressive variety (especially in big cities) of faiths and religious denominations. The following are some initial focused questions that could guide introductory discussions among future teachers:

Taking a broad view on religious and spiritual ways of living, do you find it advantageous to belong to a religious faith where the established rituals guide people in the key moments of life and death? Would you prefer to put together a ceremony in your own and/or your family's own personal ways? What do we owe the dead? We learn that Paula wrote a will where she told the way in which she wanted others to take care of her body. How helpful do you think that having a will with specific instructions upon our own death would be to our loved ones? Would Isabel's method of keeping Paula present through writing work for your mourning? If it wouldn't, what other ideas do you have for people when they need to mourn a loved one?

Isabel's family takes Paula's very young niece and nephew to the scattering of Paula's ashes. Would you take little kids to a funeral, a wake, or to this kind of ceremony? Is it important for children to participate in these ceremonies, or should we shield them from them? What is better for kids' development and why?

Jennifer and Sabrina: Drug Addiction and Adoption

Jennifer is Willie's daughter from a previous marriage. She started using drugs at a young age and was frequently in trouble with the law. She strained her health in every conceivable manner and ends up dying young, after getting pregnant and delivering a very sick and premature baby.

Jennifer's story is an opportunity for future teachers to discuss drug addiction, its consequences, and the right and wrong ways with which families and societies address the problem and try to resolve it. Discussion questions could include the following:

Why do some people use drugs to excess? After learning about Jennifer's family and personal circumstances, what in your opinion explains her choice to use drugs? Is it fair to blame Jennifer's parents for her situation? What role could parents play in their children becoming addicted? What should parents and teachers do to prevent children using drugs, or is there little that a family can do given today's environment and the ways in which drugs have become a common part in recreational activities? What has been most impactful for you about Jennifer's story?

Jennifer's death and Sabrina's birth strain Isabel's and Willie's relationship. Would it have been easier to resolve their differences had they both been from the same culture? How? The majority of intimate relationships are tested at one point or another for different circumstances. What ideas does this book give you about how to be better prepared in your future intimate relationships?

In spite of the doctors' minimal expectations about Sabrina's chances at life, she stabilizes and survives. Jennifer, however, dies, making Sabrina an orphan. Which place would have been, in your opinion, a better home for Sabrina? What advantages and disadvantages would she have living with Willie and Isabel? What about living with Nico and Celia? Would having siblings around be an advantage? How? What do you think about Sabrina's adoption by Fu and Grace? What does Sabrina bring to these two women's lives?

Nico and Celia: Personal Choices and Family Responsibilities

Nico and Celia meet in Venezuela and they are a great match. They are responsible parents and helpful family members. Nico does not have a religious education but Celia has belonged for many years to Opus Dei, an archconservative wing in the Catholic Church. She does not tolerate life choices that contradict the Catholic teachings. Slowly, as she gets to know and to love people who think differently, she changes. Relevant discussions could include the following:

What was your reaction to Celia's decision to leave Nico and start a new life with Sally? Is her decision capricious and irresponsible, or a necessary change to be "true" to herself? Is it better, in general, to be loyal and fully committed to a code, or should we always keep a door open for change, to guarantee our happiness? Should personal happiness be the principal determiner of one's choices in life? Should Celia's and Nico's previous commitment to marriage and their children have weighed more?

Isabel is trying to help Nico, Celia, and her grandchildren, but her actions cause a lot of problems. How could Isabel's help have been more beneficial and appropriate? Are Isabel's mistakes mainly due to culture or to other circumstances? Would an American grandmother have been less "intrusive" than Isabel, and if so, can you give an example?

At some point, Celia's and Nico's children will have stepparents (Nico's and Celia's new partners), so a lot more caretakers. What advantages and disadvantages does this bring to the children?

Isabel and Willie

Isabel and Willie form a marriage that needs to contend with cultural and linguistic differences and they are also bringing two families together from their previous marriages. One of their first disagreements is about helping or not helping Jennifer (Willie's youngest child from a previous marriage) after she is imprisoned for the second time because of drug use. Cultural and linguistic differences issues could be explored as follows:

Willie thinks that Jennifer needs to deal with the consequences of her actions, so he refuses to use his law firm to help her. Isabel says to him: "If she were my daughter, I would move heaven and earth to save her" (Allende, 2008, p. 11). Are these different ways to address the situation due to cultural differences, to male and female ways of responding, or to both? Which kind of help would be better for Jennifer, from your perspective, and why?

In one of Jennifer's hospitalizations, Isabel goes to see her every day and takes gifts to her. Soon she suspects that those gifts are being sold for drugs, because they disappear from the hospital room. What would you have done? Should Isabel stop bringing things that Jennifer could sell to get more drugs? What does a family member owe someone who is drug addicted?

Jennifer's addiction causes her daughter's premature birth and many grave health problems. The doctors don't think she will live very long, nor with much quality of life. Once Jennifer dies, Sabrina's future is in the hands of the U. S. legal system. In most Hispanic countries, orphans are given to extended family members, if they exist and want them. Isabel and Willie differ on what they should do with Sabrina, and Isabel says that, because of this, she and Willie "had one of those fights that make history in a couple's lives" (p. 29). They stopped speaking to each other and spending time together. Isabel even left the house for a few days and went to a friend's place to get help. Isabel did not want Sabrina to go to an institution, even after knowing how much medical care, attention she needs, and scarce possibilities for survival she has. Willie says that he and Isabel "don't have the energy to care for her or the strength to bear it if she dies" (p. 29). Willie's position seems more humble and possibly more pragmatic. Isabel can only listen to her heart. With which position do you identify more and why? Do you think that Tabra's (Isabel's friend) advice to Isabel about acknowledging that she and Willie would be overwhelmed if they adopt Sabrina is wise? In Spanish there is a saying that says, "the best is the enemy of the good." Could this refrain apply here? If so, how? Should Isabel accept the limitations that she and Willie have, and let others give Sabrina the help she needs?

Women: Spirituality, Biases, Reverence, Irreverence, Pride, and Humility

The Sum of Our Days is a meditation on women, their cultures, their belief systems, their strengths and flaws, their devotions and their irreverent ways, their nosiness, their disinterested love, and their boundless compassion. Isabel Allende hints at the diverse ways that women coexist among themselves and with men as she introduces and tells the stories of the women in her life. Future teachers can use some of her reflections and experiences with these women to guide discussions of women's diverse ways of understanding and feeling the world.

Jean Shinoda Bolen is a famous psychiatrist and writer who meets Isabel when Paula is in a coma. Bolen has written a book about "the goddesses that inhabit every woman" (p. 36), and Isabel, after reading it, tells us: "That is how I discovered that in me there was a jumble of contradictory deities that might be best not to explore" (pp. 36–37). Sometimes we find ourselves trying to harmonize or live with different and somewhat contradictory forces inside. Isabel calls them "goddesses." We may love our families, friends, job, country, and at the same time resent some of their customs, traditions, ways of doing things and expectations.

In the teacher education classroom, students could be asked: Do you sometimes feel divided inside? Can others help us resolve the contradictions or is this an individual task?

Odilia is Sabrina's nurse. Isabel describes her as "a majestic black woman with a thousand braids" and the person with the strongest faith in Sabrina's ability to survive. She sees something very powerful and special in this baby: "I told you," she says to Isabel, "that this child has an ancient and powerful soul" (p. 39). Isabel, as Catholic, doesn't believe in reincarnation, but finds great comfort in Odilia's beliefs and her reading of Sabrina. In California it is common to live surrounded by multiple faiths and spiritual beliefs.

Students could be asked: In your opinion, does this diversity enrich or impoverish an individual's spirituality? What qualities and human virtues should we cultivate when we find ourselves in an environment with very relevant differences that affect the core of individual and family beliefs?

Celia is Isabel's daughter-in-law, and she experiences major transformations, which affect her and everybody else she is related to. When she first becomes Nico's girlfriend and meets his family, she is very traditional, inflexible, and highly opinionated. Isabel is not sure Celia will be a good fit for her family and confides in her own mother, who reminds Isabel: "If your son chose this girl, there's good reason; your role is to love her and keep your mouth shut" (p. 49). Little by little, Isabel overcomes her initial dislike of Celia. "It was easy for me to love Celia, even though I was a little shocked by her bold frankness and brusque ways. We Chileans tiptoe around a subject as if we were walking on eggs" (p. 49). Celia had warned Isabel "more than once that she could not be beneath the same roof with someone whose sexual preferences did not coincide with hers" (p. 40). However, as Celia immerses herself in her new life with Nico's family and in California, she is forced to observe different lifestyles, and she slowly changes some early opinions. For instance, she gets to know Fu and Grace, the lesbian couple who ends up adopting Sabrina. "She (Celia) was so impressed with Fu and Grace, whom she came to know very well, that she ended by questioning her own views" (p. 40).

Isabel also changed some of her opinions. One example was psychotherapy. "In my opinion, therapy was a mania of North Americans, a very spoiled people unable to tolerate the normal difficulties of life. When I was young, my grandfather had instilled in me the stoic notion that life is hard, and when facing a problem there is nothing to do but grit our teeth and keep going" (p. 55). Then, at a time when her marriage to Willie was really faltering, she agrees to try: "At the time of my youth in Chile, no one visited a therapist—except for certifiable lunatics and Argentine tourists—so I strongly resisted Willie's suggestion, but he was so persistent that finally I gave in and went with him" (p. 55). Isabel humbly acknowledges how helpful therapy was for them. Humility is a very important though hard quality to achieve, and it is certainly not a virtue in which adolescents, in particular, excel.

For future teachers, the following questions could facilitate a discussion about the personal and social consequences of humility. What are the main areas in your life where you think your criteria and opinions won't change? Are there some realms where opinions/beliefs should be firm and unchangeable? Can you point at some areas where beliefs and opinions *can* and maybe *should* be modified? Would you be more willing to change your main beliefs and opinions, if you got to know people whose cultures, traditions, or religion are different from your own? Think of some things where differences may be unreconcilable and make some suggestions on what a society can do to keep a healthy, respectful, and peaceful environment where individual freedom and common responsibilities intersect to build everybody's daily life and future.

Final Thoughts

The British writer Jeannette Winterson says in her autobiography *Why Be Happy When You Could Be Normal?* (2011) that literature saved her life. "A tough life needs a tough language. . . . That is what literature offers: a language powerful enough to say how it is. It isn't a hiding place. It is a finding place" (p. 40).

The Sum of Our Days opens the door to the intimacy of Isabel's life: a very successful and wealthy writer. But these "material advantages" don't shield her from terrible pain, despair, and grief. She doesn't pretend to be perfect or to always act correctly. She shows us that life is complicated and that we can do nothing about the past, except to learn for the future.

Her stories are the stories of mature people who don't always act in mature ways. People can always repent and restart. Through this reading, the reader connects to other lives, sympathizes, and feels less isolated.

This book will serve future teachers to help their students join the not-so-perfect adult world, learn some of its secrets, anticipate difficulties in future relationships, and maybe cultivate more compassion for the adults in their lives. Some of them will be able to mourn with Isabel and quietly revisit painful and private experiences. Many will feel optimistic about their lives and will have more resources to address and balance life's ups and downs.

The Sum of Our Days will help future teachers show their students how to feel included in a world that challenges them to imagine a more realistic future. It will also facilitate giving important answers to personal questions that students find easier and safer to ask in disguise, through brave, compassionate, and well-guided class discussions.

"Reading is where the wild things are" says Winterson (2011, p. 144). Children not only need the wild nature to find the wild part of our souls. They also need "the untamed open space of our imagination" (p. 144). Literature provides many tools to tame that space and make it our own. I sincerely hope that teachers will find inspiration and abundant support in their teaching and mentoring through many works of literature, which is what this chapter and this book aim to achieve.

References

Allende, I. (2008). *The sum of our days*. (M. S. Peden, Trans.). Harper.
Winterson, J. (2011). *Why be happy when you could be normal?* Jonathan Cape.

About the Authors

Mark D. Beatham is an Associate Professor in Education at SUNY Plattsburgh, in Plattsburgh, New York, where he teaches social and psychological foundations of education and honors courses at The Honor Center. His principal research interests are in philosophy and psychology of education, and media and technology and learning.

Lynanne Black is a certified school psychologist and full professor at Indiana University of Pennsylvania (IUP). Lynanne teaches courses at the graduate and undergraduate levels in educational psychology, learning, behavior, assessment and intervention, research, and family-school relations. Lynanne began her collegiate education at The Catholic University of America (CUA) where she earned a bachelor's degree in Latin and Classical Humanities and Psychology. From there, Lynanne enrolled at Temple University where she earned her M.Ed. and Ph. D in school psychology. Lynanne's primary research interest is school psychological services in preschool settings.

Lochran C. Fallon is Assistant Professor of English at Francis Marion University, Florence, South Carolina, where he teaches courses in composition, writing, theory, and secondary education, with an emphasis on teaching English. He received his doctorate from the Pennsylvania State University in Curriculum and Instruction, with a focus on English Education. Prior to his position at the university level, he taught high school English for several years. His research interests include ways to get students and teachers to ask more questions, respectfully and attentively listen, discuss, and care for themselves and others.

Anna Gallagher is a lover of dogs, sweeping epics, breaking news, a well-turned phrase, and good conversation over coffee. She spent several decades working in chemistry labs while leisurely pursuing a bachelor's degree in English, then a master's in Liberal Arts, both from the University of Delaware. Perhaps the nicest memories from those years still spring from shared homework sessions with her son (occasionally kvetching together over the load!).

Margarita García-Notario teaches courses in Spanish, Philosophy of Education, Mythology, History of Spain, Ancient Cultures of Mesoamerica, Parenting in Evolution, and Deep Ecology at SUNY Plattsburgh. She is from Spain and received her doctorate in Philosophy of Education at the Universidad Complutense of Madrid and her Master in Philosophy and her Bachelor in Theology at the Universidad de Navarra (Pamplona). She is the author of *Filosofía Profunda y Educación*, the story of the birth of the environmental movement, its inspirational philosophies, and its key figures, as well as numerous publications and presentations at academic conferences. She is fascinated by languages, classic and medieval philosophy, ancient mythologies, religion, and literature. Her family is the center of her life, and she regularly organizes fun get-togethers with students at her house, where her Golden Retriever Bailey becomes the center of everybody's love and fun.

Frank Giuseffi is an Assistant Professor of Education and Program Manager for Ed.D. Online Programs at William Woods University. He is the author of *How the Socratic Method Engenders Authentic Educational Experiences*, a book that explores how Socratic dialogue enhances content material, learning styles, education settings, and teacher development. A former Social Studies teacher and school administrator, he received his B.A. in Philosophy and Political Science from the University of Central Missouri, an M.A. in Liberal Arts from St. John's College (Santa Fe, NM), an M.A. in Education from William Woods University, and an Ed.D. in Educational Leadership from Lindenwood University.

Cory Glenn came to education after over a decade working in the arts. He now teaches theatre at Nixa High School in southwest Missouri and is also a Per-Course Faculty member at Missouri State University in Springfield, Missouri, where he teaches educational foundations courses. His research interests include efficiency in education, arts integration in cross curricular study, and statements of purpose for academic institutions.

Brian Hibbs is Associate Professor of Education at Dalton State College. He teaches courses in applied linguistics, methods of TESOL, and culture and education designed to prepare elementary education teacher candidates to work with multilingual English learners in their instructional contexts. He has taught French and Spanish at the elementary and intermediate levels at several institutions of higher education in the United States and has taught English at the intermediate and advanced levels in Valladolid, Spain and Paris, France. His professional interests include second language acquisition, language teaching methodology, intercultural competence, teacher development, and study abroad.

Erin Hill, a former public high school English teacher, now works as a Professor of Practice in the Education Department at Wittenberg University in Springfield, Ohio. She also teaches in the English department and serves as a first reader for the Dayton Literary Peace Prize. Erin earned her B.S. in English education from Taylor University (by way of Indiana corn fields and volleyball courts) and her M.A. in English and American literature from New York University (by way of Greenwich Village park benches and coffee shops). An essayist by night, she takes her cues from the dangerous crew of poets and novelists she runs with by day.

Jeff McLaughlin is Professor Emeritus at West Chester University of Pennsylvania. A former elementary school teacher, he received his B.S.Ed. at Indiana University of Pennsylvania, M.S. (Curriculum and Instruction) at The Pennsylvania State University, and Ph.D. at Temple University (Psychological Studies in Education). His research interests have included teacher identity, teacher authority and autonomy, and unconventional teaching methods. When straying from the pedagogical universe, Jeff plays guitar and enjoys many kinds of music. He also loves to wander in the natural world, dabble in junk art creations, and write fiction. Some of these extracurricular details are available at www.moondogmotel.com.

Index

3-Stage Model, 52

A
Abolition of Man, The, 4
adolescence
  development, 1–2, 3
  expressive arts activities and, 43
  Great Ecstasy and, 1
  themes of, 6
Aeneid, 163
Adolescent Development Game, 13
adolescent identity development, 33
  For Every One and, 35–36
  lesson plans and, 34–35
afterlife, 175–76
Aladdin, 2, 8, 9
Alice in Wonderland, 8
all-but-dissertation (ABD), 129–30
Allende, I., 179–80
alternate identity, 82–83
America, 82–83
analogy, 134–35
Anterior Cingulate Cortex (ACC), 3
Areopagitica, 62
Argenti, F., 171
Aristotle, 109
Armstrong, T., 43
Atkinson-Shiffrin 3-Stage Model, 52
attention-deficit hyperactivity disorder (ADHD), 126
Auguries of Innocence, 79, 81
autism, 125
automaticity, 88

B
Bandura, A., 12
barren heath, 80
Beauty and the Beast, 2, 7, 8, 10, 14
behaviorism, 111
Bettelheim, B., 5–6
Bible, 10
biopsychospiritual homeostasis, 20
Blake, W., 71–74, 75–77, 77–79, 79–85, 89, 90
  labels for, 72
Bluebeard, 2, 10

Book of Genesis, 49
  See also Paradise Lost
Book of Urizen, The, 71, 75–77, 82, 83, 85, 86
Brannon, L., 56
Brave New World, 102–3
  educational themes in, 104–10
  efficiency in, 112–14
  five major themes in, 108
  solitude, individuality in, 116–17
  subject as access in, 115–16
Bronfenbrenner, U., 50, 51, 54, 68
Bruner, J.S., 72
Burton, S.L., 143

C
Canterbury Tales, 5
Castañeda, J.A.F., 37–38
character analysis, 135–36
Chen, P.C., 147–48, 156
Chimney Sweeper, The, 78
Christmas Carol, A, 17
chunking, 88
Cinderella, 2, 9, 11
classic stories, 1–2
  case for, 2–6
  in the college classroom, 10–12
  difficult to define, 11–12
  emotional intensity and, 5
  erotics, ecstasy and, 7–8
  four common themes in, 6–10
  power, responsibility and, 8
  seeking truth, proper authorities/order and, 8–9
  suggested assignment using, 12–14
  transformation, transcendence and, 9–10
  See also adolescence
cognition, 49, 71–75, 79
cognition-constructivism, 49, 72
cognitive development, stages of, 20, 71–75, 79
cognitive processing, 75–76, 79
cognitive reasoning, 12
Coles, R., xi
community, 106
construction of knowledge, identity and morality, 49

constructivism, 72
constructivist theory, 12
creative thinking, 77–78
creativity, 79
critical thinking, 49, 68
cultural literacy, 104, 105
Culturally Responsive Teaching Self-Efficacy (CRTSE) scale, 144
cynical teacher, 4

D
da Rimini, F., 171
Dante Alighieri, 163
Dartmouth College, 49
David Copperfield, 17
Dewey, J., 103, 104, 112, 115
Dickens, J.C.H., 17
   social criticism and, 17
   See also Great Expectations
Diehl, D.E., 104
Dindia, K., 56
disorganization, 21–22
disruption, 21–22
Divine Comedy, 45, 163, 176–77
   construction of narrative teaching lives, 164–65
   depictions of, 176
   formation of teacher identity and, 170–71
   identity and reflection in emotions and, 172–73
   limits and limitations of reflecting and, 168–70
   project-based learning (PBL) and, 174–76
   storying lives as educational practice, 165–67
   storytelling, reflection and, 163–64
   transactional learning, close reading and, 173–76
   See also Inferno
Divine Image, The, 78
disruptive reintegration, 21–22
D'Oria, B., 171
Draper, C., 144
dysfunctional reintegration, 21–22

E
ecology modeling, 50, 51, 54, 68
Economic Man, 4
Educational Existentialism, 105
educational psychology, 49–50, 120
attention, perception and, 75–77
cognition, cognitive development and, 71–75
creative thinking and, 77–78
identity development and, 80–85
limitations of perception and, 77
See also Blake
educational purpose, 104–5
efficiency, 111–12
Egan, K., 106, 115
empowerment, 62
Epic of Gilgamesh, 94
equality, 103
Erdman, D.V., 71, 72, 74, 75, 76, 77, 78, 81, 83, 84, 85, 89
Erikson, E., 20, 36, 41, 42, 54, 56, 63, 65, 80, 81, 82
Esquith, R., 11
essentialism, 103, 104–5
ethic of care, 64–5
evolutionary psychology, 12
expressive arts activities, 43
Expressive Individualism, 4
extrinsic motivation, 132

F
false self, 82–83
Fecho, B., 171
feminine marginalization, 58
feminist educational practices, 169
feminist perceptions, 61
feminist textual analysis, 50
feminist theory, 60
Fletcher, A., 3
For Every One, 33–35
   adolescent identity development and, 35–36
   James Baldwin and, 40
   as a mentor text for students, 38
   sample plans for teaching, 40–42, 42–43, 43–46
   teacher identity development and, 36–39
four-status crisis and commitment scheme, 36, 42
Four Zoas, The, 71, 83
Frozen, 6

G
Galea, S., 174
gender social theory, 64

Index

gendered linguistics, 58
gendered power dynamic, 58
general critical thinking, 49
Gilgamesh, 2, 5, 93–94
   Enkinu and, 94–96
   fate of mankind and, 97–98
   friendship and, 95–96
   guiding questions about, 98–100
   Ishtar and, 96–97
   primitive task of womanhood and, 95
Gilligan, C., 64
goal seeking, 131–32
Going to School in India, 144
Gollnick, D.M., 147, 156
good and bad authors, 4
Gopnik, A., 12
Graffiti Board, 149
Grant, L., xi
Great Expectations, 17
   biopsychospiritual homeostasis and life events in, 22–23
   disruption and disorganization in, 23–27
   reintegration in, 27–29
   teacher resiliency and, 29–30
   See also Dickins
growth stage theory, 49, 50, 54, 60, 61
Gulliver's Travels, 3

H

Hansel & Gretel, 6
Hard Times, 17
Harry Potter, 10
health education, 18
hegemonic masculinity, 169
Herbert, J., 56
hidden curriculum, 103, 114
Hobbit, The, 2
Hochschild, A.R., 172
Hollander, R., 164
homeostatic reintegration, 21–22
Homer, 119
   life of, 121
   Also see Odyssey
Huckleberry Finn, 2, 11
Human Abstract, The, 78
human identity, 80
human memory, 72–73, 87
human sexuality, 175
Huxley, A., 102, 106, 107, 108, 109, 112, 114, 116
   biography, 103
   See also Brave New World
hypothetico-deductive theory, 12

I

identity, 106
identity achievement, 82
identity construction, 34
identity development, 34, 71, 80–85
Iliad, The, 121
imagery, 88
imagination, 72
In Case You Teach English, 171
Individual Education Plan (IEP), 126
Individuals with Disabilities Education Improvement Act, 124
information processing model, 52–53, 73, 87, 89
intellectual disability (ID), 125
intelligence, 71
interaction, 21
interculturalism, 143
intrinsic motivation, 132
Irigaray, L., 169
Is This English, 171
Izadinia, M., 38

J

Jack and the Beanstalk, 11
Jerusalem, 71
Joan of Arc, 5
Johannessen, L.R., 171
John Milton Reading Room, 49
Jones, S., 56
Jungle Book, 2, 6, 9, 11

K

King Lear, 2, 8, 10
knowledge construction, 55–56
knowledge and identity development, 49–50
Kohlberg, L., 12, 20, 64, 65
Kohn, A., 111
Kramsch, C., 145

L

labeling, 125–26
Lakoff, R., 58, 59, 68
Larmer, J., 174
Latini, B., 171
learning, the "official view" of, 112
Leary, T., 103

Leshem, S., 166
Letters to a Young Poet, 40
Lewis, C.S., 4
life events, 20
limitations of rational perception and thought, 76–77
Lion King, The, 2, 7, 8, 9, 10
literary analysis, 136–38
literature
    awareness of student differences, xi
    criminal justice and, xii
    cross-cultural studies and, xii
    cultural sensitivity and, xi
    gender studies and, xii
    importance to future teachers, 101–102
    in graduate-level library science curricula, xi
    psychology and, xi–xii
    in teacher education courses, xi
Little Mermaid, 9, 11
Little Red Riding Hood, 10
long-term memory, 75, 87, 88
Lord of the Rings, 2, 9
low-resolution schemes, 8
Luster, T., 56
Lütge, C., 145–46
Luthar, S.S., 127
Luxon, T., 49

M
Mad Song, 82
maladaptive reintegration, 21–22
Malatesta, P., 171
Marcia, J., 36, 41, 42
Marek, K., xi
Marriage of Heaven and Hell, The, 71–75, 78–79, 80, 83
masculinity, four types of, 14
Matos, A., 145
McCann, T.M., 171
McLuhan, M., 103
meaning-making, 72
memory and information system model, 52
memory modeling, 49, 50
memory, notion of, 89
mentorship, 128–30
Merchant of Venice, 101
Miller, J.B., 60, 61, 63
Milton, 71, 83
Milton, J., 49–64, 64–65, 65–68

Moana, 2, 7, 10
moral development, theories on, 20, 64
moral reasoning, 71
motivation, 71
Mulan, 6, 10
multicultural children's literature, study of, 143
    analysis of data, 151
    data collection for, 150–51
    findings of study, 152–56
    research context of, 147–50
    research questions regarding, 146–47
    theoretical framework of study, 146
    See also literature
My Name is Maria Isabel, 148, 149

N
narrative (re)construction, 167
natural ecstasies, 5
Nemo, 10
Newburgh, K., 38
Nicolas III, Pope, 171
Nurse's Song, 78

O
Odyssey, The, 5, 119–20
    analogy and, 134–35
    character analysis in, 135–8
    delay of gratification in, 130–31
    educational career and, 122–23
    goal seeking in, 131–32
    labeling and, 125
    learning via, 134
    literary analysis in, 136–38
    mentorship, 128–30
    persistence, perseverance and, 132–34
    resilience in, 127–28
    special education and, 124–27
    teacher education and, 121–22
Of Mice and Men, 11
Okagaki, L., 56
Oliver Twist, 17
oral tradition, 121
other, 12

P
Paradise Lost, 49–64, 64–65, 65–68
    creation story in, 59
    empowerment in, 62
    ethic of care in, 64–65
    feminine marginalization in, 59

introduction to Eve in, 50–51
knowledge and identity development in, 49–50
knowledge construction, 55–56
memory and information system model and, 52
memory filters in, 53–54
moral development in, 64–65
Satan in, 50–51, 55, 62–63
Perennialism, 104
perseverance, 132–34
persistence, 132–34
Personal Beliefs About Diversity Scale, 151, 152, 154, 155
personal truth, 105
Peter Pan, 2, 5, 7
Piaget, J., 20, 72, 75
Pilgrim's Progress, 5
Pinocchio, 2, 5, 9, 10, 13, 14
Plato, 103, 109
Political Man, 4
Portinari, B., 171
Postman, N., 103, 115
prescriptive reflective exercises, 173
Professional Beliefs About Diversity Scale, 151, 152, 153, 154, 155
Progressivism, 105
project-based learning (PBL), 174–76
protective factors, 19
Psychological Man, 4
psychosocial development, 49

R

Rapunzel, 2
rational and reductionistic perception, 82
rational-linguistic thinking, 73
Ravid, R., 37
Reconstructionism, 105
reflective listening, 167
rehearsal, 88
Reidel, M., 143
reintegration, 21
Religious Man, 4
Republic of Plato, The, 108
Republic, The, 103
resilience, 127–28
resilient reintegration, 21
resiliency, education and, 119–20
Resiliency Model, 17–18
    definition, 18–19
    disorganization and, 21
    disruption and, 21
    importance in teaching, 18
    interaction and, 21
    protective factors, 19
    reintegration and, 21
    teacher resiliency and, 29–30
retributive justice, 176
Reynolds, J., 33–35, 36, 39–40, 41, 42, 43, 44
    awards given to him, 33
    "the meltdown" and, 39
    as a reader, 34
Richardson, G.E., 17–18, 18–20, 24, 26, 27, 28, 29
    biopsychospiritual homeostasis and, 20
    life events and, 20
Rilke, R.M., 40
Rosenblat L., 173
Rouse, D.W.H., 125, 131

S

Satiric Verses, 83–84
scheme theory, 12
School and Society, 102, 104
sensory memory, 87, 88
sensory perception, 76
Separate Peace, A, 11
seven conflicts, 36
seven stages of development, 42
Shakespeare, W., 101, 102, 115
Shattuck, R., 4
Short, K., 144–45
short term memory, 87
silencing, 58, 59
Siwatu, K.O., 144
six levels of moral development, 12
Skinner, B.F., 111
Sleeping Beauty, 9, 11
Smagorinsky, P., 173
Smith, F., 112, 115
Snow White, 2, 9, 11
Snyder, G., 7
social constructivism, 12
social-emotional competence (SEC), 119–20
social-emotional learning (SEL), 119
Solzhenitsyn, A., 14
Songs of Innocence and Experience, 71, 77, 84
special education, 124–27
specific-learning disability (SLD), 125
Speculum of the Other Woman, 169

spiritual homeostasis, 20
Spriny, 88
stability, 106
stage theory, 54–55
Star Wars, 2, 9, 10
Steiner, G., 5
stereotyping, 56
Stipek, D., 56
subject as access, 115–16
Sum of Our Days, The, 179–80, 185–86
    drug addiction and adoption in, 181
    loss in, 180–81
    personal choices and family responsibilities in, 182–83
    women in, 183–85
Swift, J., 3

T
Tale of Two Cities, A, 17
teacher identity development, 33–35, 172
    Castañeda's three components contributing to, 37–38
    For Every One and, 36
    journal writing, biographical narrative and, 38
teacher resilience, 17–18
    Resiliency Model and, 29–30
    See also Dickens, Resiliency Model
teachers' narratives, 165
Teaching English by Design, 173
Tempest, The, 102, 105, 111, 112, 114, 115, 116, 117
Teresa of Avila, St., 5
theory of self-efficacy, 12
third space, 145
This Sex Which Is Not One, 169
To Kill a Mockingbird, 2, 11
touchpoints, 145
tracking, 103, 113
Trafford, V.N., 166
transactional learning, 173
transmission and expansion of knowledge, 71–74, 75–77, 77–79, 79–85
Trusler, Reverend Dr., 81

U
Uberti, F.D., 171

V
Villegas, D.F.M., 37, 38

Virgil, 163, 168
Visions of the Daughters of Albion, 85
Vygotsky, L., 12, 72

W
Wilson, J.H., xii
Winterson, J., 185–86
working memory, 72, 87, 88
Why Be Happy When You Could Be Normal?, 185–86

Z
Zembylas, M., 172
Zur, A., 37